Education Department
General Administrative Regulations

34 Code of Federal Regulations
Parts 74, 75, 76, 77, 79, 80, 81, 82, 84, 85, 86, 97, 98, and 99

A CONDENSED GUIDE
for Program Managers & Project Directors

Printed in the United States of America.

Schoolhouse Partners, LLC
1281 Win Hentschel Boulevard
West Lafayette, Indiana 47906
Phone: 765-237-3390
Fax 765-463-3501

www.schoolhousepartners.net

Education Department General Administrative Regulations (EDGAR)
34 CFR Parts 74, 75, 76, 77, 79, 80, 81, 82, 84, 85, 86, 97, 98, 99

A Condensed Guide for Program Managers and Project Directors

Contents

PART 74—Administration of Grants and Agreements with Institutions of Higher Education, Hospitals, and Other Non-Profit Organizations

Subpart A—General

§ 74.1 Purpose.

This part establishes uniform administrative requirements for Federal grants and agreements awarded to institutions of higher education, hospitals, and other non-profit organizations. The Secretary does not impose additional or inconsistent requirements, except as provided in §§74.4 and 74.14 or required by Federal statute or E.O. This part applies to all recipients other than State and local governments and Indian tribal organizations. Non-profit organizations that implement Federal programs for States are also subject to State requirements.

§ 74.2 Definitions.

The following definitions apply to this part:

- *Accrued expenditures* - the charges incurred by the recipient during a given period requiring the provision of funds for:
    1. Goods and other tangible property received;
    2. Services performed by employees, contractors, subrecipients, and other payees; and
    3. Other amounts becoming owed under programs for which no current services or performance is required.
- *Accrued income* - the sum of earnings during a given period from delivered goods and services and the amounts owed to the recipient for which no current services or performance is required.
- *Acquisition cost of equipment* - the net invoice price of the equipment (including the cost of modifications, attachments, accessories, or apparatus necessary to make the property usable for the purpose for which it was acquired).
- *Advance* - a payment made to a recipient upon its request either before outlays are made by the recipient or through the use of predetermined payment schedules.
- *Award* - financial assistance or property awarded by the Federal Government to an eligible recipient that provides support or stimulation to accomplish a public purpose.
- *Cash contributions* - the recipient's cash outlay, including money contributed by third parties.
- *Closeout* - the process by which the Secretary determines that all applicable administrative actions and all required work of the award have been completed by the recipient and ED.
- *Contract* - a procurement contract or subcontract under an award or subaward.
- *Cost sharing or matching* - that portion of project or program costs not borne by the Government.
- *Date of completion* - the date on which all work under an award is completed or the date on the award document, or any supplement or amendment thereto, on which Federal sponsorship ends.
- *Disallowed costs* - those charges to an award that are unallowable in accordance with the applicable Federal cost principles or other terms and conditions contained in the award.
- *Equipment* - tangible nonexpendable personal property including exempt property charged directly to the award having a useful life of more than one year and an acquisition cost of $5,000 or more per unit. Lower limits may be established, consistent with recipient policy.
- *Exempt property* - tangible personal property acquired in whole or part with Federal funds, where the Secretary has authority to vest title in recipient without further obligation to the Government.
- *Federal awarding agency* - the Federal agency that provides an award to the recipient.
- *Federal funds authorized* - the total Federal funds obligated by the Federal Government for use by the recipient. This amount may include any authorized carryover of unobligated funds from prior funding periods when permitted by ED regulations or implementing instructions.
- *Federal share of real property, equipment, or supplies* - that percentage of the property's acquisition costs and any improvement expenditures paid with Federal funds.

- *Intangible property and debt instruments* - trademarks, copyrights, patents and patent applications and such property as loans, notes and other debt instruments, lease agreements, stock, and other instruments of property ownership, whether considered tangible or intangible.
- *Obligations* - the amounts of orders placed, contracts and grants awarded, services received, and similar transactions that require payment by the recipient during the same or a future period.
- *Outlays or expenditures* - charges made to the project or program.
- *Personal property* - property of any kind except real property. It may be tangible, having physical existence, or intangible, having no physical existence, such as copyrights, patents, or securities.
- *Prior approval* - written approval by an authorized official evidencing prior consent.
- *Program income* - gross income earned by the recipient that is directly generated by an activity or earned as a result of the award (see exclusions in §74.24(e) and (h)).
- *Project costs* - all allowable costs incurred by a recipient and the value of the contributions made by third parties in accomplishing the objectives of the award during the project period.
- *Project period* - the period stated in the award during which Federal sponsorship begins and ends.
- *Property* - real property, equipment, intangible property, and debt instruments.
- *Real property* - land, including land improvements, structures and appurtenances thereto, but excludes movable machinery and equipment.
- *Recipient* - an organization receiving financial assistance to carry out a project or program.
- *Research and development* - all research activities, both basic and applied, and all development activities supported at universities, colleges, and other non-profit institutions. "Research" is defined as a systematic study directed toward fuller scientific knowledge or understanding of the subject studied. "Development" is the systematic use of knowledge and understanding gained from research directed toward the production of useful materials, devices, systems, or methods, including design and development of prototypes and processes. The term "research" also includes activities involving training individuals in research techniques where these activities utilize the same facilities as other research and development activities and where these activities are not included in the instruction function.
- *Small awards* - a grant or cooperative agreement not exceeding the small purchase threshold fixed at 41 U.S.C. 403(11) (currently $25,000).
- *Subaward* - a financial assistance award in the form of money (or property in lieu of money) made under an award by a recipient to an eligible subrecipient or by a subrecipient to a lower tier subrecipient.
- *Subrecipient* - the legal entity to which a subaward is made and which is accountable to the recipient for the use of the funds provided.
- *Supplies* - all personal property excluding equipment, intangible property, and debt instruments as defined in this section, and inventions of a contractor conceived or first actually reduced to practice in the performance of work under a funding agreement ("subject inventions").
- *Suspension* - an action that temporarily withdraws Federal sponsorship under an award, pending corrective action by the recipient or pending a decision to terminate the award by the Secretary.
- *Termination* - the cancellation of Federal sponsorship, in whole or in part, under an agreement at any time prior to the date of completion.
- *Third party in-kind contributions* - the value of non-cash contributions provided by non-Federal third parties. Such contributions may be in the form of real property, equipment, and supplies, and the value of goods and services benefiting and specifically identifiable to the project.
- *Unliquidated obligations for financial reports prepared on a cash basis* - the amount of obligations incurred by the recipient that have not been paid.
- *Unobligated balance* - authorized funds that have not been obligated by the recipient.
- *Unrecovered indirect cost* - the difference between the amount awarded and the amount which could have been awarded under the recipient's approved negotiated indirect cost rate.
- *Working capital advance* - a procedure whereby funds are advanced to the recipient to cover its estimated disbursement needs for a given initial period.

§ 74.3 Effect on other issuances.
For awards subject to this part, all administrative requirements of codified program regulations, program manuals, handbooks, and other non-regulatory materials which are inconsistent with the requirements of this part are superseded, except to the extent they are required by statute, or authorized in accordance with the deviations provision in §74.4.

§ 74.4 Deviations.
The Secretary may grant exceptions for classes of grants or recipients subject to the requirements of this part when exceptions are not prohibited by statute. These are permitted only in unusual circumstances. The Secretary may apply more or less restrictive requirements to a class of recipients. Exceptions may be made by the Secretary on a case-by-case basis.

§ 74.5 Subawards.
Unless sections of this part exclude subrecipients from coverage, this part shall be applied to subrecipients performing work under awards if the subrecipients are institutions of higher education, hospitals, or other non-profit organizations. State and local government subrecipients are subject to the provisions of Part 80.

Subpart B—Pre-Award Requirements

§ 74.10 Purpose.
Sections §§ 74.11 through 74.17 prescribe forms, instructions, and other pre-award matters to be used in applying for awards.

§ 74.11 Pre-award policies.
Use of grants, cooperative agreements, and contracts. In each instance, the Secretary decides on the appropriate type of award in accordance with The Federal Grant and Cooperative Agreement Act (31 U.S.C. 6301–08). The statutory criterion for choosing between grants and cooperative agreements is that for the latter, substantial involvement is expected between ED and the recipient when carrying out the activity contemplated in the agreement. Contracts shall be used when the principal purpose is acquisition of property or services for the direct benefit or use of the Federal Government. In any case, the Secretary notifies the public of intended funding priorities for discretionary grant programs, unless funding priorities are established by Federal statute.

§ 74.12 Forms for applying for Federal assistance.
Applicants shall use the SF–424 series or those forms and instructions prescribed by the Secretary. For Federal programs covered by E.O. 12372 (Intergovernmental Review of Federal Programs), the applicant shall complete the appropriate sections indicating whether the application was subject to review by the State Single Point of Contact (SPOC). If ED does not use the SF–424 form, the Secretary may indicate whether the application is subject to review by the State under E.O. 12372.

§ 74.13 Debarment and suspension.
The non-procurement debarment and suspension common rule (implemented in Part 85) restricts subawards and contracts with parties that are debarred, suspended, excluded from, or ineligible for participation in Federal assistance programs or activities.

§ 74.14 Special award conditions.
The Secretary may impose special award conditions if an applicant or recipient has a history of poor performance, is not financially stable, has a management system that does not meet the standards of this part, has not conformed to the terms/conditions of a previous award, or is not generally responsible. Any special

conditions are promptly removed once the conditions that prompted them have been corrected. If special award conditions are established, the Secretary notifies the applicant or recipient of:

1. The nature of the additional requirements;
2. The reason why the additional requirements are being imposed;
3. The nature of the corrective action needed;
4. The time allowed for completing the corrective actions; and
5. The method for requesting reconsideration of the additional requirements imposed.

§ 74.15 Metric system of measurement.
The Metric Conversion Act, as amended by the Omnibus Trade and Competitiveness Act (15 U.S.C. 205) declares that the metric system is the preferred measurement system for U.S. trade and commerce.

§ 74.16 Resource Conservation and Recovery Act.
Recipients receiving direct Federal awards or funds shall give preference to purchasing recycled products pursuant to the EPA guidelines (40 CFR Parts 247–254) and the Resource Conservation and Recovery Act (RCRA) (42 U.S.C. 6962).

§ 74.17 Certifications and representations.
Unless prohibited by statute or regulation, recipients may submit certifications and representations required by statute, E.O., or regulation on an annual basis (if the recipients have ongoing and continuing relationships with ED). Such certifications and representations shall be signed by responsible officials with the authority to ensure compliance with the pertinent requirements.

Subpart C—Post-Award Requirements

Financial and Program Management

§ 74.20 Purpose of financial and program management.
Sections 74.21 through 74.28 prescribe standards for financial management systems, methods for making payments and rules for satisfying cost sharing and matching requirements, accounting for program income, approving budget revisions, making audits, determining allowability of cost, and establishing fund availability.

§ 74.21 Standards for financial management systems.
A recipient's financial management systems shall provide for the following:

1. Accurate, current, and complete disclosure of the financial results of each federally-sponsored project in accordance with requirements established in §74.52.
2. Records that identify the source, application, and accountability of funds, property, and other assets for federally-sponsored activities. These records shall contain information pertaining to awards, authorizations, obligations, unobligated balances, assets, outlays, income, and interest.
3. Comparison of outlays with budget amounts for each award. Whenever appropriate, financial information should be related to performance and unit cost data.
4. Written procedures to minimize the time elapsing between the transfer of funds to the recipient from the U.S. Treasury and the issuance or redemption of checks, warrants, or payments by other means for program purposes by the recipient.
5. Written procedures for determining the reasonableness, allocability, and allowability of costs in accordance with the provisions of applicable Federal cost principles and the terms of the award.
6. Documentation including cost accounting records that is supported by source documentation.

Where the Federal Government guarantees or insures the repayment of money borrowed by the recipient, the Secretary may require adequate bonding and insurance to protect the interest of the Federal Government. Fidelity bond coverage may also be required.

§ 74.22 Payment.

Recipients are paid in advance, provided they have financial management systems that meet the standards for fund control and accountability (as established in §74.21) as well as minimize the time elapsing between the transfer of funds from the U.S. Treasury and disbursement by the recipient. When such requirements cannot be met, the reimbursement method is preferred, whereby ED makes payment within 30 days after receipt of the billing (unless the billing is improper). Recipients are authorized to submit request for reimbursement at least monthly when electronic funds transfers are not used.

Cash advances are limited to the minimum amounts needed and should be timed with the actual, immediate cash requirements of the recipient to carry out the approved project. Whenever possible, advances are consolidated to cover cash needs for all awards made by the Secretary. Recipients are authorized to submit requests for advances and reimbursements at least monthly when electronic fund transfers are not used.

Unless required by statute, the Secretary does not withhold payments for proper charges made by recipients at any time during the project period unless:

1. A recipient has failed to comply with the project objectives, the terms and conditions of the award, or Federal reporting requirements; or
2. The recipient or subrecipient is delinquent in a Federal debt as defined in OMB A–129.

Under these conditions, the Secretary may inform the recipient that ED does not make payments for obligations incurred after a specified date until the conditions are corrected or the indebtedness to the Government is liquidated.

The standards governing the use of banks require recipients to account for the receipt, obligation, and expenditure of funds. Advances of Federal funds shall be deposited and maintained in insured accounts whenever possible. Interest bearing accounts are also encouraged unless the banking institution requires a minimum balance so high that it would not be feasible based on the expected cash resources. Recipients are also encouraged to use women- and minority-owned banks (a bank which is owned at least 50% by women or minority group members).

Except as noted elsewhere, only the following forms (one original and two copies) are authorized to request advances and reimbursements:

1. SF–270—Request for Advance or Reimbursement; or
2. SF–271—Outlay Report and Request for Reimbursement for Construction Programs.

§ 74.23 Cost sharing or matching.

All contributions, including cash and third party in-kind, are accepted as part of the recipient's cost sharing or matching when contributions are:

1. Verifiable from the recipient's records;
2. Are not included as contributions for any other federal project;
3. Are necessary to accomplish the program objectives;
4. Are allowable and conform to applicable cost principles;
5. Are not paid by the Federal Government under another award; and
6. Are provided for in the budget. Unrecovered indirect costs may also be included as part of cost sharing or matching only with prior approval.

The value of the donated property for cost sharing or matching shall be in accordance with applicable cost principles and will be the lesser of:

1. The certified value of the remaining life of the property recorded in the recipient's accounting records at the time of donation; or
2. The current fair market value.

Volunteer services furnished by professional and technical personnel, consultants, and other skilled and unskilled labor may be counted as cost sharing or matching if the service is an integral and necessary part of an approved project or program. Rates for volunteer services must be consistent with those paid for similar work in the recipient's organization or the labor market. Paid fringe benefits that are reasonable, allowable, and allocable may be included in the valuation. When an employer other than the recipient furnishes the services of an employee, these services are valued at the employee's regular rate of pay (plus appropriate fringes, but exclusive of overhead costs), provided these services are in the same skill for which the employee is normally paid. Volunteer services must be documented by the same methods used by the recipient's own employees.

Value assessed to donated supplies included in the cost sharing or matching share shall be reasonable and not exceed the fair market value of the property at the time of the donation. The value of donated land and buildings may not exceed its fair market value at the time of donation to the recipient as established by an independent appraiser and certified by a responsible official of the recipient. The value of donated or loaned equipment may not exceed the fair market value of equipment of the same age and condition at the time of donation. The value of donated space may not exceed the fair rental value of comparable space as established by an independent appraisal of comparable space and facilities in a privately-owned building in the same locality.

§ 74.24 Program income.

Program income earned during the project period must be retained by the recipient and, in accordance with ED regulations or the award terms, must be used in one or more of the following ways:

1. Added to funds committed to the project by the Secretary and recipient to further eligible project or program objectives (this rule automatically applies to research projects unless specified otherwise);
2. Used to finance the non-Federal share of the project or program; and/or
3. Deducted from the total project or program allowable cost in determining the net allowable costs on which the Federal share of costs is based (this applies automatically to all projects, except research, when rules for program income are not specified).

Unless ED regulations or the terms and conditions of the award provide otherwise, recipients have no obligation to the Government regarding program income earned after the end of the project period or to program income earned from license fees and royalties for copyrighted material, patents, patent applications, trademarks, and inventions produced under an award. Patent and Trademark Amendments (35 U.S.C. 18) apply to inventions made under an experimental, developmental, or research award.

§ 74.25 Revision of budget and program plans.

The budget plan is the financial expression of the approved project or program. Recipients must report deviations from budget and program plans, and request prior approvals for revisions. When requesting approval for budget revisions, recipients shall generally use the budget forms that were used in the application.

Non-Construction Awards. For non-construction awards, recipients shall request prior approvals from ED for one or more of the following program or budget related reasons:

1. Change in the scope or the objective of the project or program (even if there is no associated budget revision requiring prior written approval).
2. Change in a key person specified in the application or award document.

3. The absence for more than three months, or a 25% reduction in time devoted to the project, by the approved project director or principal investigator.
4. The need for additional Federal funding.
5. The transfer of amounts budgeted for indirect costs to absorb increases in direct costs, or vice versa (if approval is required by the Secretary).
6. The transfer of funds allotted for direct payment to trainees into other categories of expense.
7. The subaward, transfer, or contracting out of any work under an award (unless described in the application and funded in the approved awards). This does not apply to the purchase of supplies, material, equipment, or general support services.

Waivers. The Secretary may waive cost-related and administrative prior written approvals (required by this part and OMB A–21 and A–122) to authorize recipients to:

1. Incur pre-award costs 90 calendar days prior to award at the recipient's risk (i.e., the Secretary is under no obligation to reimburse these costs if for any reason the recipient does not receive an award or if the award is less than anticipated and inadequate to cover these costs);
2. Initiate a one-time extension of the expiration date of the award of up to 12 months; and/or
3. Carry forward unobligated balances to subsequent funding periods.

Cost Transfer. ED may restrict the transfer of funds among direct cost categories or activities for awards in which the Federal share of the project exceeds $100,000 and the cumulative amount of the transfers exceeds 10% of the total budget. Transfers that would cause any Federal appropriation or part thereof to be used for purposes other than those consistent with the original intent of the appropriation are not permitted.

Construction Awards. For construction awards, recipients shall request prior written approval promptly from the Secretary for budget revisions whenever:

1. The revision results from changes in the scope or the objective of the project or program;
2. The need arises for additional federal funds to complete the project; or
3. A revision is desired which involves specific costs for which prior written approval requirements may be imposed consistent with applicable OMB cost principles listed in §74.27.

For awards that support both construction and non-construction work, the Secretary may require the recipient to request prior approval before making any fund transfers between the two types of work supported. For these types of awards, ED must also be notified in writing when Federal funds are expected to exceed the recipient's needs for the project period by more than $5,000 or 5% of the Federal award, whichever is greater.

§ 74.26 Non-Federal audits.

Recipients and subrecipients that are institutions of higher education or other non-profit organizations (including hospitals) shall be subject to the audit requirements contained in 31 U.S.C. 7501–7507 and revised OMB A–133. State and local governments shall be subject to the audit requirements contained in the Single Audit Act Amendments of 1996 within 31 U.S.C. 7501–7507 and revised OMB A–133. For-profit hospitals not covered by the audit provisions of revised OMB A–133 shall be subject to the audit requirements of the Federal awarding agencies. Commercial organizations are subject to the audit requirements established by the Secretary or the prime recipient as incorporated into the award document.

§ 74.27 Allowable costs.

OMB A-122 is to be used by private nonprofit organizations (other than institutions of higher education, hospitals, or an organization named in OMB A–122 as not subject to that circular). OMB A-21 is to be used by educational institutions. Appendix E to 45 CFR Part 74 is to be used by hospitals. 48 CFR Part 31 (Contract Cost Principles and Procedures or uniform cost accounting standards that comply with cost principles acceptable to ED) is to be used by commercial for-profit organization other than a hospital and an educational institution. Cost principles applicable to a State, a local government, or Federally recognized Indian tribal government are specified at 34 CFR §80.22.

§ 74.28 Period of availability of funds.
Where a funding period is specified, a recipient may charge to the grant only allowable costs resulting from obligations incurred during the funding period and any pre-award costs authorized by the Secretary.

Property Standards

§ 74.30 Purpose of property standards.
Sections 74.31 through 74.37 establish uniform standards governing management and disposition of property furnished by ED whose cost was charged to a project supported by a Federal award. The Secretary does not impose additional requirements unless specifically required by Federal statute. The recipient may use its own property management standards and procedures provided it observes the provisions of §§74.31 through 74.37.

§ 74.31 Insurance coverage.
Recipients shall, at a minimum, provide the equivalent insurance coverage for real property and equipment acquired with Federal funds as provided to property owned by the recipient. Federally-owned property need not be insured unless required by the terms and conditions of the award.

§ 74.32 Real property.
Title. Title to real property must vest in the recipient so long as the recipient shall use the real property for the authorized purpose of the project as long as it is needed and shall not encumber the property without approval of the Secretary. Use of real property in other projects shall be limited to those under federally-sponsored awards that have purposes consistent with those authorized for support by the Secretary.

Disposition. When the real property is no longer needed, the recipient shall request disposition instructions from ED or its successor Federal awarding agency. The recipient may be permitted to:

1. Retain title without further obligation after it compensates the Government for that percentage of the current fair market value of the property attributable to the Federal participation in the project;
2. Sell the property and pay the Government for that percentage of the current fair market value of the property attributable to the Federal participation in the project (after deducting actual and reasonable selling and fix-up expenses, if any, from the sales proceeds); or
3. Transfer title to the property to the Government or to an eligible third party. The recipient is entitled to compensation for its attributable percentage of the current fair market value of the property.

§ 74.33 Federally-owned and exempt property.
Federally-owned property. Title to federally-owned property remains vested in the Federal Government. Recipients shall submit an annual inventory of federally-owned property in their custody. Upon completion of the award or when the property is no longer needed, the recipient shall report the property to the Secretary. If ED has no further need for the property, it shall be declared excess and reported to the General Services Administration. Appropriate instructions shall be issued to the recipient by ED.

Exempt property. The Secretary may vest title to property acquired with Federal funds in the recipient without further obligation to the Government and under conditions the Secretary considers appropriate. This property is "exempt property." Should the Secretary not establish conditions, title to exempt property upon acquisition vests in the recipient without further obligation to the Federal Government.

§ 74.34 Equipment.
Title to equipment acquired by a recipient with Federal funds shall vest in the recipient (subject to conditions). A recipient may not use equipment acquired with Federal funds to provide services to non-Federal outside organizations for a fee that is less than private companies charge for equivalent services. The recipient shall use the equipment in the project for which it was acquired, whether or not the project or program continues to be supported by Federal funds and may not encumber the property without prior approval. When no longer needed for the original project, the recipient shall use the equipment in connection with its other federally-sponsored activities. When acquiring replacement equipment, the recipient may sell or trade-in equipment and use proceeds to offset costs of replacement equipment (subject to approval). Adequate maintenance procedures must be implemented to keep the equipment in good condition. The recipient's shall maintain property management standards for equipment acquired with Federal funds and/or owned (in whole or in part) by the Federal Government.

§ 74.35 Supplies and other expendable property.
Title to supplies and expendable property shall vest in the recipient upon acquisition. If residual unused supplies exist that exceed $5,000 in total aggregate value upon project termination or completion and the supplies are not needed for any other federally-sponsored project or program, the recipient shall retain the supplies for use on non-Federal sponsored activities or sell them. In either case, the Government must be compensated for its share. Such compensation shall be computed in the same manner as for equipment.

§ 74.36 Intangible property.
Recipients may copyright any work that is subject to copyright and was developed, or for which ownership was purchased, under an award. ED and any other Federal awarding agency reserve a royalty-free, nonexclusive, and irrevocable right to reproduce, publish, or otherwise use the work for Federal purposes, and to authorize others to do so (or use such data for Federal purposes). Title to intangible property and debt instruments acquired under an award or subaward vests upon acquisition in the recipient. The recipient shall use that property for the originally-authorized purpose, and the recipient shall not encumber the property without approval of the Secretary. When no longer needed for the originally authorized purpose, disposition of intangible property shall occur in accordance with the provisions of §74.34(g).

In response to a Freedom of Information Act (FOIA) request for research data relating to published research findings produced under a Federal award, ED shall request the research data so that they can be made available to the public through the procedures established under the FOIA. The recipient shall provide data requested by ED within a reasonable time.

§ 74.37 Property trust relationship.
Real property, equipment, intangible property, and debt instruments that are acquired or improved with Federal funds must be held in trust by the recipient as trustee for the beneficiaries of the project or program under which the property was acquired or improved. The Secretary may require recipients to record liens or other appropriate notices of record to indicate that personal or real property has been acquired or improved with Federal funds and that use and disposition conditions apply to the property.

Procurement Standards

§ 74.40 Purpose of procurement standards.
Sections 74.41 through 74.48 contain standards for recipients in establishing procedures for the procurement of supplies and other expendable property, equipment, real property, and other services with Federal funds. The Secretary does not impose additional procurement standards upon recipients unless required by Federal statute or E.O. or as authorized in §74.4 or §74.14.

§ 74.41 Recipient responsibilities.

The recipient is the responsible authority, without recourse to the Secretary, regarding the settlement and satisfaction of all contractual and administrative issues arising out of procurements entered into in support of an award or other agreement. This includes disputes, claims, protests of award, source evaluation, or other matters of a contractual nature.

§ 74.42 Codes of conduct.

The recipient shall maintain written standards of conduct governing the performance of its employees engaged in the award and administration of contracts. No employee, officer, or agent shall participate in the selection, award, or administration of a contract supported by Federal funds if a real or apparent conflict of interest would be involved. A conflict would arise when the employee, officer, or agent, any member of his or her immediate family, his or her partner, or an organization which employs or is about to employ any of the parties indicated herein, has a financial or other interest in the firm selected for an award. The officers, employees, and agents of the recipient shall neither solicit nor accept gratuities, favors, or anything of monetary value from contractors or parties to subagreements. The standards of conduct shall provide for disciplinary actions to be applied for violations of these standards by officers, employees, or agents of the recipient.

§ 74.43 Competition.

All procurement transactions shall be conducted in a manner to provide, to the maximum extent practical, open and free competition. Recipients shall be alert to organizational conflicts of interest as well as noncompetitive practices among contractors that may restrict or eliminate competition or restrain trade. In order to ensure objective contractor performance (and eliminate unfair competitive advantage), contractors that develop specifications, requirements, statements of work, invitations for bids, or requests for proposals shall be excluded from competing for procurements. Awards must be made to the bidder whose bid is responsive to the solicitation and is most advantageous to the recipient, price, quality, and other factors considered. Any bid may be rejected when it is in the recipient's best interest to do so.

§ 74.44 Procurement procedures.

Written procurement procedures. All recipients shall establish written procurement procedures to ensure that unnecessary items are not purchased as well as provide analyses regarding lease and purchase alternatives to determine which would be the most economical and practical procurement for the Federal Government.

Solicitations for goods and services. Solicitations for goods and services provide for all of the following:

1. A clear and accurate description of the technical requirements for the material, product, or service to be procured. In competitive procurements, a description shall not contain features which unduly restrict competition.
2. Requirements which the bidder/offeror must fulfill and all other factors to be used in evaluating bids or proposals.
3. A description, whenever practicable, of technical requirements in terms of functions to be performed, including the range of acceptable characteristics or minimum acceptable standards.
4. The specific features of brand name or equal descriptions that bidders are required to meet when these items are included in the solicitation.
5. The acceptance, to the extent practicable and economically feasible, of products and services dimensioned in the metric system of measurement.
6. Preference, to the extent practicable and economically feasible, for products and services that conserve natural resources and protect the environment, and are energy efficient.

Women- and Minority-Owned Business. Efforts shall be made by recipients to utilize small businesses, minority-owned firms, and women's business enterprises, whenever possible. Recipients must:

1. Ensure that small businesses, minority-owned firms, and women's business enterprises are used to the fullest extent practicable.
2. Make information on forthcoming opportunities available and arrange time frames for purchases and contracts to encourage and facilitate participation by small businesses, minority-owned firms, and women's business enterprises.
3. Consider in the contract process whether firms competing for larger contracts intend to subcontract with small businesses, minority-owned firms, and women's business enterprises.
4. Encourage contracting with consortiums of small businesses, minority-owned firms and women's business enterprises when a contract is too large for one of these firms to handle individually.
5. Use the services and assistance, as appropriate, of organizations such as the Small Business Administration and the Department of Commerce's Minority Business Development Agency in the solicitation and utilization of small businesses, minority-owned firms and women's business enterprises.

Contracts. The type of procuring instruments used (e.g., fixed price contracts, cost reimbursable contracts, purchase orders, and incentive contracts) shall be determined by the recipient but must be appropriate for the particular procurement and promote the best interest of the project. The "cost-plus-a-percentage-of-cost" or "percentage of construction cost" methods of contracting must not be used. Contracts are made only with responsible contractors who possess the potential ability to perform successfully under the procurement conditions. Consideration is given to contractor integrity, record of past performance, financial and technical resources, and/or accessibility to other necessary resources.

Documentation. Recipients shall, on request, make available for the Secretary, pre-award review and procurement documents, such as request for proposals or invitations for bids, independent cost estimates, etc., when any of the following conditions apply:

1. A recipient's procurement procedures fail to comply with the procurement standards in this part.
2. The procurement is expected to exceed the small purchase threshold fixed at 41 U.S.C. 403 (11) (currently $25,000) and is to be awarded without competition or only one bid or offer is received in response to a solicitation.
3. The procurement, which is expected to exceed the small purchase threshold, specifies a "brand name" product.
4. The proposed award over the small purchase threshold is to be awarded to a bidder other than the apparent low bidder under a sealed bid procurement.
5. A proposed contract modification changes the scope of a contract or increases the contract amount by more than the amount of the small purchase threshold.

Faith-Based Organizations. A faith-based organization is eligible to contract with recipients on the same basis as any other private organization. Recipients shall not discriminate for or against a private organization on the basis of the organization's religious character or affiliation. A private organization that engages in religious activities must offer those services separately in time or location from any programs or services supported by a contract with a recipient, and participation in any such religious activities by beneficiaries of the supported programs must be voluntary. A faith-based organization that contracts with a recipient may retain its independence, autonomy, right of expression, religious character, and authority over its governance.

§ 74.45 Cost and price analysis.

Some form of cost or price analysis must be made and documented in the procurement files in connection with every procurement action. Price analysis may be accomplished in various ways, including the comparison of price quotations submitted, market prices and similar indicia, together with discounts.

§ 74.46 Procurement records.

At a minimum, procurement records and files for purchases in excess of the small purchase threshold must include the basis for contractor selection, the justification for lack of competition when competitive bids or offers are not obtained, and the basis for award cost or price.

§ 74.47 Contract administration.

A system for contract administration must be maintained to ensure contractor conformance with the terms, conditions and specifications of the contract, and to ensure adequate and timely follow up of all purchases. Recipients shall evaluate contractor performance and document, as appropriate, whether contractors have met the terms, conditions, and specifications of the contract.

§ 74.48 Contract provisions.

In addition to provisions to define a sound and complete agreement, the recipient shall include the following provisions in all contracts and subcontracts:

1. Contracts in excess of the small purchase threshold shall contain contractual conditions that allow for administrative, contractual, or legal remedies in instances in which a contractor breaches the contract terms, and provide for appropriate remedial actions;
2. Contracts exceeding the small purchase threshold must provide for termination by the recipient;
3. For those contracts or subcontracts exceeding $100,000, the Secretary may accept the bonding policy and requirements of the recipient, provided that the government's interest is protected;
4. All negotiated contracts (except those for less than the small purchase threshold) awarded by recipients must include provisions allowing the recipient, ED, or the Comptroller General access to any books, documents, and records of the contractor which are directly pertinent to a specific program for the purpose of making audits, examinations, excerpts and transcriptions.

All contracts, including small purchases, awarded by recipients and contractors must contain procurement provisions of Appendix A to this part, as appropriate.

Reports and Records

§ 74.50 Purpose of reports and records.

Sections 74.51 through 74.53 establish the procedures for record retention, monitoring and reporting on the recipient's financial and program performance, and the necessary standard forms.

§ 74.51 Monitoring and reporting program performance.

Recipients are responsible for managing, monitoring, and reporting on each project, program, subaward, or activity supported by the award at the frequency prescribed by the Secretary. Recipients shall also monitor subawards to ensure subrecipients have met audit requirements in §74.26. When required, each performance report must generally contain brief information on actual accomplishments (with the goals and objectives for the period), reasons why goals were not met, and other pertinent information (including cost overruns and other appropriate data). The Secretary is also authorized to make site visits, as needed.

§ 74.52 Financial reporting.

SF–269 and SF–269A. The Secretary requires recipients to submit the SF–269 or SF–269A (an original and no more than two copies) no later than 30 days after the end of each specified reporting period for quarterly and semi-annual reports, and 90 calendar days for annual and final reports. The Secretary determines the frequency of the Financial Status Report for each program, but does not require submission more frequently than quarterly or less than annually (but a final report is required upon completion of the grant). Extensions of reporting due dates may be approved by the Secretary.

SF–272 and SF–272A. When funds are advanced to recipients, the Secretary requires each recipient to submit the SF–272 and, when necessary, its continuation sheet, SF–272A. These are used to monitor cash advanced to recipients and to obtain disbursement information for each agreement with the recipients. Forecasts of Federal cash requirements may be required in the "Remarks" section of the report as well as the amount of cash advances received in excess of three days. Recipients shall provide short narrative explanations of actions taken to reduce excess balances. Recipients are required to submit no more than one original and two copies of the SF–272 15 calendar days following the end of each quarter. A monthly report may be required from those recipients receiving advances totaling $1 million or more per year.

§ 74.53 Retention and access requirements for records.

Retention. Financial records, supporting documents, statistical records, and all other records pertinent to an award shall be retained for a period of three years from the date of submission of the final expenditure report or, for awards that are renewed quarterly or annually, from the date of the submission of the quarterly or annual financial report. The only exceptions are the following:

1. If any litigation, claim, or audit is started before the expiration of the three-year period, the records shall be retained until all such actions and findings have been resolved and final action taken.
2. Records for real property and equipment acquired with Federal funds shall be retained for 3 years after final disposition.
3. When records are transferred to or maintained by ED, the three-year retention requirement is not applicable to the recipient.
4. Indirect cost rate proposals, cost allocations plans, etc. as specified in §74.53(g).

The Secretary requests transfer of certain records to its custody from recipients when it determines that the records possess long term retention value. However, in order to avoid duplicate recordkeeping, the Secretary may make arrangements for recipients to retain any records that are continuously needed for joint use.

Access. The Secretary, Inspector General, Comptroller General of the U.S., or any of their duly authorized representatives, have the right of timely and unrestricted access to any books, documents, papers, or other records of recipients pertinent to the awards, in order to make audits, examinations, excerpts, transcripts, and copies of documents. This includes access to a recipient's personnel for interview. The rights of access in this paragraph are not limited to the required retention period, but shall last as long as records are retained.

Freedom of Information Act. Unless required by statute, the Secretary does not place restrictions on recipients that limit public access to recipient records that are pertinent to an award. The Secretary may limit access when it can be demonstrated that the records must be kept confidential and would have been exempted from disclosure pursuant to FOIA (5 U.S.C. 552) if the records had belonged to ED.

Termination and Enforcement

§ 74.60 Purpose of termination and enforcement.

Sections 74.61 and 74.62 establish uniform suspension, termination, and enforcement procedures.

§ 74.61 Termination.

Awards may be terminated in whole or in part only by:

1. The Secretary, if a recipient fails to comply with the terms and conditions of an award;
2. The Secretary with the consent of the recipient, in which case the two parties shall agree upon the termination conditions or portions; or
3. The recipient, upon sending the written notification containing the reasons for termination and effective date (and in the case of partial termination, the portion to be terminated).

§ 74.62 Enforcement.

Remedies for noncompliance. If a recipient materially fails to comply with the stated terms and conditions of an award (including Federal statute or regulation), the Secretary may impose special conditions (outlined in §74.14) and take one or more of the following actions:

1. Temporarily withhold cash payments;
2. Disallow costs of the activity or action not in compliance;
3. Wholly or partly suspend or terminate the current award; and/or
4. Withhold further awards for the project or program.

Hearings and appeals. In taking an enforcement action, the Secretary provides the recipient an opportunity for a hearing, appeal, or other administrative proceeding to which the recipient is entitled under any statute or regulation applicable to the action involved.

Effects of suspension and termination. Costs of a recipient resulting from obligations incurred by the recipient during a suspension or after termination of an award are not allowable unless authorized in the notice of suspension or termination or by the Secretary under certain circumstances.

Relationship to debarment and suspension. Enforcement remedies, including suspension and termination, do not preclude ED from initiating debarment or suspension under 34 CFR Part 85 (see §74.13).

Subpart D—After-the-Award Requirements

§ 74.70 Purpose.

Sections 74.71 through 74.73 contain closeout procedures for subsequent disallowances and adjustments.

§ 74.71 Closeout procedures.

Recipients shall submit all financial, performance, and other required reports within 90 calendar days after the award completion date. Unless an extension is authorized, a recipient shall liquidate all obligations incurred under the award not later than 90 calendar days after the funding period or the date of completion as specified in the award conditions or in ED implementing instructions. The recipient shall refund any balances of unobligated or advanced cash that is not authorized to be retained by the recipient. The recipient shall account for any real and personal property acquired with Federal funds or received from the Federal Government in accordance with §§74.31 through 74.37. In the event a final audit has not been performed prior to grant closeout, ED retains the right to recover an appropriate amount after fully considering the recommendations on disallowed costs resulting from the final audit.

§ 74.72 Subsequent adjustments and continuing responsibilities.

The closeout of an award does not affect the Secretary's right to disallow costs and recover funds on the basis of a later audit or review, or the recipient's obligation to return any funds due as a result of later refunds, corrections, or other transactions. Closeouts also do not affect the requirements of audits in §74.26, property management in §§74.31 through 74.37, or records retention in §74.53.

§ 74.73 Collection of amounts due.

Funds paid to a recipient in excess of the amount to which the recipient is determined to be entitled under the terms of the award constitute a debt to the Government. If not paid within a reasonable period after the demand for payment, the Secretary may reduce the debt by making an administrative offset against other requests for reimbursements or withholding advance payments due to the recipient. Except as otherwise provided by law, the Secretary charges interest on overdue debts in accordance with 4 CFR Chapter II—Federal Claims Collection Standards.

Appendix A to Part 74—Contract Provisions

All contracts shall contain the following provisions as applicable:

1. *Equal Employment Opportunity*—All contracts must contain a provision requiring compliance with E.O. 11246, as amended by E.O. 11375—Amending E.O. 11246 relating to Equal Employment Opportunity, and as supplemented by regulations at 41 CFR Part 60—Office of Federal Contract Compliance Programs, Equal Employment Opportunity.
2. *Copeland "Anti-Kickback" Act* (18 U.S.C. 874 and 40 U.S.C. 276c) —All construction or repair awards in excess of $2,000 must comply with the Copeland "Anti-Kickback" Act. The Act provides that each contractor or subrecipient shall be prohibited from inducing any person employed in the construction, completion, or repair of public work to give up any part of the compensation to which he is otherwise entitled.
3. *Davis-Bacon Act*, as amended (40 U.S.C. 276a to a-7) —When required by legislation, all construction contracts awarded by the recipients and subrecipients of more than $2,000 must comply with the Davis-Bacon Act and as supplemented by DOL regulations (29 CFR Part 5). Under this Act, contractors are required to pay wages to laborers (not less than once a week) at a rate not less than the minimum wages specified in a wage determination made by the Secretary of Labor. The recipient must place a copy of the current prevailing DOL wage determination in each solicitation; an award shall be conditioned upon the acceptance of the wage determination.
4. *Contract Work Hours and Safety Standards Act* (40 U.S.C. 327–333) —Where applicable, all contracts awarded by recipients in excess of $2,000 for construction contracts and in excess of $2,500 for other contracts employing mechanics or laborers must comply with Sections 102 and 107 of 40 U.S.C. 327–333, as supplemented by DOL regulations (29 CFR Part 5). These requirements do not apply to the purchases of supplies or materials or articles ordinarily available on the open market, or contracts for transportation or transmission of intelligence.
5. *Rights to Inventions Made Under a Contract or Agreement* — Contracts or agreements for the performance of experimental, developmental, or research work must provide for the rights of the Federal Government and the recipient in any resulting invention in accordance with 37 CFR Part 401 and any implementing regulations issued by the awarding agency.
6. *Clean Air Act* (42 U.S.C. 7401 et seq.) and the Federal Water Pollution Control Act (33 U.S.C. 1251 et seq.), as amended — Contracts and subgrants in excess of $100,000 require the recipient to agree to comply with all applicable standards, orders, or regulations issued pursuant to the Clean Air Act and the Federal Water Pollution Control Act as amended.
7. *Byrd Anti-Lobbying Amendment* (31 U.S.C. 1352) —Contractors who apply or bid for an award of $100,000 or more shall file the required certification. Each tier certifies to the tier above that it will not and has not used Federal funds to pay any person or organization for influencing or attempting to influence an officer or employee of any agency, a member of Congress, officer or employee of Congress, or an employee of a member of Congress in connection with obtaining any Federal contract, grant, or any other award covered by 31 U.S.C. 1352. Each tier shall also disclose any lobbying with non-Federal funds that takes place in connection with obtaining any Federal award. The disclosures are forwarded from tier to tier up to the recipient.
8. *Debarment and Suspension* (E.O. 12549 and E.O. 12689) —No contract may be made to parties listed on the General Services Administration's List of Parties Excluded from Federal Procurement or Non-procurement Programs. This list contains the names of parties and contractors declared suspended, ineligible, debarred, or excluded by agencies.
9. Contractors with awards that exceed the small purchase threshold must provide the required certification regarding its exclusion status and that of its principal employees.

PART 75—DIRECT GRANT PROGRAMS

Subpart A—General

Regulations That Apply to Direct Grant Programs

§ 75.1 Programs to which Part 75 applies.
The regulations in Part 75 apply to each ED direct grant program. If a direct grant program does not have implementing regulations, the Secretary implements the program under the authorizing statute, the General Education Provisions Act (GEPA), and the regulations in this part. For the purposes of this part, the term "direct grant program" includes any ED grant program other than a program whose authorizing statute or regulations provide a formula for allocating program funds among eligible States. With respect to Public Law 81–874 (the Impact Aid Program), "direct grant program" includes only the entitlement increase for children with disabilities under section 3(d)(2)(C) of Public Law 81–874 (20 U.S.C. 238(d)(2)(C) and disaster assistance under section 7 of that law (20 U.S.C. 241–1).

§ 75.2 Exceptions in program regulations to Part 75.
If a program has regulations that are not consistent with Part 75, the implementing regulations for that program identify the sections of Part 75 that do not apply.

§ 75.4 Department contracts.
ED contracts are governed by:
1. Chapters 1 and 34 of Title 48 CFR,
2. Applicable program regulations, and
3. The request for proposals for the procurement, if any, referenced in Commerce Business Daily.

The regulations in Part 75 do not apply to an ED contract unless regulations in Part 75 or a program's regulations specifically provide otherwise.

Eligibility for a Grant

§ 75.50 How to find out whether you are eligible.
Eligibility to apply for a grant under a program of the Department is governed by the authorizing statute and implementing regulations for that program.

§ 75.51 How to prove nonprofit status.
An applicant may be required to show proof that it is a nonprofit organization. Such proof may include:
1. Recognition by the IRS under Section 501(c)(3) of the Internal Revenue Code;
2. A statement from a State taxing body or the State attorney general certifying that the nonprofit organization operates within the State and no part of its net earnings lawfully benefit any private shareholder or individual; or
3. A certified copy of the applicant's certificate of incorporation if it establishes the nonprofit status of the applicant.

§ 75.52 Eligibility of faith-based organizations for a grant.
A faith-based organization is eligible to apply for and receive a grant under an ED program on the same basis as any other private organization. ED does not discriminate for or against a private organization on the basis of the organization's religious character or affiliation in the selection of grantees. The provisions of §75.532 apply to a faith-based organization that receives a grant under a program of the Department.

A private organization that engages in inherently religious activities, such as religious worship, instruction, or proselytization, must offer those services separately in time or location from any programs or services supported by a grant from ED, and participation in any such inherently religious activities by beneficiaries of the programs supported by the grant must be voluntary.

A faith-based organization that applies for or receives a grant under an ED program may retain its independence, autonomy, right of expression, religious character, and authority over its governance. A faith-based organization may, among other things:

1. Retain religious terms in its name;
2. Continue to carry out its mission, including the definition, development, practice, and expression of its religious beliefs;
3. Use its facilities to provide services without removing or altering religious art, icons, scriptures, or other symbols from these facilities;
4. Select its board members and otherwise govern itself on a religious basis; and
5. Include religious references in its mission statement and other chartering or governing documents.

If a grantee contributes its own funds in excess of those required by a grant agreement to supplement federally funded activities, the grantee has the option to segregate those additional funds or commingle them with the funds required by the matching requirements or grant agreement. However, if the additional funds are commingled, this section applies to all of the commingled funds.

Ineligibility of Certain Individuals To Receive Assistance

§ 75.60 Individuals ineligible to receive assistance.

An individual is ineligible to receive a fellowship, scholarship, or discretionary grant funded by ED if the individual is not current in repaying a debt or is in default on a debt under a fellowship, scholarship, discretionary grant, loan program, or a Federal non-procurement transaction.

§ 75.61 Certification of eligibility; effect of ineligibility.

An individual who applies for a fellowship, scholarship, or discretionary grant from the ED shall provide a certification, under penalty of perjury, that he or she is eligible under §75.60 and has not been debarred or suspended by a judge under section 5301 of the Anti-Drug Abuse Act of 1988 (21 U.S.C. 853a). If a fellowship, scholarship, or discretionary grant is made to an individual who provided a false certification, the individual is liable for recovery of the funds made available under the certification, for civil damages or penalties imposed for false representation, and for criminal prosecution under 18 U.S.C. 1001.

§ 75.62 Requirements applicable to entities making certain awards.

An entity that provides a fellowship, scholarship, or discretionary grant to an individual under a grant from, or an agreement with, the Secretary shall require the individual who applies for such an award to provide with his or her application a certification under the penalty of perjury, that the individual is eligible under §75.60 and that the individual has not been debarred or suspended by a judge under section 5301 of the Anti-Drug Abuse Act of 1988 (21 U.S.C. 853a). The Secretary may require an entity subject to this section to provide a list of the individuals to whom fellowship, scholarship, or discretionary grant awards have been made or are proposed to be made by the entity.

Subpart B [Reserved]

Subpart C—How To Apply for a Grant

The Application Notice

§ 75.100 Publication of an application notice; content of the notice.
Each fiscal year, the Secretary publishes application notices in the Federal Register that explain what kind of assistance is available for new grants under the programs that the Secretary administers. The application notice for a program explains one or more of the following:

1. How to apply for a new grant; and
2. How to pre-apply for a new grant (if preapplications are used under the program).

§ 75.101 Information in the application notice that helps an applicant apply.
The Secretary may include such information as the following in an application notice:

1. How an applicant can get an application package that contains information about the program and the application form (and preapplication form, if appropriate) that the applicant must use.
2. The amount of funds available for grants, the estimated number of those grants, the estimated amounts of those grants and, if appropriate, the maximum award amounts of those grants.
3. If the Secretary plans to approve multi-year projects, the project period that will be approved.
4. Priorities established by the Secretary for the program for that year and the method the Secretary will use to implement the priorities.
5. Where to find the regulations that apply to the program.
6. The statutory authority for the program.
7. The deadlines established under §75.102 (Deadline date for applications) and 34 CFR 79.8.

§ 75.102 Deadline date for applications.
The application notice for a program sets a deadline date for the transmittal of applications to the Department. If the Secretary allows an applicant to submit a paper application, the applicant must show one of the following as proof of mailing by the deadline date:

1. A legibly dated U.S. Postal Service postmark;
2. A legible mail receipt with the date of mailing stamped by the U.S. Postal Service; and/or
3. A dated shipping label, invoice, or receipt from a commercial carrier.

If an application is mailed through the U.S. Postal Service, the Secretary does not accept a private metered postmark or mail receipt that is not dated by the U.S. Postal service as proof of mailing.

§ 75.103 Deadline date for preapplications.
If the Secretary invites or requires preapplications under a program, the application notice for the program sets a deadline date for preapplications. An applicant shall submit its preapplication in accordance with the procedures for applications in §75.102(b) and (d).

§ 75.104 Applicants must meet procedural rules.
The Secretary may make a grant only to an eligible party that submits an application. If a maximum award amount is established in the Federal Register notice, the Secretary may reject any application that proposes a project funding level that exceeds the stated maximum award amount.

§ 75.105 Annual priorities.
What programs are covered by this section? This section applies to any program for which the Secretary establishes priorities for selection of applications in a particular fiscal year.

How does the Secretary establish annual priorities? The Secretary establishes final annual priorities by publishing the priorities in a notice in the Federal Register (usually in the application notice for that program). The Secretary also publishes proposed annual priorities for public comment, unless:

1. The final annual priorities will be implemented only by inviting applications that meet the priorities;
2. The final annual priorities are chosen from a list of priorities already established in the program's regulations;
3. Publishing proposed annual priorities would seriously interfere with an orderly, responsible grant award process or would otherwise be impracticable, unnecessary, or contrary to the public interest;
4. The program statute requires or authorizes the Secretary to establish specified priorities; or
5. The annual priorities are chosen from allowable activities specified in the program statute.

How does the Secretary implement an annual priority? The Secretary may choose one or more of the following methods to implement an annual priority:

1. *Invitations.* ED may simply invite applications that meet a priority. If this method is chosen, an application that meets the priority receives no competitive or absolute preference over applications that do not meet the priority.
2. *Competitive preference.* Competitive preference may be given to applications that meet determined priorities.
3. *Absolute preference.* Absolute preference may be given to applications that meet a priority. The Secretary may establish a separate competition for applications that meet a priority and reserve all or part of a program's funds solely for that competition. The amount reserved for a priority may be adjusted after determining the number of high quality applications received.

Application Contents

§ 75.109 Changes to application; number of copies.

Each applicant that submits a paper application shall submit an original and two copies to the Department, including any voluntarily supplied information. An applicant may make changes to its application on or before the deadline date for submitting applications under the program.

§ 75.112 Include a proposed project period and a timeline.

An application must propose a project period for the project as well as a narrative that describes how and when, in each budget period of the project, the applicant plans to meet each objective of the project.

§ 75.117 Information needed for a multi-year project.

An applicant that proposes a multi-year project shall include in its application information that shows why a multi-year project is needed as well as a budget narrative (accompanied by a budget form prescribed by the Secretary) that provides budget information for each budget period of the proposed project period.

§ 75.118 Requirements for a continuation award.

A recipient that wants to receive a continuation award shall submit a performance report that provides the most current performance and financial expenditure information that meets the reporting requirements of 34 CFR 74.51, 75.590, 75.720, and 80.40. If a recipient fails to submit a performance report that meets such requirements, the Secretary denies continued funding for the grant.

§ 75.119 Information needed if private school students participate.

If a program requires applicants to provide an opportunity for participation of students enrolled in private schools, applications must include the information required of subgrantees under 34 CFR 76.656.

Separate Applications—Alternative Programs

§ 75.125 Submit a separate application to each program.
An applicant shall submit a separate application to each program under which it wants a grant.

§ 75.126 Application must list all programs to which it is submitted.
If an applicant submits an application for the same project under more than one Federal program, they shall list these programs in its application. The Secretary uses this information to avoid duplicate grants for the same project.

Group Applications

§ 75.127 Eligible parties may apply as a group.
Eligible parties may apply as a group for a grant. A group may be made of eligible parties which can include institutions of higher education, consortiums, joint applications, and cooperative arrangements.

§ 75.128 Who acts as applicant; the group agreement.
If a group of eligible parties applies for a grant, the members of the group shall either designate one member of the group to apply for the grant or establish a separate and eligible legal entity to apply for the grant. The members of the group shall enter into an agreement that details the activities that each member of the group plans to perform and binds each member of the group to every statement and assurance made by the applicant in the application. The applicant shall submit the agreement with its application.

§ 75.129 Legal responsibilities of each member of the group.
If a grant is awarded to a group of eligible applicants, the applicant for the group is the grantee and is legally responsible for the use of all grant funds, ensuring that the project is carried out by the group in accordance with Federal requirements, and ensuring that indirect costs are determined as required under §75.564(e). Each member of the group is legally responsible to carry out the activities it agrees to perform and use funds under the agreement in accordance with applicable Federal requirements.

State Comment Procedures

§ 75.155 Review procedures if State may comment on applications: Purpose of §§75.156–75.158.
If the authorizing statute for a program requires that a specific State agency be given an opportunity to comment on each application, the State and the applicant shall use the procedures in §§75.156–75.158.

§ 75.156 When an applicant under §75.155 must submit its application to the State; proof of submission.
Each applicant under a program covered by §75.155 shall submit a copy of its application to the State on or before the deadline date for submitting its application to the Department. The applicant shall attach to its application a copy of its letter that requests the State to comment on the application.

§ 75.157 The State reviews each application.
A State that receives an application under §75.156 may review and comment on the application.

§ 75.158 Deadlines for State comments.
The Secretary may establish a deadline date for receipt of State comments on applications. The State shall make its comments in a written statement signed by an appropriate State official. The appropriate State official shall submit comments to the Secretary by the deadline date for State comments.

§ 75.159 Effect of State comments or failure to comment.
The Secretary considers those comments of the State that relate to any selection criterion that applies under the program, or any other matter that affects the selection of projects for funding under the program. If the State fails to comment on an application on or before the deadline date for the appropriate program, the State waives its right to comment. If the applicant does not give the State an opportunity to comment, the Secretary does not select that project for a grant.

Development of Curricula or Instructional Materials

§ 75.190 Consultation.
Each applicant that intends to develop curricula or instructional materials under a grant is encouraged to assure that such materials will be developed in a manner conducive to dissemination, through continuing consultations with publishers, personnel of State and local educational agencies, teachers, administrators, community representatives, and other individuals experienced in dissemination.

§ 75.191 Consultation costs.
An applicant may budget reasonable consultation fees or planning costs in connection with the development of curricula or instructional materials.

§ 75.192 Dissemination.
If an applicant proposes to publish and disseminate curricula or instructional materials under a grant, the applicant shall include an assurance in its application that the curricula or materials will reach the populations for which the curricula or materials were developed.

Subpart D—How Grants Are Made

Selection of New Projects

§ 75.200 How applications for new grants and cooperative agreements are selected for funding; standards for use of cooperative agreements.
Direct grant programs. The Department administers two kinds of direct grant programs: a discretionary grant or a formula grant.

Discretionary grant programs. A discretionary grant program is one in which the Secretary is permitted to select applications for funding based, in part, on:

1. Selection criteria established under §75.209;
2. Selection criteria established under §75.210; or
3. Selection criteria in program-specific regulations.

Cooperative agreements. The Secretary may award a cooperative agreement instead of a grant if the Secretary determines that substantial involvement between ED and the recipient is necessary to carry out a collaborative project. The Secretary uses the selection procedures in this subpart to select recipients of cooperative agreements.

Formula grant programs. A formula grant program is one that entitles certain applicants to receive grants if they meet the requirements of the program. Applicants do not compete with each other for the funds, and each grant is either for a set amount or for an amount determined under a formula. The Secretary applies the program statute and regulations to fund projects under a formula grant program.

§ 75.201 How the selection criteria will be used.
In the Federal Register notice or application package, applicants are informed of the selection criteria chosen and any factors selected for considering the selection criteria. If points are assigned to the selection criteria, applicants are also notified of the total possible score for all of the criteria for a program and the assigned weight or the maximum possible score for each criterion.

§ 75.209 Selection criteria based on statutory provisions.
The Secretary may evaluate applications by:

1. Establishing selection criteria based on statutory provisions that apply to the authorized program (which may include, but are not limited to specific statutory selection criteria, allowable activities, application content requirements, or other pre-award and post-award conditions); and
2. Assigning the maximum possible score for each of the criteria established under paragraph (a)(1) of the full Federal section.

§ 75.210 General selection criteria.
In determining selection criteria to be used in each grant competition, the Secretary may select one or more of the following criteria (and may select among the list of optional factors under each criterion):

Need for project. In determining the need for the proposed project, the Secretary considers one or more of the following factors:

1. The magnitude or severity of the problem to be addressed by the proposed project.
2. The magnitude of the need for the services to be provided or the activities to be carried out by the proposed project.
3. The extent to which the proposed project will provide services or otherwise address the needs of students at risk of educational failure.
4. The extent to which the proposed project will focus on serving or otherwise addressing the needs of disadvantaged individuals.
5. The extent to which specific gaps or weaknesses in services, infrastructure, or opportunities have been identified and will be addressed by the proposed project, including the nature and magnitude of those gaps or weaknesses.
6. The extent to which the proposed project will prepare personnel for fields in which shortages have been demonstrated.

Significance. In determining the significance of the proposed project, the Secretary considers one or more of the following factors:

1. The national significance of the proposed project.
2. The significance of the problem or issue to be addressed by the proposed project.
3. The potential contribution of the proposed project to increased knowledge or understanding of educational problems, issues, or effective strategies.
4. The potential contribution of the proposed project to increased knowledge or understanding of rehabilitation problems, issues, or effective strategies.
5. The likelihood that the proposed project will result in system change or improvement.
6. The potential contribution of the proposed project to the development and advancement of theory, knowledge, and practices in the field of study.
7. The potential for generalizing from the findings or results of the proposed project.
8. The extent to which the proposed project is likely to yield findings that may be utilized by other appropriate agencies and organizations.
9. The extent to which the proposed project is likely to build local capacity to provide, improve, or expand services that address the needs of the target population.

10. The extent to which the proposed project involves the development or demonstration of promising new strategies that build on, or are alternatives to, existing strategies.
11. The likely utility of the products (such as information, materials, processes, or techniques) that will result from the proposed project, including the potential for their being used effectively in a variety of other settings.
12. The extent to which the results of the proposed project are to be disseminated in ways that will enable others to use the information or strategies.
13. The potential replicability of the proposed project or strategies, including, as appropriate, the potential for implementation in a variety of settings.
14. The importance or magnitude of the results or outcomes likely to be attained by the proposed project, especially improvements in teaching and student achievement.
15. The importance or magnitude of the results or outcomes likely to be attained by the proposed project, especially improvements in employment, independent living services, or both, as appropriate.
16. The importance or magnitude of the results or outcomes likely to be attained by the project.

Quality of the project design. In determining the quality of the design of the proposed project, the Secretary considers one or more of the following factors:

1. The extent to which the goals, objectives, and outcomes to be achieved by the proposed project are clearly specified and measurable.
2. The extent to which the design of the proposed project is appropriate to, and will successfully address, the needs of the target population or other identified needs.
3. The extent to which there is a conceptual framework underlying the proposed research or demonstration activities and the quality of that framework.
4. The extent to which the proposed activities constitute a coherent, sustained program of research and development in the field, including, as appropriate, a substantial addition to an ongoing line of inquiry.
5. The extent to which the proposed activities constitute a coherent, sustained program of training in the field.
6. The extent to which the proposed project is based upon a specific research design, and the quality and appropriateness of that design, including the scientific rigor of the studies involved.
7. The extent to which the proposed research design includes a thorough, high-quality review of the relevant literature, a high-quality plan for research activities, and the use of appropriate theoretical and methodological tools, including those of a variety of disciplines, if appropriate.
8. The extent to which the design of the proposed project includes a thorough, high-quality review of the relevant literature, a high-quality plan for project implementation, and the use of appropriate methodological tools to ensure successful achievement of project objectives.
9. The quality of the proposed demonstration design and procedures for documenting project activities and results.
10. The extent to which the design for implementing and evaluating the proposed project will result in information to guide possible replication of project activities or strategies, including information about the effectiveness of the approach or strategies employed by the project.
11. The extent to which the proposed development efforts include adequate quality controls and, as appropriate, repeated testing of products.
12. The extent to which the proposed project is designed to build capacity and yield results that will extend beyond the period of Federal financial assistance.
13. The extent to which the design of the proposed project reflects up-to-date knowledge from research and effective practice.
14. The extent to which the proposed project represents an exceptional approach for meeting statutory purposes and requirements.

15. The extent to which the proposed project represents an exceptional approach to the priority or priorities established for the competition.
16. The extent to which the proposed project will be coordinated with similar or related efforts, and with other appropriate community, State, and Federal resources.
17. The extent to which the proposed project will establish linkages with other appropriate agencies and organizations providing services to the target population.
18. The extent to which the proposed project is part of a comprehensive effort to improve teaching and learning and support rigorous academic standards for students.
19. The extent to which the proposed project encourages parental involvement.
20. The extent to which the proposed project encourages consumer involvement.
21. The extent to which performance feedback and continuous improvement are integral to the design of the proposed project.
22. The quality of the methodology to be employed in the proposed project.
23. The extent to which fellowship recipients or other project participants are to be selected on the basis of academic excellence.

Quality of project services. In determining the quality of the services to be provided by the proposed project, the Secretary considers the quality and sufficiency of strategies for ensuring equal access and treatment for eligible project participants who are members of groups that have traditionally been underrepresented based on race, color, national origin, gender, age, or disability. This is mandatory within this criterion. In addition, the Secretary considers one or more of the following factors:

1. The extent to which the services to be provided by the proposed project are appropriate to the needs of the intended recipients or beneficiaries of those services.
2. The extent to which entities that are to be served by the proposed technical assistance project demonstrate support for the project.
3. The extent to which the services to be provided by the proposed project reflect up-to-date knowledge from research and effective practice.
4. The likely impact of the services to be provided by the proposed project on the intended recipients of those services.
5. The extent to which the training or professional development services to be provided by the proposed project are of sufficient quality, intensity, and duration to lead to improvements in practice among the recipients of those services.
6. The extent to which the training or professional development services to be provided by the proposed project are likely to alleviate the personnel shortages that have been identified or are the focus of the proposed project.
7. The likelihood that the services to be provided by the proposed project will lead to improvements in the achievement of students as measured against rigorous academic standards.
8. The likelihood that the services to be provided by the proposed project will lead to improvements in the skills necessary to gain employment or build capacity for independent living.
9. The extent to which the services to be provided by the proposed project involve the collaboration of appropriate partners for maximizing the effectiveness of project services.
10. The extent to which the technical assistance services to be provided by the proposed project involve the use of efficient strategies, including the use of technology, as appropriate, and the leveraging of non-project resources.
11. The extent to which the services to be provided by the proposed project are focused on those with greatest needs.
12. The quality of plans for providing an opportunity for participation in the proposed project of students enrolled in private schools.

Quality of project personnel. In determining the quality of project personnel, the Secretary considers the extent to which the applicant encourages applications for employment from persons who are members of groups that have traditionally been underrepresented based on race, color, national origin, gender, age, or disability. This is mandatory within this criterion. In addition, the Secretary considers one or more of the following factors:

1. The qualifications, including relevant training and experience, of the project director or principal investigator.
2. The qualifications, including relevant training and experience, of key project personnel.
3. The qualifications, including relevant training and experience, of project consultants or subcontractors.

Adequacy of resources. In determining the adequacy of resources for the proposed project, the Secretary considers one or more of the following factors:

1. The adequacy of support, including facilities, equipment, supplies, and other resources, from the applicant organization or the lead applicant organization.
2. The relevance and demonstrated commitment of each partner in the proposed project to the implementation and success of the project.
3. The extent to which the budget is adequate to support the proposed project.
4. The extent to which the costs are reasonable in relation to the objectives, design, and potential significance of the proposed project.
5. The extent to which the costs are reasonable in relation to the number of persons to be served and to the anticipated results and benefits.
6. The potential for continued support of the project after Federal funding ends, including, as appropriate, the demonstrated commitment of appropriate entities to such support.
7. The potential for the incorporation of project purposes, activities, or benefits into the ongoing program of the agency or organization at the end of Federal funding.

Quality of the management plan. In determining the quality of the management plan for the proposed project, the Secretary considers one or more of the following factors:

1. The adequacy of the management plan to achieve the objectives of the proposed project on time and within budget, including clearly defined responsibilities, timelines, and milestones for accomplishing project tasks.
2. The adequacy of procedures for ensuring feedback and continuous improvement in the operation of the proposed project.
3. The adequacy of mechanisms for ensuring high-quality products and services from the proposed project.
4. The extent to which the time commitments of the project personnel are appropriate and adequate to meet the objectives of the proposed project.
5. How the applicant will ensure that a diversity of perspectives are brought to bear in the operation of the proposed project, including those of parents, teachers, the business community, a variety of disciplinary and professional fields, recipients or beneficiaries of services, or others, as appropriate.

Quality of the project evaluation. In determining the quality of the evaluation, the Secretary considers one or more of the following factors:

1. The extent to which the methods of evaluation are thorough, feasible, and appropriate to the goals, objectives, and outcomes of the proposed project.
2. The extent to which evaluation methods are appropriate to the context within which the project operates.
3. The extent to which the methods of evaluation provide for examining the effectiveness of project implementation strategies.
4. The extent to which the methods of evaluation include the use of objective performance measures that are clearly related to the intended outcomes of the project and will produce quantitative and

qualitative data to the extent possible.

5. The extent to which the methods of evaluation will provide timely guidance for quality assurance.
6. The extent to which the methods of evaluation will provide performance feedback and permit periodic assessment of progress toward achieving intended outcomes.
7. The extent to which the evaluation will provide guidance about effective strategies suitable for replication or testing in other settings.

§ 75.211 Selection criteria for unsolicited applications.

If the Secretary considers an unsolicited application, the Secretary uses the selection criteria and factors used for the competition under which the application could have been funded and/or any other criteria that are appropriate to evaluate the activities proposed in the unsolicited application.

Selection Procedures

§ 75.215 How the Department selects a new project: purpose of §§75.216–75.222.

Sections 75.216–75.222 describe the process used by the Secretary to select applications for new discretionary grants. Section 75.216 applies also to formula grant programs.

§ 75.216 Applications not evaluated for funding.

The Secretary does not evaluate an application if:

1. The applicant is not eligible;
2. The applicant does not comply with procedural rules that govern the submission of the application;
3. The application does not contain the information required under the program; or
4. The proposed project cannot be funded under the authorizing statute or implementing regulations for the program.

§ 75.217 How the Secretary selects applications for new grants.

The Secretary selects applications for new grants on the basis of the authorizing statute, the selection criteria, priorities, or other applicable requirements published in the Federal Register. The Secretary may use experts to evaluate the applications submitted under a program, which may include persons who are not employees of the Federal Government. A rank order of the applications will be prepared based solely on the evaluation of their quality according to the selection criteria. The order in which applications will be selected for grants is then determined, considering the information in each application, the rank ordering of the applications, and any other pertinent information (including information specific to the applicant and prior performance history).

§ 75.218 Applications not evaluated or selected for funding.

The Secretary informs an applicant if its application is not evaluated or selected for funding and can provide explanation why the application was not evaluated or selected (if requested by the applicant).

§ 75.219 Exceptions to the procedures under §75.217.

The Secretary may select an application for funding without following the procedures in §75.217 if:

1. The objectives of the project cannot be achieved unless the Secretary makes the grant before the date grants can be made under the procedures in §75.217;
2. The application was evaluated under the preceding competition of the program;
3. The application rated high enough to deserve selection under §75.217; and
4. The application was not selected for funding because the application was mishandled by ED; or
5. The Secretary receives an unsolicited application that meets the requirements of §75.222.

§ 75.220 Procedures the Department uses under §75.219(a).

If special circumstances of §75.219(a) appear to exist for an application, the Secretary may assemble a board to review the application. Such a board will consist of:

1. A program officer of the program under which the applicant wants a grant;
2. An employee from the Office of the Chief Financial Officer (OCFO) with responsibility for grant policy; and
3. An ED employee who is not a program officer of the program but who is qualified to evaluate the application.

The board reviews the application to decide if:

1. The special circumstances under §75.219(a) are satisfied;
2. The application rates high enough to deserve selection; and
3. Application selection will not have an adverse impact on the program budget.

§ 75.221 Procedures the Department uses under §75.219(b).

If the special circumstances of §75.219(b) appear to exist for an application, the application may be selected for funding if the Secretary:

1. Has documentary evidence that special circumstances of §75.219(b) exist; and
2. Has a statement that explains the circumstances of the mishandling.

§ 75.222 Procedures the Department uses under §75.219(c).

If the Secretary receives an unsolicited application, the application may be considered under certain procedures unless the Secretary has published a notice in the Federal Register stating that the program that would fund the application would not consider unsolicited applications.

The Secretary determines whether the application could be funded under a competition planned or conducted for the fiscal year under which funds would be used to fund the application. If the application could be funded under a competition and the deadline for submission of applications has not passed, the Secretary refers the application to the appropriate competition for consideration under the procedures in §75.217. If the deadline has passed, however, the Secretary may consider the application only in exceptional circumstances.

If an application may be considered, the Secretary determines if:

1. There is a substantial likelihood that it is of exceptional quality and national significance for a program administered by ED;
2. It meets the requirements of all applicable statutes and codified regulations that apply to the program; and
3. Selection of the project will not have an adverse impact on funds available for other program awards.

If it is determined that necessary criteria have been met, the Secretary assembles a panel of experts (not including any ED employees) to review the application. If the experts highly rate the application and determine that the application is of such exceptional quality and national significance that it should be funded as an unsolicited application, the Secretary may fund the application.

Note: Applicants submitting unsolicited applications should send the application, marked "Unsolicited Application" on the outside, to the Chief, Application Control Center, U.S. Department of Education, Washington, DC 20202–4725.

§ 75.224 What are the procedures for using a multiple tier review process to evaluate applications?
The Secretary may use a multiple tier review process to evaluate applications and may refuse to review applications in any tier that do not meet a minimum cut-off score established for the prior tier. Cut-off scores may be established in the application notice published in the Federal Register or after reviewing the applications to determine the overall range in the quality of applications received.

§ 75.225 What procedures does the Secretary use if the Secretary decides to give special consideration to novice applications?
As used in this section, "novice applicant" means any applicant for a grant from ED that has:

1. Never received a grant or subgrant under the program from which it seeks funding;
2. Never been a member of a group application submitted in accordance with §§75.127–75.129 that received a grant under the program from which it seeks funding; and
3. Not had an active discretionary grant from the Federal Government in the five years before the deadline date for applications under the program. Before making a grant to a novice applicant, the Secretary imposes special conditions, if necessary, to ensure the grant is managed effectively and project objectives are achieved.

Procedures To Make a Grant

§ 75.230 How the Department makes a grant; purpose of §§75.231–75.236.
If an application is selected under §§75.217, 75.220, or 75.222, the Secretary follows the procedures in §§75.231–75.236 to set the amount and determine the conditions of a grant.

§ 75.231 Additional information.
After selecting an application for funding, the applicant may be required to submit additional information.

§ 75.232 The cost analysis; basis for grant amount.
Before the Secretary sets the amount of a new grant, he or she does a cost analysis of the project to verify the cost data in the detailed budget for the project, evaluate specific elements of costs, and examine costs to determine if they are necessary, reasonable, and allowable under applicable statutes and regulations. The cost analysis serves as a basis for determining the amount of the grant to the applicant and shows whether the applicant can achieve the objectives with reasonable efficiency and economy under the budget.

§ 75.233 Setting the amount of the grant.
Subject to any applicable matching or cost-sharing requirements, the Secretary may fund up to 100% of the allowable costs in the applicant's budget. The Secretary may also consider any other financial resources available to the applicant.

§ 75.234 The conditions of the grant.
The Secretary makes a grant to an applicant only after determining the approved costs and any special conditions. In awarding a cooperative agreement, the Secretary includes conditions that state the explicit character and extent of anticipated collaboration between ED and the recipient.

§ 75.235 The notification of grant award.
To make a grant, the Secretary sends a grant award notification to the grantee, which sets the amount of the grant award and establishes other specific conditions, if any.

§ 75.236 Effect of the grant.
The grant obligates both the Government and the grantee to the requirements that apply to the grant.

Approval of Multi-Year Projects

§ 75.250 Project period can be up to 60 months.
The Secretary may approve a project period of up to 60 months.

§ 75.251 The budget period.
The Secretary usually approves a budget period of not more than 12 months, even if the project has a multi-year period. If a multi-year project is approved, the Secretary makes a grant for the initial budget period and indicates his/her intention to make continuation awards to fund the remainder of the project period.

§ 75.253 Continuation of a multi-year project after the first budget period.
In selecting applications for funding, the Secretary gives priority to continuation awards over new grants subject to the criteria in this section. The Secretary may make a continuation award for a budget period after the first budget period of an approved multi-year project if:

1. Congress has appropriated sufficient funds under the program;
2. The recipient has made substantial progress toward meeting the objectives in its approved application or obtained approval of changes in the project that do not increase the cost of the grant and enable the recipient to meet those objectives in succeeding budget periods;
3. The recipient has submitted all reports as required by §75.118; and
4. Continuation of the project is in the best interest of the Federal Government.

Notwithstanding any regulatory requirements in 34 CFR Part 80, a grantee may expend funds that have not been obligated at the end of a budget period for obligations of the subsequent budget period if the obligation falls within the scope and objectives of the project and ED regulations (other than 34 CFR Part 80, or the grant conditions do not prohibit the obligation). The Secretary may require a grantee to send a written statement describing how funds made available under this section will be used, and determine the amount of new funds that ED will make available for the subsequent budget period after considering the statement the grantee provides under paragraph (c)(2)(i) of the full Federal section. In determining the amount of new funds to make available to a grantee, the Secretary considers whether the unobligated funds made available are needed to complete activities that were planned for completion in the prior budget period.

If the Secretary decides not to make a continuation award, he or she may authorize a no-cost extension of the last budget period of the grant in order to provide for the orderly closeout of the grant. If the Secretary does decide to make a continuation award under this section, it is made under §§75.231–75.236 and the new budget period begins on the day after the previous budget period ends. Unless prohibited by program regulations, a recipient that is in the final budget period of a project period may seek continued assistance for the project under the procedures for selecting new projects.

Miscellaneous

§ 75.260 Allotments and reallotments.
Under some of the programs covered by this part, the Secretary allots funds under a statutory or regulatory formula. Any reallotment to other grantees will be made in accordance with the authorizing statute for that program.

§ 75.261 Extension of a project period.
General rule. A grantee may, notwithstanding any regulatory requirement in 34 CFR Part 80, extend the project period of an award one time for a period up to 12 months without prior approval of the Secretary, if the grantee meets the requirements for extension of 34 CFR 74.25(e)(2) and ED regulations other than regulations in 34 CFR Part 80, statutes, or the conditions of an award do not prohibit the extension.

Specific rule for certain programs of the National Institute on Disability and Rehabilitation Research. Notwithstanding the above paragraph, grantees under some selected NIDRR programs must request prior approval to extend their grants under the next paragraph of this section.

Other regulations. If ED regulations (other than the regulations in 34 CFR Part 80 or the conditions of the award) require the grantee to get prior approval to extend the project period, the Secretary may permit the grantee to extend the project period if:

1. The extension does not violate any statute or regulations;
2. The extension does not involve the obligation of additional federal funds; and
3. The extension is to carry out the activities in the approved application.

Waiver. The Secretary may waive some requirements of this section if a grantee could not reasonably have known of the need for the extension on or before the start of the 45-day time period, or the failure to give notice on or before the start of the 45-day time period was unavoidable.

§ 75.262 Conversion of a grant or a cooperative agreement.

The Secretary may convert a grant to a cooperative agreement or a cooperative agreement to a grant at the time a continuation award is made under §75.253. In deciding whether to convert a grant to a cooperative agreement or a cooperative agreement to a grant, the factors included in §75.200 are considered. The Secretary and a recipient may agree at any time to such a conversion.

§ 75.263 Pre-award costs; waiver of approval.

A grantee may, notwithstanding any requirement in 34 CFR Part 80, incur pre-award costs as specified in 34 CFR 74.25(e)(1) unless ED regulations other than 34 CFR Part 80 or a statute prohibit these costs, or the conditions of the award prohibit these costs.

§ 75.264 Transfers among budget categories.

A grantee may, notwithstanding any requirement in 34 CFR Part 80, make transfers as specified in 34 CFR 74.25 unless ED regulations other than 34 CFR Part 80 or a statute prohibit these transfers, or the conditions of the grant prohibit these transfers.

Subpart E—What Conditions Must Be Met by a Grantee?

Nondiscrimination

§ 75.500 Federal statutes and regulations on nondiscrimination.

Each grantee shall comply with the following statutes and regulations:

Subject	Statute	Regulations
Discrimination on the basis of race, color or national origin	Title VI of the Civil Rights Act of 1964 (42 U.S.C. 2000d through 2000d–4)	34 CFR Part 100.
Discrimination on the basis of sex	Title IX of the Education Amendments of 1972 (20 U.S.C. 1681–1683)	34 CFR Part 106.
Discrimination on the basis of handicap	Section 504 of the Rehabilitation Act of 1973 (29 U.S.C. 794)	34 CFR Part 104.
Discrimination on the basis of age	The Age Discrimination Act (42 U.S.C. 6101 et seq.)	34 CFR Part 110.

Project Staff

§ 75.511 Waiver of requirement for a full-time project director.
If program regulations require a full-time project director, the Secretary may waive that requirement if the project will not be adversely affected by the waiver, the project director is needed to coordinate two or more related projects, or the project director must teach a minimum number of hours to retain faculty status. The waiver either permits a grantee to use a part-time project director or not to use any.

§ 75.515 Use of consultants.
Subject to Federal statutes and regulations, a grantee shall use its general policies and practices when it hires, uses, and pays a consultant as part of the project staff. The grantee may not use its grant to pay a consultant unless there is a need in the project for the services of that consultant and the grantee cannot meet that need by using an employee rather than a consultant.

§ 75.516 Compensation of consultants—employees of institutions of higher education.
If an institution of higher education receives a grant for research or for educational services, it may pay a consultant's fee to one of its employees only in unusual circumstances and only if the work performed by the consultant is in addition to his or her regular departmental load, the consultation is across departmental lines, or the consultation involves a separate or remote operation.

§ 75.517 Changes in key staff members.
A grantee shall comply with 34 CFR 74.25 concerning replacement or lesser involvement of any key project staff, whether or not the grant is for research.

§ 75.519 Dual compensation of staff.
A grantee may not use its grantee to pay a project staff member for time or work for which that staff member is compensated from some other source of funds.

Conflict of Interest

§ 75.524 Conflict of interest: Purpose of §75.525.
The conflict of interest regulations of the Department that apply to a grant are listed below in §75.525; however, those regulations do not apply to a grantee's procurement contracts (the conflict of interest regulations that cover those procurement contracts are in 34 CFR Part 74). These conflict of interest regulations do not apply to a "government" as defined in 34 CFR 80.3.

§ 75.525 Conflict of interest: Participation in a project.
A grantee may not permit any person participating in the project to use his or her position for a purpose that is—or gives the appearance of being—motivated by a desire for a private financial gain for that person or for others. A grantee may also not permit a person to participate in an administrative decision regarding a project if the decision is likely to benefit that person or a member of his or her immediate family, the person is a public official, or the person has a family or business relationship with the grantee.

Allowable Costs

§ 75.530 General cost principles.
The general principles to be used in determining costs applicable to grants and cost-type contracts under grants are specified at 34 CFR 74.27 (for institutions of higher education and other non-profit organizations) and 34 CFR 80.22 (for grants and cooperative agreements to State and local governments).

§ 75.531 Limit on total cost of a project.
A grantee shall ensure that the total cost to the Federal Government is not more than the amount stated in the notification of grant award.

§ 75.532 Use of funds for religion prohibited.
No grantee may use its grant to pay for religious worship, instruction, or proselytization. Additionally, grantees may not use its grant equipment or supplies for any such activity.

§ 75.533 Acquisition of real property; construction.
No grantee may use its grant for acquisition of real property or for construction unless specifically permitted by the authorizing statute or implementing regulations for the program.

§ 75.534 Training grants—automatic increases for additional dependents.
The Secretary may increase a grant to cover the cost of additional dependents not specified in the notice of award under §75.235 if appropriations are available to cover such costs and allowances for dependents are authorized by the program statute and are allowable under the grant.

Indirect Cost Rates

§ 75.560 General indirect cost rates; exceptions.
The differences between direct and indirect costs and the principles for determining the general indirect cost rate that a grantee may use under most programs are specified in 34 CFR §§ 74.27 and 80.22. If the grantee has a federally recognized indirect cost rate agreement, the Secretary accepts the rate, but may impose restrictions to satisfy any statutory ED program requirements. If a grantee does not have a federally recognized indirect cost rate agreement, the Secretary may permit the grantee to charge its grant for indirect costs at a temporary rate of 10% of budgeted direct salaries and wages.

§ 75.561 Approval of indirect cost rates.
If the ED is the cognizant agency, the Secretary approves an indirect cost rate for a grantee other than a local educational agency (LEA). For the purposes of this section, LEA does not include a State agency. Each State educational agency, on the basis of a plan approved by the Secretary, shall approve an indirect cost rate for each LEA that requests it to do so. These rates may be for periods longer than a year if rates are sufficiently stable to justify a longer period. The Secretary generally approves indirect cost rate agreements annually; however, they may be approved for periods longer than one year if the Secretary determines that rates will be sufficiently stable to justify a longer rate period.

§ 75.562 Indirect cost rates for educational training projects.
Educational training grants provide funding for training or other educational services (i.e., summer institutes, the introduction of new or expanded courses, and similar instructional undertakings separately budgeted and accounted for). These grants do not usually support activities involving research, development, and dissemination of new educational materials and methods. Training grants largely implement previously developed materials and methods and require no significant adaptation of techniques or instructional services to fit different circumstances.

Indirect cost reimbursement on a training grant or subgrant is limited to the recipient's actual indirect costs (as determined in its negotiated indirect cost rate agreement) or 8% of a modified total direct cost (MTDC) base, whichever amount is less. For the purposes of this section, a MTDC base consists of total direct costs minus:

1. The amount of each sub-award in excess of $25,000;
2. Stipends;
3. Tuition and related fees; and
4. Equipment.

The 8% limit does not apply to agencies of State or local governments, including federally recognized Indian tribal governments, as defined in 34 CFR 80.3. Indirect costs in excess of the 8% limit may not be charged directly, used to satisfy matching or cost-sharing requirements, or charged to another Federal award. A grantee using the training rate of 8% is required to have documentation available for audit that shows that its negotiated indirect cost rate is at least 8%.

§ 75.563 Restricted indirect cost rate—programs covered.
If a grantee decides to charge indirect costs to a program that has a statutory requirement prohibiting the use of Federal funds to supplant non-Federal funds, the grantee shall use a restricted indirect cost rate computed under 34 CFR 76.564 through 76.569.

§ 75.564 Reimbursement of indirect costs.
Reimbursement of indirect costs is subject to the availability of funds and statutory or administrative restrictions. The application of the rates and the determination of the direct cost base by a grantee must be in accordance with the indirect cost rate agreement approved by the grantee's cognizant agency. Indirect cost reimbursement is not allowable under grants for:

1. Fellowships and similar awards if Federal financing is exclusively in the form of fixed amounts such as scholarships, stipend allowances, or the tuition and fees of an institution;
2. Construction grants;
3. Grants to individuals;
4. Grants to organizations located outside the territorial limits of the United States;
5. Grants to Federal organizations; and
6. Grants made exclusively to support conferences.

Groups of eligible parties. Indirect costs for a group of eligible parties (See §§75.127 through 75.129) are limited to the amount derived by applying the rate of the applicant, or a restricted rate when applicable, to the direct cost base for the grant in keeping with the terms of the applicant's federally recognized indirect cost rate agreement. If a group of eligible parties applies for a training grant under the group application procedures in §§75.127 through 75.129, the grant funds allocated among the members of the group are not considered sub-awards for the purposes of applying the indirect cost rate in §75.562(c).

§ 75.580 Coordination with other activities.
A grantee shall, to the extent possible, coordinate its project with other activities that are in the same geographic area served by the project and that serve similar purposes and target groups.

Evaluation

§ 75.590 Evaluation by the recipient.
A recipient shall submit an annual performance report (or final report for the last year of a project) that evaluates:

1. The recipient's progress in achieving the objectives in its approved application;
2. The effectiveness of the project in meeting the purposes of the program; and
3. The effect of the project on participants being served by the project.

§ 75.591 Federal evaluation—cooperation by a grantee.
A grantee shall cooperate in any evaluation of the program by the Secretary.

§ 75.592 Federal evaluation—satisfying requirement for grantee evaluation.
If a grantee cooperates in a Federal evaluation of a program, the Secretary may determine that the grantee meets the evaluation requirements of the program, including §75.590.

Construction

§ 75.600 Use of a grant for construction: Purpose of §§75.601–75.615.
Sections 75.601–75.615 apply to an applicant that requests funds for construction and a grantee whose grant includes funds for construction.

§ 75.601 Applicant's assessment of environmental impact.
An applicant shall include with its application its assessment of the impact of the proposed construction on the quality of the environment in accordance with section 102(2)(C) of the National Environmental Policy Act of 1969 and E.O. 11514 (34 FR 4247).

§ 75.602 Preservation of historic sites must be described in the application.
An applicant shall describe in its application the relationship of the proposed construction to and probable effect on any district, site, building, structure, or object that is included in the National Register of Historic Places or eligible under criteria established by the Secretary of Interior for such inclusion. In deciding whether to make a grant, the Secretary considers the information provided by the applicant and any comments by the Advisory Council on Historic Preservation.

§ 75.603 Grantee's title to site.
A grantee must have or obtain a full title or other interest in the site, including right of access, that is sufficient to ensure the grantee's undisturbed use and possession of the facilities for 50 years or the useful life of the facilities, whichever is longer.

§ 75.604 Availability of cost-sharing funds.
A grantee shall ensure that sufficient funds are available to meet any non-Federal share of the cost of constructing the facility.

§ 75.605 Beginning the construction.
A grantee shall begin work on construction within a reasonable time after the grant for the construction is made. Before construction is advertised or placed on the market for bidding, the grantee shall get approval by the Secretary of the final working drawings and specifications.

§ 75.606 Completing the construction.
A grantee shall complete its construction within a reasonable time, in accordance with the application and approved drawings and specifications.

§ 75.607 General considerations in designing facilities and carrying out construction.
A grantee shall ensure that the construction is functional, economical, and not elaborate in design (or extravagant in the use of materials) as compared with facilities of a similar type constructed in the geographic area. In developing plans for the facilities, the grantee shall consider excellence of architecture and design and inclusion of works of art (however, the grantee may not spend more than 1% of the cost of the project on inclusion of works of art).

§ 75.608 Areas in the facilities for cultural activities.
A grantee may make reasonable provision, consistent with the other uses to be made of the facilities, for areas in the facilities that are adaptable for artistic and other cultural activities.

§ 75.609 Comply with safety and health standards.
In planning for and designing facilities, grantees shall observe OSHA standards (Pub. L. 91–576) and all applicable state and local codes (to the extent that they are more stringent).

§ 75.610 Access by the handicapped.
A grantee shall comply with the Federal regulations on access by the handicapped that apply to construction and alteration of facilities. These regulations are:

1. For residential facilities: 24 CFR Part 40; and
2. For non-residential facilities: 41 CFR Subpart 101–19.6.

§ 75.611 Avoidance of flood hazards.
In planning the construction, a grantee shall:

1. Evaluate flood hazards in connection with the construction; and
2. As far as practicable, avoid uneconomic, hazardous, or unnecessary use of flood plains in connection with the construction.

§ 75.612 Supervision and inspection by the grantee.
A grantee shall maintain competent architectural engineering supervision and inspection at the construction site to ensure that the work conforms to the approved drawings and specifications.

§ 75.613 Relocation assistance by the grantee.
Grantees are subject to regulations on relocation assistance and real property acquisition in 34 CFR Part 15.

§ 75.614 Grantee must have operational funds.
A grantee shall ensure that sufficient funds will be available for the effective operation and maintenance of the facilities when construction is completed.

§ 75.615 Operation and maintenance by the grantee.
Grantees shall operate and maintain facilities in accordance with Federal, State, and local requirements.

§ 75.616 Energy conservation.
To the extent feasible, a grantee shall design and construct facilities (built with Federal project funds) to maximize the efficient use of energy (see the standards of the American Society of Heating, Refrigerating, and Air Conditioning Engineers as listed in the full section).

§ 75.617 Compliance with the Coastal Barrier Resources Act.
A recipient may not use, within the Coastal Barrier Resources System, funds made available under a program administered by ED for any purpose prohibited by 31 U.S.C. Chapter 55 (sections 3501–3510).

Equipment and Supplies

§ 75.618 Charges for use of equipment or supplies.
A grantee may not charge students or school personnel for the ordinary use of equipment or supplies purchased with grant funds.

Publications and Copyrights

§ 75.620 General conditions on publication.
Subject to any specific requirements that apply to its grant, a grantee may decide the format and content of project materials that it publishes or arranges to have published. The grantee shall ensure that any publication that contains project materials also contains the following statements:

> *"The contents of this (insert type of publication; e.g., book, report, film) were developed under a grant from the Department of Education. However, those contents do not necessarily represent the policy of the Department of Education, and you should not assume endorsement by the Federal Government."*

§ 75.621 Copyright policy for grantees.
A grantee may copyright project materials in accordance with 34 CFR Part 74 or 80, as appropriate.

§ 75.622 Definition of "project materials."
As used in §§75.620–75.621, "project materials" means a copyrightable work developed with funds from a grant of the Department.

Inventions and Patents

§ 75.626 Show Federal support; give papers to vest title.
Any patent application filed by a grantee for an invention made under a grant must include the following statement in the first paragraph: "The invention described in this application was made under a grant from the Department of Education."

Other Requirements for Certain Projects

§ 75.650 Participation of students enrolled in private schools.
If the authorizing statute for a program requires a grantee to provide for participation by students enrolled in private schools, the grantee shall provide a genuine opportunity for equitable participation in accordance with the requirements that apply to subgrantees under 34 CFR 76.650–76.662.

§ 75.681 Protection of human research subjects.
If a grantee uses a human subject in a research project, the grantee shall protect the person from physical, psychological, or social injury resulting from the project. Cross reference: 34 CFR Part 97.

§ 75.682 Treatment of animals.
If a grantee uses an animal in a project, the grantee shall provide the animal with proper care and humane treatment in accordance with the Animal Welfare Act of 1970.

§ 75.683 Health or safety standards for facilities.
A grantee shall comply with any Federal health or safety requirements that apply to the facilities that the grantee uses for the project.

Subpart F—What Are the Administrative Responsibilities of a Grantee?

General Administrative Responsibilities

§ 75.700 Compliance with statutes, regulations, and applications.
A grantee shall comply with applicable statutes, regulations, and approved applications, and shall use Federal funds in accordance with those statutes, regulations, and applications.

§ 75.701 The grantee administers or supervises the project.
A grantee shall directly administer or supervise the administration of the project.

§ 75.702 Fiscal control and fund accounting procedures.
A grantee shall use fiscal control and fund accounting procedures that ensure proper disbursement of and accounting for Federal funds.

§ 75.703 Obligation of funds during the grant period.
A grantee may use grant funds only for obligations it makes during the grant period.

§ 75.707 When obligations are made.
The following table shows when a grantee makes obligations for various kinds of property and services:

If the obligation is for—	The obligation is made—
1. Acquisition of real or personal property	On the date the grantee makes a binding written commitment to acquire the property.
2. Personal services by an employee of the grantee	When the services are performed.
3. Personnal services by a contractor who is not an employee of the grantee	On the date on which the grantee makes a binding written commitment to obtain the services.
4. Performance of work other than personal services	On the date on which the grantee makes a binding written commitment to obtain the work.
5. Public utility services	When the grantee receives the services.
6. Travel	When the travel is taken.
7. Rental of real or personal property	When the grantee uses the property.
8. A preagreement cost that was properly approved by the Secretary under the cost principles identified in 34 CFR 74.171 or 80.22	

§ 75.708 Prohibition of subgrants.
A grantee may not make a subgrant under a program covered by this part unless specifically authorized by statute. A grantee may contract for supplies, equipment, construction, and other services, in accordance with 34 CFR Part 74, Subpart C—Post-Award Requirements (Procurement Standards §§74.40–74.48) and 34 CFR Part 80, Subpart C—Post-Award Requirements (§80.36 Procurement).

Reports

§ 75.720 Financial and performance reports.
This section applies to the reports required under 34 CFR 74.51, 34 CFR 74.52, 34 CFR 80.40, and 34 CFR 80.41. A grantee shall submit these reports annually, unless the Secretary allows less frequent reporting.

However, the Secretary may require a grantee of a grant made under 34 CFR Part 700, 706, 707, or 708 (certain programs of the Office of Educational Research and Improvement) to submit performance reports more often than annually. The Secretary may require a grantee to report more frequently than annually under 34 CFR 74.14 (Special award conditions), 34 CFR 74.21 (Standards for financial management systems), 34 CFR 80.12 (Special grant or subgrant conditions for "high-risk" grantees) or 34 CFR 80.20 (Standards for financial management systems).

Records

§ 75.730 Records related to grant funds.
A grantee shall keep records that fully show the amount of funds under the grant, how the grantee uses the funds, the total cost of the project, the share of that cost provided from other sources, and other records to facilitate an effective audit.

§ 75.731 Records related to compliance.
A grantee shall keep records to show its compliance with program requirements.

§ 75.732 Records related to performance.
A grantee shall keep records of significant project experiences and results and use the records to determine progress in accomplishing project objectives (and revise those objectives, if necessary).

Privacy

§ 75.740 Protection of and access to student records; student rights in research, experimental programs, and testing.
Most records on present or past students are subject to the requirements of section 444 of GEPA and its implementing regulations in 34 CFR Part 99 (Family Educational Rights and Privacy Act of 1974.) Under most programs administered by the Secretary, research, experimentation, and testing are subject to the requirements of section 445 of GEPA and its implementing regulations at 34 CFR Part 98.

Subpart G—What Procedures Does the Department Use To Get Compliance?

§ 75.900 Waiver of regulations prohibited.
No official, agent, or employee of ED may waive any regulation that applies to a Department program, unless the regulation specifically provides that it may be waived. No act or failure to act by an official, agent, or employee of ED can affect the authority of the Secretary to enforce regulations.

§ 75.901 Suspension and termination.
The Secretary may use the Education Appeal Board to resolve disputes not subject to other procedures.

§ 75.903 Effective date of termination.
Termination is effective on the latest of:

1. The date of delivery to the grantee of the notice of termination;
2. The termination date given in the notice of termination; or
3. The date of a final decision of the Secretary under Part 78 of this title.

§ 75.910 Cooperation with audits.
A grantee shall cooperate with the Secretary and U.S. Comptroller General (or any duly authorized representatives) in the conduct of Federally authorized audits. This includes access without unreasonable restrictions to records and personnel of the grantee for the purpose of obtaining relevant information.

PART 76—STATE-ADMINISTERED PROGRAMS

Subpart A—General

Regulations That Apply to State-Administered Programs

§ 76.1 Programs to which Part 76 applies.
The regulations in Part 76 apply to each State-administered program of ED. If a State formula grant program does not have implementing regulations, the Secretary implements the program under the authorizing statute, GEPA, and the regulations in this part. For the purposes of this part, the term State formula grant program means a program whose authorizing statute or implementing regulations provide a formula for allocating program funds among eligible States.

§ 76.2 Exceptions in program regulations to Part 76.
If a program has regulations that are not consistent with Part 76, the implementing regulations for that program will identify the sections of Part 76 that do not apply.

Eligibility for a Grant or Subgrant

§ 76.50 Statutes determine eligibility and whether subgrants are made.
Under a program covered by this part, the Secretary makes a grant to the State agency designated by the authorizing statute for the program, or to the State agency designated by the State in accordance with the authorizing statute. The authorizing statute determines the extent to which a State may use grant funds directly and make subgrants to eligible applicants. The regulations in Part 76 on subgrants apply to a program only if subgrants are authorized under that program. The authorizing statute determines the eligibility of an applicant for a subgrant.

§ 76.51 A State distributes funds by formula or competition.
If a program statute authorizes a State to make subgrants, the statute:

1. Requires the State to use a formula to distribute funds;
2. Gives the State discretion to select subgrantees through a competition among the applicants or through some other procedure; or
3. Allows some combination of these procedures.

§ 76.52 Eligibility of faith-based organizations for a subgrant.
A faith-based organization is eligible to apply for and receive a subgrant under an ED program on the same basis as any other private organization. A private organization that engages in inherently religious activities, such as religious worship, instruction, or proselytization, must offer those services separately in time or location from programs /services supported by a subgrant from a State under a State-administered program of ED, and participation in any such inherently religious activities by beneficiaries of the programs supported by the subgrant must be voluntary (see § 76.532). A faith-based organization may:

1. Retain religious terms in its name;
2. Continue to carry out its mission, including the definition, development, practice, and expression of its religious beliefs;
3. Use its facilities to provide services without removing or altering religious art, icons, scriptures, or other symbols from these facilities;
4. Select its board members and otherwise govern itself on a religious basis; and
5. Include religious references in its mission statement and other chartering or governing documents.

Subpart B—How a State Applies for a Grant

State Plans and Applications

§ 76.100 Effect of this subpart.

This subpart establishes general requirements that a State must meet to apply for a grant under a program covered by this part. Additional requirements are in the authorizing statute and implementing program regulations.

§ 76.101 The general State application.

A State that makes subgrants to local educational agencies under a program subject to this part shall have on file with the Secretary a general application that meets the requirements of section 441 of the GEPA.

§ 76.102 Definition of "State plan" for Part 76.

As used in this part, State plan means any of the following documents:

Document	Program	Authorizing statute	Principal Office
State plan	Assistance to States for Education of Handicapped Children	Part B (except section 619), Individuals with Disabilities Education Act (20 U.S.C. 1411–1420)	OSERS
Application	Preschool Grants	Section 619, Individuals with Disabilities Education Act (20 U.S.C. 1419)	OSERS
Application	Handicapped Infants and Toddlers	Part H, Individuals with Disabilities Education Act (20 U.S.C. 1471–1485)	OSERS
Application or written request for assistance	Client Assistance Program	Section 112, Rehabilitation Act of 1973 (29 U.S.C. 732)	OSERS
Application	Removal of Architectural Barriers to the Handicapped Program	Section 607, Individuals with Disabilities Education Act (20 U.S.C. 1406)	OSERS
State plan	State Vocational Rehabilitation Services Program	Title I, Parts A-C, Rehabilitation Act of 1973 (29 U.S.C. 720–741)	OSERS
State plan supplement	State Supported Employment Services Program	Title VI, Part C, Rehabilitation Act of 1973 (29 U.S.C. 795j–795r)	OSERS
State plan	State Independent Living Services Program	Title VII, Part A, Rehabilitation Act of 1973 (29 U.S.C. 796–796d)	OSERS
State plan	State Vocational Education Program	Title I, Part B, Carl D. Perkins Vocational Education Act (20 U.S.C. 2321–2325)	OVAE
State plan and application	State-Administered Adult Education Program	Section 341, Adult Education Act (20 U.S.C. 1206)	OVAE
State plan	Even Start Family Literacy Program	Title I, Chapter 1, Part B of the Elementary and Secondary Education Act of 1965 (20 U.S.C. 2741–2749)	OESE
State application	State Grants for Strengthening Instruction in Mathematics and Science	Title II, Part A, Elementary and Secondary Education Act of 1965, as amended (20 U.S.C. 2981–2993)	OESE

State application	Federal, State and Local Partnership for Educational Improvement	Title I, Chapter 2, Elementary and Secondary Education Act of 1965, as amended (20 U.S.C. 2911–2952 and 2971–2976)	OESE
State plan or application	Migrant Education Program	Sections 1201, 1202, Chapter 1, Title I, Elementary and Secondary Education Act of 1965, as amended (20 U.S.C. 2781 and 2782)	OESE
Application	State Student Incentive Grant Program	Section 415C, Higher Education Act of 1965 (20 U.S.C. 1070c–2)	OPE
Application	Paul Douglas Teacher Scholarship Program	Section 553, Higher Education Act of 1965 (20 U.S.C. 1111b)	OPE
Basic State plan, long-range program, and annual program	The Library Services and Construction Act State-Administered Program	Library Services and Construction Act (20 U.S.C. 351–355e–3)	OERI
Application	Emergency Immigrant Education Program	Emergency Immigrant Education Act (20 U.S.C. 3121–3130)	OBEMLA
Application	Transition Program for Refugee Children	Section 412(d) Immigration and Naturalization Act (8 U.S.C. 1522 (d))	OBEMLA
Any document that the authorizing statute for a State-administered program requires a State to submit to receive funds	Any State-administered program without implementing regulations	Section 408(a)(1), GEPA and Section 414, ED Organization Act (20 U.S.C. 1221e–3(a)(1) and 3474)	Dept-wide

§ 76.103 Multi-year State plans.

Each State plan will be effective for a period of more than one fiscal year, determined by the Secretary or by regulations. If the Secretary determines that the multi-year State plans should be submitted by the States on a staggered schedule, the Secretary may require groups of States to submit or resubmit their plans in different years. If a State submits an annual plan under the Vocational Education Act, this section does not apply.

§ 76.104 A State shall include certain certifications in its State plan.

A State shall include the following certifications in each State plan:

1. That the plan is submitted by the State agency that is eligible to submit the plan.
2. That the State agency has authority under State law to perform the functions of the State under the program.
3. That the State legally may carry out each provision of the plan.
4. That all provisions of the plan are consistent with State law.
5. That a State officer, specified by title in the certification, has authority under State law to receive, hold, and disburse Federal funds made available under the plan.
6. That the State officer who submits the plan, specified by title in the certification, has authority to submit the plan.
7. That the agency that submits the plan has adopted or otherwise formally approved the plan.
8. That the plan is the basis for State operation and administration of the program.

§ 76.106 State documents are public information.
A State shall make the following documents available for public inspection:

1. All State plans and related official materials;
2. All approved subgrant applications; and
3. All documents that the Secretary transmits to the State regarding a program.

Consolidated Grant Applications for Insular Areas

§ 76.125 What is the purpose of these regulations?
Sections 76.125 through 76.137 contain requirements for the submission of an application by an Insular Area for the consolidation of two or more grants under an annual consolidated grant to assist an Insular Area in carrying out one or more State-administered formula grant programs of ED. For the purpose of these sections, the term Insular Area means the Virgin Islands, Guam, American Samoa, the Trust Territory of the Pacific Islands, or the Commonwealth of the Northern Mariana Islands.

§ 76.126 What regulations apply to the consolidated grant applications for insular areas?
The following regulations apply to those programs included in a consolidated grant:

1. The regulations in §§76.125 through 76.137; and
2. The regulations that apply to each specific program included in a consolidated grant for which funds are used.

§ 76.127 What is the purpose of a consolidated grant?
An Insular Area may apply for a consolidated grant for two or more of the programs listed in §76.125(c). This procedure is intended to:

1. Simplify the application and reporting procedures that would otherwise apply for each of the programs included in the consolidated grant; and
2. Provide the insular area with flexibility in allocating the funds under the consolidated grant to achieve any of the purposes to be served by the programs that are consolidated.

§ 76.128 What is a consolidated grant?
A consolidated grant is a grant to an Insular Area for any two or more of the programs listed in §76.125(c). The amount of the consolidated grant is the sum of the allocations the Insular Area receives under each of the programs included in the consolidated grant if there had been no consolidation.

§ 76.129 How does a consolidated grant work?
An Insular Area shall use funds it receives under a consolidated grant to carry out, in its jurisdiction, one or more programs included in the grant. An Insular Area shall comply with the statutory and regulatory requirements that apply to each program under which funds from the consolidated grant are expended.

§ 76.130 How are consolidated grants made?
The Secretary annually makes a single consolidated grant to each Insular Area that meets the requirements of §§76.125 through 76.137 and each program under which the grant funds are to be used and administered. The Secretary may decide that one or more programs cannot be included in the consolidated grant if it is determined that the Insular Area failed to meet the program objectives stated in its plan for the previous fiscal year in which it carried out the programs.

§ 76.131 How does an insular area apply for a consolidated grant?
An Insular Area that desires to apply for a grant consolidating two or more programs listed in §76.125(c) shall submit to the Secretary an application that contains the assurances in §76.132 and meets the appropri-

ate application requirements. An Insular Area shall include in its consolidated grant application a program plan that:

1. Contains a list of the programs in §76.125(c) to be included in the consolidated grant;
2. Describes the program or programs in §76.125(c) under which the consolidated grant funds will be used and administered;
3. Describes the goals, objectives, activities, and the means of evaluating program outcomes for the programs for which the Insular Area will use the funds received under the consolidated grant during the fiscal year for which it submits the application, including needs of the population that will be met by the consolidation of funds; and
4. Contains a budget that includes a description of the allocation of funds—including any anticipated carryover funds of the program in the consolidated grant from the preceding year—among the programs to be included in the consolidated grant.

§ 76.132 What assurances must be in a consolidated grant application?

An Insular Area shall include in its consolidated grant application assurances to the Secretary that it will:

1. Follow policies and use administrative practices that will ensure that non-Federal funds will not be supplanted by Federal funds made available under the authority of the programs in the consolidated grant;
2. Comply with the requirements (except those relating to the submission of State plans or similar documents) in the authorizing statutes and implementing regulations for the programs under which funds are to be used and administered, (except requirements for matching funds);
3. Provide for proper and efficient administration of funds in accordance with the authorizing statutes and implementing regulations for those programs under which funds are to be used and administered;
4. Provide for fiscal control and fund accounting procedures to assure proper disbursement of, and accounting for, Federal funds received under the consolidated grant;
5. Submit an annual report to the Secretary containing information covering the program or programs for which the grant is used and administered, including the financial and program performance information required under 34 CFR 74.51–74.52 and 34 CFR 80.40–80.41.
6. Provide that funds received under the consolidated grant will be under control of, and that title to property acquired with these funds will be in, a public agency, institution, or organization. The public agency shall administer these funds and property;
7. Keep records, including a copy of the State Plan or application document under which funds are to be spent, which show how the funds received under the consolidated grant have been spent.
8. Adopt and use methods of monitoring and providing technical assistance to any agencies, organizations, or institutions that carry out the programs under the consolidated grant and enforce any obligations imposed on them under the applicable statutes and regulations.
9. Evaluate the effectiveness of these programs in meeting the purposes and objectives in the authorizing statutes under which program funds are used and administered;
10. Conduct evaluations of these programs at intervals and in accordance with procedures the Secretary may prescribe; and
11. Provide appropriate opportunities for participation by local agencies, representatives of the groups affected by the programs, and other interested institutions, organizations, and individuals in planning and operating the programs.

§ 76.133 What is the reallocation authority?

After an Insular Area receives a consolidated grant, it may reallocate the funds in a manner different from the allocation described in its consolidated grant application. Funds cannot be used for purposes not authorized under the programs in the applicable consolidated grant. If an Insular Area decides to reallocate the funds received under a consolidated grant, it shall notify the Secretary by amending its original application to include updated information required under §76.131.

§ 76.134 What is the relationship between consolidated and non-consolidated grants?
An Insular Area may request that any number of programs in §76.125(c) be included in its consolidated grant and may apply separately for assistance under any other programs listed in §76.125(c) for which it is eligible.

§ 76.135 Are there any requirements for matching funds?
The Secretary waives all requirements for matching funds for those programs that are consolidated by an Insular Area in a consolidated grant application.

§ 76.136 Under what programs may consolidated grant funds be spent?
Insular Areas may only use and administer funds under programs described in §76.125(c) during a fiscal year for which the Insular Area is entitled to receive funds under an appropriation for that program.

§ 76.137 How may carryover funds be used under the consolidated grant application?
Funds under any applicable program available for obligation and expenditure in the year succeeding the fiscal year for which they are appropriated must be obligated and expended in accordance with the consolidated grant application submitted by the Insular Area for that program for the succeeding fiscal year.

Amendments

§ 76.140 Amendments to a State plan.
If the Secretary determines that an amendment to a State plan is essential during the effective period of the plan, the State shall make the amendment. A State shall also amend a State plan if there is a significant and relevant change in:

1. The information or the assurances in the plan;
2. The administration or operation of the plan; or
3. The organization, policies, or operations of the State agency that received the grant, if the change materially affects the information or assurances in the plan.

§ 76.141 An amendment requires the same procedures as the document being amended.
If a State amends a plan under §76.140, the State shall use the same procedures as those it must use to prepare and submit a State plan.

§ 76.142 An amendment is approved on the same basis as the document being amended.
The Secretary uses the same procedures to approve an amendment to a State plan—or any other document a State submits—as the Secretary uses to approve the original document.

Subpart C—How a Grant Is Made to a State

Approval or Disapproval by the Secretary

§ 76.201 A State plan must meet all statutory and regulatory requirements.
The Secretary approves a State plan if it meets the requirements of the Federal statutes and regulations that apply to the plan.

§ 76.202 Opportunity for a hearing before a State plan is disapproved.
The Secretary may disapprove a State plan only after:

1. Notifying the State;
2. Offering the State a reasonable opportunity for a hearing; and
3. Holding the hearing, if requested by the State.

§ 76.235 The notification of grant award.
To make a grant to a State, the Secretary issues and sends to the State a notification of grant award, which identifies the amount of the grant and provides other information about the grant.

Allotments and Reallotments of Grant Funds

§ 76.260 Allotments are made under program statute or regulations.
The Secretary allots program funds to a State in accordance with the authorizing statute or implementing regulations for the program. Any reallotment to other States will be made by the Secretary in accordance with the authorizing statute or implementing regulations for that program.

§ 76.261 Reallotted funds are part of a State's grant.
Funds that a State receives as a result of a reallotment are part of the State's grant for the appropriate fiscal year. However, the Secretary does not consider a reallotment in determining the maximum or minimum amount to which a State is entitled for a following fiscal year.

Subpart D—How To Apply to the State for a Subgrant

§ 76.300 Contact the State for procedures to follow.
An applicant for a subgrant can find out the procedures it must follow by contacting the State agency that administers the program.

§ 76.301 Local educational agency general application.
A local educational agency that applies for a subgrant under a program subject to this part shall have on file with the State a general application that meets the requirements of Section 442 of GEPA.

§ 76.302 The notice to the subgrantee.
A State shall notify a subgrantee in writing of the amount of the subgrant, the period during which the subgrantee may obligate the funds, and the Federal requirements that apply to the subgrant.

§ 76.303 Joint applications and projects.
Two or more eligible parties may submit a joint application for a subgrant. If the State must use a formula to distribute subgrant funds (see §76.51), it may not make a subgrant that exceeds the sum of the entitlements of the separate subgrantees. If the State funds the application, each subgrantee shall carry out the activities that the subgrantee agreed to carry out, and use the funds in accordance with Federal requirements. Each subgrantee shall use an accounting system that permits identification of the costs paid for under its subgrant.

§ 76.304 Subgrantee shall make subgrant application available to the public.
A subgrantee shall make any application, evaluation, periodic program plan, or report relating to each program available for public inspection.

Subpart E—How a Subgrant Is Made to an Applicant

§ 76.400 State procedures for reviewing an application.
A State that receives an application for a subgrant shall take the following steps:

1. *Review.* The State shall review the application.
2. *Approval—entitlement programs.* The State shall approve an application if first, the application is submitted by an applicant that is entitled to receive a subgrant under the program; and second, the applicant meets the requirements of the Federal statutes and regulations that apply to the program.

3. *Approval—discretionary programs.* The State may approve an application if first, the application is submitted by an eligible applicant under a program in which the State has the discretion to select subgrantees; second, the applicant meets the requirements of the Federal statutes and regulations that apply to the program; and third, the State determines that the project should be funded under the authorizing statute and implementing regulations for the program.
4. *Disapproval—entitlement and discretionary programs.* If an application does not comply with applicable Federal statutes and regulations, the State shall not approve the application.

§ 76.401 Disapproval of an application—opportunity for a hearing.
State agency hearing before disapproval. Under the programs listed in the chart below, the State agency that administers the program shall provide an applicant with notice and an opportunity for a hearing before it may disapprove the application.

Program	Authorizing statute	34 CFR Part
Chapter 1, Program in Local Educational Agencies	Title I, Chapter 1, Elementary and Secondary Education Act of 1965, as amended (20 U.S.C. 2701–2731, 2821–2838, 2851–2854, and 2891–2901)	200
Chapter 1, Program for Neglected and Delinquent Children	Title 1, Chapter 1, Elementary and Secondary Education Act of 1965, as amended (20 U.S.C. 2801–2804)	203
State Grants for Strengthening Instruction in Mathematics and Science	Title II, Part A, Elementary and Secondary Education Act of 1965, as amended (20 U.S.C. 2981–2993)	208
Federal, State, and Local Partnership for Educational Improvement	Title I, Chapter 2, Elementary and Secondary Education Act of 1965, as amended (20 U.S.C. 2911–2952 and 2971–2976)	298
Assistance to States for Education of Handicapped Children	Part B, Individuals with Disabilities Education Act (except Section 619) (20 U.S.C. 1411–1420)	300
Preschool Grants	Section 619, Individuals with Disabilities Education Act (20 U.S.C. 1419)	301
Chapter 1, State-Operated or Supported Programs for Handicapped Children	Title 1, Chapter 1, Elementary and Secondary Education Act of 1965, as amended (20 U.S.C. 2791–2795)	302
Transition Program for Refugee Children	Section 412(d), Immigration and Naturalization Act (8 U.S.C. 1522(d))	538
Emergency Immigrant Education Program	Emergency Immigrant Education Act (20 U.S.C. 3121–3130)	581
Financial Assistance for Construction, Reconstruction, or Renovation of Higher Education Facilities	Section 711, Higher Education Act of 1965 (20 U.S.C. 1132b)	617

Other programs—hearings not required. Under other programs covered by this part, a State agency (other than a SEA) is not required to provide a hearing regarding the agency's disapproval of an application. If a subgrant applicant alleges that any of the following actions of a State educational agency violates a State or Federal statute or regulation, the SEA and the applicant shall follow the procedures in paragraph (d) of the full section:

1. Disapproval of or failure to approve the application or project in whole or in part; or
2. Failure to provide funds in amounts in accordance with the requirements of statutes and regulations.

State educational agency hearing procedures.

1. If the applicant applied under a program listed in the above table, the SEA shall provide an opportunity for a hearing before the agency disapproves the application.
2. If the applicant applied under a program not listed in the table, the SEA shall provide an opportunity for a hearing either before or after the agency disapproves the application.
3. The applicant shall request the hearing within 30 days of the action of the SEA.
4. Within 30 days after it receives a request, the SEA shall hold a hearing on the record and shall review its action. No later than 10 days after the hearing, the agency shall issue its written ruling, including findings of fact and reasons for the ruling. If the agency determines that its action was contrary to State or Federal statutes or regulations that govern the applicable program, the agency shall rescind its action.
5. If the SEA does not rescind its final action after a review under this paragraph, the applicant may appeal by filing a notice of the appeal to the Secretary within 20 days after the applicant has been notified by the SEA of the results of the review.
6. The Secretary may also issue interim orders to SEAs as appropriate. If the Secretary determines that the action of the SEA was contrary to Federal statutes or regulations that govern the applicable program, he or she issues an order that requires the SEA to take appropriate action.
7. Each SEA shall make available to each applicant all records pertaining to any review or appeal the applicant is conducting under this section, including records of other applicants.
8. If a SEA does not comply with any provision of this section, or with any order, the Secretary terminates all assistance to the SEA under the applicable program or issues such other orders as he or she deems appropriate to achieve compliance.

Other State agency hearing procedures. State agencies that are required to provide a hearing under the first paragraph of this section (other than SEAs) are not required to use the State educational agency hearing procedures of this section.

Subpart F—What Conditions Must Be Met by the State and Its Subgrantees?

Nondiscrimination

§ 76.500 Federal statutes and regulations on nondiscrimination.

A State and a subgrantee shall comply with the following statutes and regulations:

Subject	Statute	Regulation
Discrimination on the basis of race, color, or national origin	Civil Rights Act of 1964 Title VI (45 U.S.C. 2000d through 2000d–4)	34 CFR Part 100
Discrimination on the basis of sex	Education Amendments of 1972 Title IX (20 U.S.C. 1681–1683)	34 CFR Part 106
Discrimination on the basis of handicap	Rehabilitation Act of 1973 Section 504 (29 U.S.C. 794)	34 CFR Part 104
Discrimination on the basis of age	The Age Discrimination Act (42 U.S.C. 6101 et seq.)	34 CFR Part 110

Allowable Costs

§ 76.530 General cost principles.
Both 34 CFR 74.27 and 34 CFR 80.22 reference the general cost principles that apply to grants, subgrants and cost type contracts under grants and subgrants.

§ 76.532 Use of funds for religion prohibited.
No State or subgrantee may use its grant or subgrant to pay for religious worship, instruction, or proselytization (or any equipment or supplies used for such activities).

§ 76.533 Acquistion of real property; construction.
No State or subgrantee may use its grant or subgrant for acquisition of real property or for construction unless specifically permitted by the authorizing statute or implementing regulations for the program.

§ 76.534 Use of tuition and fees restricted.
No State or subgrantee may count tuition and fees collected from students toward meeting matching, cost sharing, or maintenance of effort requirements of a program.

Indirect Cost Rates

§ 76.560 General indirect cost rates; exceptions.
The differences between direct and indirect costs and the principles for determining the general indirect cost rate that a grantee may use for grants under most programs are specified in the cost principles at 34 CFR 74.27 and 80.22. A grantee must have a current indirect cost rate agreement to charge indirect costs to a grant. The Secretary accepts an indirect cost rate negotiated by a grantee's cognizant agency, but may establish a restricted indirect cost rate for a grantee to satisfy the statutory requirements of certain programs administered by ED.

§ 76.561 Approval of indirect cost rates.
If ED is the cognizant agency, the Secretary approves an indirect cost rate for a State agency and a subgrantee (other than a local educational agency, or LEA). For the purposes of this section, LEA does not include a State agency. Each SEA, on the basis of a plan approved by the Secretary, shall approve an indirect cost rate for each LEA that requests it to do so. These rates may be for longer than a year if rates are sufficiently stable to justify a longer period. The Secretary generally approves indirect cost rate agreements annually, but may be approved for periods longer than a year if the rates will be sufficiently stable to justify a longer rate period.

§ 76.563 Restricted indirect cost rate—programs covered.
Sections 76.564 through 76.569 apply to agencies of State and local governments that are grantees under programs with a statutory requirement prohibiting the use of Federal funds to supplant non-Federal funds.

§ 76.564 Restricted indirect cost rate—formula.
An indirect cost rate for a grant covered by §76.563 or 34 CFR 75.563 is determined by the following formula:

Restricted indirect cost rate=
(General management costs + Fixed costs)÷(Other expenditures)

General management costs, fixed costs, and other expenditures must be determined under §§76.565 through 76.567. Indirect costs that are unrecovered as a result of these restrictions may not be charged directly, used to satisfy matching or cost-sharing requirements, or charged to another Federal award.

§ 76.565 General management costs—restricted rate.
General management costs (as used in§76.564) means the costs of activities that are for the direction and control of the grantee's affairs that are organization-wide. An activity is not organization-wide if it is limited to one activity, one component of the grantee, one subject, one phase of operations, or other single responsibility. General management costs include service functions (such as accounting, payroll preparation, or personnel management) that are normally at the grantee's level even if the function is physically located elsewhere for convenience or better management. The term also includes certain occupancy and space maintenance costs as determined under §76.568. The term does not include expenditures for:

1. Divisional administration that is limited to one component of the grantee;
2. The governing body of the grantee;
3. Compensation of the chief executive officer of the grantee;
4. Compensation of the chief executive officer of any component of the grantee; and
5. Operation of the immediate offices of these officers.

§ 76.566 Fixed costs—restricted rate.
As used in §76.564, fixed costs means contributions of the grantee to fringe benefits and similar costs, but only those associated with salaries and wages that are charged as indirect costs, including:

1. Retirement, including State, county, or local retirement funds, Social Security, and pension payments;
2. Unemployment compensation payments; and
3. Property, employee, health, and liability insurance.

§ 76.567 Other expenditures—restricted rate.
As used in §76.564, other expenditures means the grantee's total expenditures for its federally- and non-federally-funded activities in the most recent year for which data are available. The term also includes direct occupancy and space maintenance costs as determined under §76.568 and costs related to the chief executive officers of the grantee and components of the grantee and their offices. The term does not include:

1. General management costs determined under §76.565;
2. Fixed costs determined under §76.566;
3. Subgrants;
4. Capital outlay;
5. Debt service;
6. Fines and penalties;
7. Contingencies; and
8. Election expenses.

§ 76.568 Occupancy and space maintenance costs—restricted rate.
As used in the calculation of a restricted indirect cost rate, occupancy and space maintenance costs means such costs as:

1. Building costs whether owned or rented;
2. Janitorial services and supplies;
3. Building, grounds, and parking lot maintenance;
4. Guard services;
5. Light, heat, and power;
6. Depreciation, use allowances, and amortization; and
7. All other related space costs.

Occupancy and space maintenance costs associated with organization-wide service functions (accounting, payroll, and personnel) may be included as general management costs if a space allocation or use study supports the allocation. Occupancy and space maintenance costs associated with functions that are not organization-wide must be included with other expenditures in the indirect cost formula (these costs may be charged directly to affected programs only to the extent that statutory supplanting prohibitions are not violated). This reimbursement must be approved in advance by the Secretary.

§ 76.569 Using the restricted indirect cost rate.
Under the programs referenced in §76.563, the maximum amount of indirect costs under a grant is determined by the following formula:

Indirect costs=(Restricted indirect cost rate)×(Total direct costs of the grant minus capital outlays, subgrants, and other distorting or unallowable items as specified in the grantee's indirect cost rate agreement)

§ 76.580 Coordination with other activities.
A State and a subgrantee shall, to the extent possible, coordinate each of its projects with other activities that are in the same geographic area served by the project and that serve similar purposes and target groups.

Evaluation

§ 76.591 Federal evaluation—cooperation by a grantee.
A grantee shall cooperate in any evaluation of the program by the Secretary.

§ 76.592 Federal evaluation—satisfying requirement for State or subgrantee evaluation.
If a State or a subgrantee cooperates in a Federal evaluation of a program, the Secretary may determine that the State or subgrantee meets the evaluation requirements of the program.

Construction

§ 76.600 Where to find construction regulations.
A State or a subgrantee that requests program funds for construction shall comply with the rules on construction that apply to applicants under 34 CFR 75.600–75.617. The State shall also perform and submit the functions that the Secretary performs under §§75.602 (Preservation of historic sites) and 75.605 (Approval of drawings and specifications) of this title.

Participation of Students Enrolled in Private Schools

§ 76.650 Private schools; purpose of §§76.651–76.662.
Under some programs, the authorizing statute requires that a State and its subgrantees provide for participation by students enrolled in private schools. Sections 76.651–76.662 apply to those programs and provide rules for participation. These sections do not affect the authority of the State or a subgrantee to enter into a contract with a private party. If any other rules for participation of students enrolled in private schools apply under a particular program, they are in the authorizing statute or implementing regulations for that program.

§ 76.651 Responsibility of a State and a subgrantee.
State. A State shall ensure that each subgrantee complies with the requirements in §§76.651–76.662. If a State carries out a project directly, it shall comply with these requirements as if it were a subgrantee.

Subgrantee. A subgrantee shall provide students enrolled in private schools with a genuine opportunity for equitable participation in accordance with the requirements in §§76.652–76.662 and in the authorizing statute and implementing regulations for a program. The subgrantee shall provide that opportunity to participate in a manner that is consistent with the number of eligible private school students and their needs. The subgrantee shall also maintain continuing administrative direction and control over funds and property that benefit students enrolled in private schools.

§ 76.652 Consultation with representatives of private school students.
An applicant for a subgrant shall consult with appropriate representatives of students enrolled in private schools during all development and design phases of the project covered by the application, including consideration of:

1. Which children will receive benefits under the project;
2. How the children's needs will be identified;
3. What benefits will be provided;
4. How the benefits will be provided; and
5. How the project will be evaluated.

§ 76.653 Needs, number of students, and types of services.
A subgrantee shall determine the following matters on a basis comparable to that used by the subgrantee in providing for participation of public school students:

1. The needs of students enrolled in private schools;
2. The number of those students who will participate in a project; and
3. The benefits that the subgrantee will provide under the program to those students.

§ 76.654 Benefits for private school students.
Comparable benefits. The program benefits that a subgrantee provides for students enrolled in private schools must be comparable in quality, scope, and opportunity for participation to the program benefits that the subgrantee provides for students enrolled in public schools.

Same benefits. If a subgrantee uses funds under a program for public school students in a particular attendance area, or grade or age level, the subgrantee shall ensure equitable opportunities for participation by students enrolled in private schools who have the same needs as the public school students to be served and are in that group, attendance area, or age or grade level.

Different benefits. If the needs of students enrolled in private schools are different from the needs of students enrolled in public schools, a subgrantee shall provide program benefits for the private school students that are different from the benefits the subgrantee provides for the public school students.

§ 76.655 Level of expenditures for students enrolled in private schools.
A subgrantee shall spend the same average amount of program funds on a student enrolled in:

1. A private school who receives benefits under the program; and
2. A public school who receives benefits under the program.

However, the subgrantee shall spend a different average amount on program benefits for students enrolled in private schools if the average cost of meeting the needs of those students is different from the average cost of meeting the needs of students enrolled in public schools.

§ 76.656 Information in an application for a subgrant.
An applicant for a subgrant shall include the following information in its application:

1. A description of how the applicant will meet the Federal requirements for participation of students enrolled in private schools.

2. The number of students enrolled in private schools who have been identified as eligible to benefits under the program.
3. The number of students enrolled in private schools who will receive benefits under the program.
4. The basis the applicant used to select the students.
5. The manner and extent to which the applicant complied with §76.652 (consultation).
6. The places and times that the students will receive benefits under the program.
7. The differences, if any, between the program benefits the applicant will provide to public and private school students, and the reasons for the differences.

§ 76.657 Separate classes prohibited.
A subgrantee may not use program funds for classes that are organized separately on the basis of school enrollment or religion of the students if the classes are at the same site and the classes include students enrolled in public schools and students enrolled in private schools.

§ 76.658 Funds not to benefit a private school.
The subgrantee shall use program funds to meet the specific needs of students enrolled in private schools, rather than the needs of a private school or the general needs of the students enrolled in a private school. A subgrantee may not use program funds to finance the existing level of instruction in a private school or to otherwise benefit the private school.

§ 76.659 Use of public school personnel.
A subgrantee may use program funds to make public personnel available in other than public facilities to the extent necessary to provide equitable program benefits designed for students enrolled in a private school and if those benefits are not normally provided by the private school.

§ 76.660 Use of private school personnel.
A subgrantee may use program funds to pay for the services of a private school employee if such services are performed outside of regular duty hours and is under public supervision and control.

§ 76.661 Equipment and supplies.
Under some program statutes, a public agency must keep title to and exercise continuing administrative control of all equipment and supplies that the subgrantee acquires with program funds. This public agency is usually the subgrantee.

The subgrantee may place equipment and supplies in a private school for the period of time needed only for the project and can be removed without remodeling the private school facilities. The subgrantee shall remove equipment or supplies from a private school if the equipment or supplies are no longer needed for the purposes of the project or removal is necessary to avoid use of the equipment of supplies for other than project purposes.

§ 76.662 Construction.
A subgrantee shall not use program funds for the construction of private school facilities.

Procedures for Bypass

§ 76.670 Applicability and filing requirements.
The regulations in §§76.671 to 76.677 apply to the following programs under which the Secretary may waive the requirements for providing services to private school children and to implement a bypass:

CFDA #	Authorizing statute	34 CFR Part
84.010	Chapter 1, Title I, Elementary and Secondary Education Act of 1965, as amended (20 U.S.C. 2701 et seq.)	200
84.151	Chapter 2, Title I, Elementary and Secondary Education Act of 1965, as amended (20 U.S.C. 2911–2952, 2971–2976)	298
84.164	Title II, Part A, Elementary and Secondary Education Act of 1965, as amended (20 U.S.C. 2981–2993)	208
84.186	Part B, Drug Free Schools and Communities Act of 1986 (20 U.S.C. 3191–3197)	None

Filing requirements. Any written submission under §§76.671 to 76.675 must be filed by hand-delivery, mail, or facsimile transmission. The Secretary discourages the use of facsimile transmission for documents longer than five pages. If agreed upon by the parties, service of a document may be made upon the other party by facsimile transmission. A party filing by facsimile transmission is responsible for confirming that a complete and legible copy of the document was received by ED. If a document is filed by facsimile transmission, the Secretary or the hearing officer, as applicable, may require the filing of a follow-up hard copy by hand-delivery or by mail within a reasonable period of time.

§ 76.671 Notice by the Secretary.

Before taking any final action to implement a bypass under a program listed in §76.670, the Secretary provides the affected grantee and any subgrantee with written notice (via certified mail with return receipt requested) indicating:

1. The reasons for the proposed bypass in sufficient detail to allow the grantee and subgrantee to respond; and
2. The requirement that is the basis for the alleged failure to comply.

The Secretary advises the grantee and subgrantee that they:

1. Have at least 45 days after receiving the written notice to submit written objections to the proposed bypass; and
2. May request in writing the opportunity for a hearing to show cause why the bypass should not be implemented.

§ 76.672 Bypass procedures.

Sections 76.673 through 76.675 contain procedures used in conducting a show cause hearing. The hearing officer may modify procedures for a particular case if all parties agree modification is appropriate.

§ 76.673 Appointment and functions of a hearing officer.

If a grantee or subgrantee requests a hearing to show cause why the Secretary should not implement a bypass, the Secretary appoints a hearing officer and notifies appropriate representatives of the affected private school children that they may participate in the hearing. The hearing officer has no authority to require or conduct discovery or to rule on the validity of any statute or regulation. The hearing officer notifies the grantee, subgrantee, and representatives of the private school children of the time and place of the hearing.

§ 76.674 Hearing procedures.

The following procedures apply to a show cause hearing regarding implementation of a bypass:

1. The hearing officer arranges for a transcript to be taken; and
2. The grantee, subgrantee, and representatives of the private school children each may be represented by legal counsel and submit oral or written evidence and arguments at the hearing.

Within 10 days after the hearing, the hearing officer:

1. Indicates that a decision will be issued on the basis of the existing record; or
2. Requests further information from the grantee, subgrantee, representatives of the private school children, or ED officials.

§ 76.675 Posthearing procedures.
Within 120 days after the record a hearing is closed, the hearing officer issues a written decision on whether a bypass should be implemented. Copies of the written decision are sent to the grantee, subgrantee, representatives of the private school children, and the Secretary. Within 30 days after receiving the hearing officer's decision, these parties may each submit to the Secretary written comments on the decision. The Secretary may adopt, reverse, modify, or remand the hearing officer's decision.

§ 76.676 Judicial review of a bypass action.
If a grantee or subgrantee is dissatisfied with the Secretary's final action after a proceeding under §§76.672 through 76.675, it may, within 60 days after receiving notice of that action, file a petition for review with the U.S. Court of Appeals for the circuit in which the State is located.

§ 76.677 Continuation of a bypass.
The Secretary continues a bypass until the Secretary determines that the grantee or subgrantee will meet the requirements for providing services to private school children.

Other Requirements for Certain Programs

§ 76.681 Protection of human subjects.
If a State or a subgrantee uses a human subject in a research project, the State or subgrantee shall protect the person from physical, psychological, or social injury resulting from the project.

§ 76.682 Treatment of animals.
If a State or a subgrantee uses an animal in a project, the State or subgrantee shall provide the animal with proper care and humane treatment in accordance with the Animal Welfare Act of 1970.

§ 76.683 Health or safety standards for facilities.
A State and a subgrantee shall comply with any Federal health or safety requirements that apply to the facilities that the State or subgrantee uses for a project.

Subpart G—What Are the Administrative Responsibilities of the State and Its Subgrantees?

General Administrative Responsibilities

§ 76.700 Compliance with statutes, regulations, State plan, and applications.
A State and a subgrantee shall comply with the State plan and applicable statutes, regulations, and approved applications, and shall use Federal funds in accordance with those statutes, regulations, plan, and applications.

§ 76.701 The State or subgrantee administers or supervises each project.
A State or a subgrantee shall directly administer or supervise the administration of each project.

§ 76.702 Fiscal control and fund accounting procedures.
A State and a subgrantee shall use fiscal control and fund accounting procedures that ensure proper disbursement of and accounting for Federal funds.

§ 76.703 When a State may begin to obligate funds.

Submission date. For a program subject to this part, the Secretary may establish a submission date for the State plan and any other required documents. If no such date is established, the date for submission is three months before the date the Secretary may begin to obligate funds under the program. The Secretary does not determine whether a State plan is substantially approvable until the plan and any required documents have been submitted. The Secretary notifies a State when ED has received the plan.

Obligation. If a State submits a State plan in substantially approvable form (or an amendment), and submits any other required documentation on or before the due date, the State may begin to obligate funds on the date that the funds are first available for obligation by the Secretary. If the State plan is submitted after the due date, ED determines the date that the State plan is substantially approvable.

§ 76.704 New State plan requirements that must be addressed in a State plan.

This section specifies the State plan requirements that must be addressed in a State plan if the State plan requirements established in statutes or regulations change on a date close to the date that State plans are due for submission to the Department. A State plan must meet the following requirements:

1. Every State plan requirement in effect three months before the date the State plan is due to be submitted to the Department under 34 CFR 76.703; and
2. Every State plan requirement included in statutes or regulations that will be effective on or before the date that funds become available for obligation by the Secretary and that have been signed into law or published in the Federal Register as final regulations three months before the date the State plan is due to be submitted to the Department under 34 CFR 76.703.

If a State plan does not have to meet a new State plan requirement of this section, ED takes one of the following actions:

1. Require the State to submit assurances and appropriate documentation to show that the new requirements are being followed under the program; or
2. Extend the submission date of State plans and approve pre-award costs to hold the State harmless.

§ 76.707 When obligations are made.

This table shows when a State or a subgrantee makes obligations for various kinds of property and services:

If the obligation is for:	The obligation is made:
Acquisition of real or personal property	On the date the State or subgrantee makes a binding written commitment to acquire the property.
Personal services by an employee of the State or subgrantee	When the services are performed.
Personal services by a contractor who is not an employee of the State or subgrantee	On the date the State or subgrantee makes a binding written commitment to obtain the services.
Performance of work other than personal services	On the date the State or subgrantee makes a binding written commitment to obtain the work.
Public utility services	When the State or subgrantee receives services.
Travel	When the travel is taken.
Rental of real or personal property	When the State or subgrantee uses the property.
A pre-agreement cost that was properly approved by the State under the cost principals identified in 34 CFR 74.171 and 80.22.	

§ 76.708 When certain subgrantees may begin to obligate funds.

If the authorizing statute for a program requires a State to make subgrants on the basis of a formula, the State may not authorize a subgrantee applicant to obligate funds until the later of:

1. The date that the State may begin to obligate funds under §76.703; or
2. The date that the applicant submits its application to the State in substantially approvable form.

If the authorizing statute for a program gives the State discretion to select subgrantees, it may not authorize a subgrantee applicant to obligate funds until the subgrant is made. However, the State may approve pre-agreement costs in accordance with the cost principles in 34 CFR Part 74 (Appendices C–F).

§ 76.709 Funds may be obligated during a "carryover period."

If a State or a subgrantee does not obligate all grant or subgrant funds by the end of the fiscal year for which Congress appropriated the funds, it may obligate the remaining funds during a carryover period of one additional fiscal year. The State shall return to the Federal Government any carryover funds not obligated by the end of the carryover period by the State and its subgrantees.

§ 76.710 Obligations made during a carryover period are subject to current statutes, regulations, and applications.

A State and a subgrantee shall use carryover funds in accordance with Federal statutes and regulations that apply to the program and are in effect for the carryover period as well as any State plan, or application for a subgrant, that the State or subgrantee is required to submit for the carryover period.

§ 76.711 Requesting funds by CFDA number.

If a program is listed in the CFDA, a State shall identify that program by the CFDA number when requesting funds under the program.

Reports

§ 76.720 State reporting requirements.

This section applies to a State's reports required under 34 CFR 80.40 (Monitoring and reporting of program performance) and 34 CFR 80.41 (Financial reporting), and other reports required by the Secretary and approved by the OMB. A State must submit these reports annually unless the Secretary allows less frequent reporting or requires a State to report more than annually.

1. A State must submit these reports in the manner prescribed by the Secretary at the quality level specified in the data collection instrument.
2. Failure by a State to submit reports in accordance with this section constitutes a failure, under section 454 of GEPA, 20 U.S.C. 1234c, to comply substantially with a requirement of law applicable to the funds made available under that program.

§ 76.722 Subgrantee reporting requirements.

A State may require a subgrantee to submit reports in any way that assists the State in complying with the requirements under 34 CFR 76.720 and in carrying out other responsibilities under the program.

Records

§ 76.730 Records related to grant funds.

A State and a subgrantee shall keep records that show:

1. The amount of funds under the grant or subgrant;
2. How funds are used;

3. The total cost of the project;
4. The share costs provided from other sources; and
5. Other records to facilitate an effective audit.

§ 76.731 Records related to compliance.
A State and a subgrantee shall keep records to show its compliance with program requirements.

Privacy

§ 76.740 Protection of and access to student records; student rights in research, experimental programs, and testing.
Most records on present or past students are subject to the requirements of section 438 of GEPA and 34 CFR Part 99 regulations. Under most programs administered by the Secretary, research, experimentation, and testing are subject to GEPA requirements and implementing regulations at 34 CFR Part 98.

Use of Funds by States and Subgrantees

§ 76.760 More than one program may assist a single activity.
A State or a subgrantee may use funds under more than one program to support different parts of the same project if the State or subgrantee complies with the requirements of each program (with respect to the part of the project assisted with funds under that program) and has an accounting system that permits identification of the costs paid for under each program.

§ 76.761 Federal funds may pay 100% of cost.
A State or a subgrantee may use program funds to pay up to 100% of the cost of a project if they are not required to match the funds and the project can be assisted under the authorizing statute and implementing regulations for the program.

State Administrative Responsibilities

§ 76.770 A State shall have procedures to ensure compliance.
Each State shall have procedures for reviewing and approving applications for subgrants and amendments to those applications, for providing technical assistance, for evaluating projects, and for performing other administrative responsibilities that are necessary to ensure compliance with applicable regulations.

§ 76.783 State educational agency action—subgrantee's opportunity for a hearing.
A subgrantee may request a hearing if it alleges that any of the following actions by the State educational agency violated a State or Federal statute or regulation:

1. Ordering, in accordance with a final State audit resolution determination, the repayment of misspent or misapplied Federal funds; or
2. Terminating further assistance for an approved project.

Subpart H—How Does a State or Local Educational Agency Allocate Funds to Charter Schools?

General

§ 76.785 What is the purpose of this subpart?
The regulations in this subpart implement section 10306 of the Elementary and Secondary Education Act of 1965 (ESEA), requiring States to ensure that each charter school in the State receives the funds for which it

is eligible under a covered program during its first year of operation and during subsequent years in which the charter school expands its enrollment.

§ 76.786 What entities are governed by this subpart?

The regulations in this subpart apply to:

1. State educational agencies (SEAs) and local educational agencies (LEAs) that fund charter schools under a covered program, including SEAs and LEAs located in States that do not participate in the Department's Public Charter Schools Program;
2. State agencies that are not SEAs, if they are responsible for administering a covered program; and
3. Charter schools that are scheduled to open or significantly expand their enrollment during the academic year and wish to participate in a covered program.

§ 76.787 What definitions apply to this subpart?

- *Academic year* - the regular school year (as defined by State law, policy, or practice) in which the State allocates funds under a covered program.
- *Charter school* - has the same meaning as provided in title X, Part C of the ESEA.
- *Charter school LEA* - a charter school treated as an LEA for the applicable covered program.
- *Covered program* - an elementary or secondary education program administered by ED under which funds are allocated to States on a formula basis. The term does not encompass subgrants awarded by an SEA on a discretionary or noncompetitive basis.
- *Local educational agency* - has the same meaning as provided in authorizing program statutes.
- *Significant expansion of enrollment* - a substantial increase in the number of students attending a charter school due to a significant event that is unlikely to occur on a regular basis, such as the addition of one or more grades or educational programs in major curriculum areas. The term also includes any other expansion of enrollment that the SEA determines to be significant.

Responsibilities for Notice and Information

§ 76.788 What are a charter school LEA's responsibilities under this subpart?

Notice. At least 120 days before the date a charter school LEA is scheduled to open or significantly expand its enrollment, the charter school LEA or its authorized public chartering agency must provide its SEA with written notification of that date.

Information. In order to receive funds, a charter school LEA must provide to the SEA any available data or information that may assist it in estimating the amount of funds the LEA may be eligible to receive under a covered program. Once the LEA has opened or significantly expanded its enrollment, it must provide actual enrollment and eligibility data to the SEA. An SEA is not required to provide funds to a charter school LEA until the LEA provides required actual enrollment and eligibility data.

Compliance. Except as provided in §76.791, or the authorizing statute or implementing regulations for the applicable covered program, a charter school LEA must establish its eligibility and comply with all applicable program requirements on the same basis as other LEAs.

§ 76.789 What are an SEA's responsibilities under this subpart?

Information. Upon receiving notice under §76.788(a) of the date a charter school LEA is scheduled to open or significantly expand its enrollment, an SEA must provide the charter school LEA with timely and meaningful information about each covered program in which the charter school LEA may be eligible to participate, including notice of any upcoming competitions under the program.

Allocation of Funds. An SEA must allocate funds under a covered program in accordance with this subpart to any charter school LEA that:

1. Opens for the first time or significantly expands its enrollment during an academic year for which the State awards funds by formula or through a competition under the program;
2. Establishes eligibility and complies with all program requirements (in accordance with §76.791(a)); and
3. Meets the requirements of §76.788(a).

In order to meet the requirements of this subpart, an SEA may allocate funds to, or reserve funds for, an eligible charter school LEA based on reasonable estimates of projected enrollment at the charter school LEA.

Allocation of Funds by State Educational Agencies

§ 76.791 On what basis does an SEA determine whether a charter school LEA that opens or significantly expands its enrollment is eligible to receive funds under a covered program?

For purposes of this subpart, an SEA must determine whether a charter school LEA is eligible to receive funds under a covered program based on actual enrollment or other eligibility data for the charter school LEA on or after the date the charter school LEA opens or significantly expands its enrollment. For the year the charter school LEA opens or significantly expands its enrollment, determination may not be based on enrollment or eligibility data from a prior year, even if the SEA makes eligibility determinations for other LEAs under the program based on enrollment or eligibility data from a prior year.

§ 76.792 How does an SEA allocate funds to eligible charter school LEAs under a covered program in which the SEA awards subgrants on a formula basis?

For each eligible charter school LEA that opens or significantly expands enrollment on or before November 1 of an academic year, the SEA must implement procedures that ensure that the LEA receives a proportionate amount of funds they are eligible for under each covered program. For those that open or expand enrollment after November 1 (but before February 1), the SEA must implement procedures ensuring the charter school LEA receives at least a pro rata portion of the proportionate amount of funds for which the LEA is eligible under each covered program. For each eligible charter school LEA that opens or expands enrollment on or after February 1 of an academic year, the SEA may implement procedures to provide the LEA with a pro rata portion of the proportionate amount of funds for which the LEA is eligible under each program.

§ 76.793 When is an SEA required to allocate funds to a charter school LEA under this subpart?

Except as provided in §§76.788(b) and 76.789(b)(3):

1. The SEA must allocate funds to the charter school LEA within five months of the date the charter school LEA opens or significantly expands its enrollment for each eligible charter school LEA that opens or significantly expands its enrollment on or before November 1 of an academic year.
2. For those that open or significantly expand enrollment after November 1 (but before February 1 of an academic year), the SEA must allocate funds to the charter school LEA on or before the date the SEA allocates funds to LEAs under the applicable covered program for the succeeding academic year.

§ 76.794 How does an SEA allocate funds to charter school LEAs under a covered program in which the SEA awards subgrants on a discretionary basis?

Competitive programs. For covered programs in which the SEA awards subgrants on a competitive basis, the SEA must provide each eligible charter school LEA in the State that is scheduled to open on or before the closing date of any competition under the program a full and fair opportunity to apply in the program.

Noncompetitive discretionary programs. The requirements in this subpart do not apply to discretionary programs or portions of programs under which the SEA does not award subgrants through a competition.

Adjustments

§ 76.796 What are the consequences of an SEA allocating more or fewer funds to a charter school LEA under a covered program than the amount for which the charter school LEA is eligible when the charter school LEA actually opens or significantly expands its enrollment?

An SEA that allocates more or fewer funds to a charter school LEA than the amount for which the charter school LEA is eligible must make appropriate adjustments to the amount of funds allocated to the LEA as well as to other LEAs under the applicable program. Adjustments to to charter school LEA allocations must be based on actual enrollment or other eligibility data for the LEA on or after the date the LEA first opens or significantly expands enrollment.

§ 76.797 When is an SEA required to make adjustments to allocations under this subpart?

The SEA must make any necessary adjustments to allocations under a covered program on or before the date the SEA allocates funds to LEAs under the program for the succeeding academic year. In allocating funds to a charter school LEA based on any such necessary adjustments made, the SEA may use funds from the SEA's allocation under the applicable covered program for the academic year in which the charter school LEA opened or significantly expanded its enrollment, or from the SEA's allocation under the program for the succeeding academic year.

Applicability of This Subpart to Local Educational Agencies

§ 76.799 Do the requirements in this subpart apply to LEAs?

Each LEA responsible for funding a charter school under a covered program must comply with the requirements in this subpart on the same basis as SEAs are required to comply with the requirements in this subpart. In applying the requirements in this subpart (except for §§76.785, 76.786, and 76.787) to LEAs, references to SEA (or State), charter school LEA, and LEA must be read as references to LEA, charter school, and public school, respectively.

Subpart I—What Procedures Does the Secretary Use To Get Compliance?

§ 76.900 Waiver of regulations prohibited.

No official, agent, or employee of ED may waive any regulation that applies to an ED program unless the regulations specifically provide that it may be waived. No act or failure to act by an official, agent, or employee of ED can affect the authority of the Secretary to enforce regulations.

§ 76.901 Office of Administrative Law Judges.

The Office of Administrative Law Judges (established under Part E of GEPA and whose regulations are at 34 CFR Part 81) has the jurisdiction to conduct:

1. Recovery of Funds hearings under section 452 of GEPA;
2. Withholding Hearings under section 455 of GEPA;
3. Cease and Desist hearings under section 456 of GEPA; and any other proceeding designated by the Secretary under section 451 of GEPA.

§ 76.902 Judicial review.

After a hearing, a State is usually entitled to judicial review of the Secretary's decision.

§ 76.910 Cooperation with audits.

A grantee or subgrantee shall cooperate with the Secretary and the U.S. Comptroller General (or any of their authorized representatives) in the conduct of audits authorized by Federal law. This cooperation includes access without unreasonable restrictions to records and personnel of the grantee or subgrantee for the purpose of obtaining relevant information.

PART 77—DEFINITIONS THAT APPLY TO DEPARTMENT REGULATIONS

§ 77.1 Definitions that apply to all Department programs.

The definitions provided in Parts 74 and/or 80 apply to the regulations in Title 34 of the Code of Federal Regulations. Unless a statute or regulation provides otherwise, the following definitions also apply to the regulations in this title:

- *Acquisition* - taking ownership of property, receiving property as a gift, entering into a lease-purchase arrangement, leasing property, or the processing, delivery, and installation of property.
- *Applicant* - a party requesting a grant or subgrant under an ED program.
- *Application* - a request for a grant or subgrant under an ED program.
- *Budget* - that recipient's financial plan for carrying out the project or program.
- *Budget period* - an interval of time into which a project period is divided for budgetary purposes.
- *Department* and *ED* - the United States Department of Education.
- *Elementary school* - a day or residential school providing elementary education under State law.
- *Facilities* - one or more structures in one or more locations.
- *Fiscal year* - the Federal fiscal year begins on October 1 and ends on the following September 30.
- *Grant period* - the period for which funds have been awarded.
- *Grantee* - the entire legal entity to which a grant is awarded and which is accountable to the Government for the use of the funds provided. The term does not include secondary recipients such as subgrantees, contractors, etc., who may receive funds from a grantee pursuant to a grant.
- *Local educational agency* (LEA)- a public board of education or other public authority that performs service functions for public elementary, secondary schools, or vocational education programs in a city, county, township, school district, or other political subdivision of a State.
- *Minor remodeling* - minor alterations in a previously completed building. The term also includes the extension of utility lines from points beyond the confines of the space in which the minor remodeling is undertaken but within the confines of the previously completed building. The term does not include building construction, stuctural alterations to buildings, maintenance, or repairs.
- *Nonprofit* - an agency, organization, or institution that it is owned and operated by one or more corporations or associations whose net earnings do not benefit, and cannot lawfully benefit, any private shareholder or entity.
- *Nonpublic* - an agency, organization or institution not under Federal or public supervision or control.
- *Preschool* - the educational level from a child's birth to the time at which the State provides elementary education.
- *Private* - an agency, organization, or institution that it is not under Federal or public control.
- *Public* - the agency, organization, or institution that is under the administrative supervision or control of a government other than the Federal Government.
- *Secondary school* - a day or residential school that provides secondary education as determined under State law.
- *Secretary* - the Secretary of Education or an official acting under authority for the Secretary.
- *Service function* - an educational service that is performed by a legal entity whose jurisdiction does not extend to the whole State and that is authorized to provide consultative, advisory, or educational services to public elementary or secondary schools.
- *State* - any of the 50 States, Puerto Rico, the District of Columbia, Guam, American Samoa, the Virgin Islands, the Northern Mariana Islands, or the Trust Territory of the Pacific Islands.
- *State educational agency (SEA)* - the State board of education or other agency primarily responsible for the supervision of public elementary and secondary schools in a State.
- *Work of art* - an item that is incorporated into facilities primarily because of its aesthetic value.

PART 79—INTERGOVERNMENTAL REVIEW OF ED PROGRAMS AND ACTIVITIES

§ 79.1 What is the purpose of these regulations?

The regulations in this part implement E.O. 12372, "Intergovernmental Review of Federal Programs." These regulations foster an intergovernmental partnership and strengthen Federalism by relying on state processes and on state, areawide, regional, and local coordination for review of proposed federal financial assistance.

§ 79.2 What definitions apply to these regulations?

- *Department* or *ED* - the United States Department of Education
- Order - Executive Order 12372, issued July 14, 1982, amended April 8, 1983, and titled "Intergovernmental Review of Federal Programs."
- *Secretary* - the Secretary of the U.S. Department of Education or an official or employee of the Department acting for the Secretary under a delegation of authority.
- *State* - any of the 50 states, the District of Columbia, the Commonwealth of Puerto Rico, the Commonwealth of the Northern Mariana Islands, Guam, American Samoa, the U.S. Virgin Islands, or the Trust Territory of the Pacific Islands.

§ 79.3 What programs and activities of the Department are subject to these regulations?

The Federal Register lists the Department's programs and activities that are subject to these regulations and identifies which are subject to the requirements of Section 204 of the Demonstration Cities and Metropolitan Development Act. If an ED program does not have implementing regulations, the regulations in this part apply to that program or activity. The following programs and activities are excluded from coverage under this part:

1. Proposed legislation.
2. Regulation and budget formulation.
3. National security matters.
4. Procurement.
5. Direct payments to individuals.
6. Financial transfers for which ED has no funding discretion to approve sites or projects.
7. Research and development national in scope.
8. Assistance to federally recognized Indian tribes.

§ 79.4 What are the Secretary's general responsibilities under the Order?

The Secretary provides opportunities for consultation by elected officials of those state and local governments that would provide the nonfederal funds for (or would be directly affected by) proposed federal financial assistance from ED. If a state adopts a process under the Order to review and coordinate proposed federal financial assistance, the Secretary:

1. Uses the state process to determine official views of state and local elected officials;
2. Communicates with state and local elected officials as early in a program planning cycle as is reasonably feasible to explain specific plans and actions;
3. Makes efforts to accommodate concerns with proposed federal financial assistance that are communicated through the state process;
4. Allows the states to simplify and consolidate existing federally required state plan submissions;
5. encourages the substitution of state plans for federally required state plans, if permitted by law;
6. Seeks the coordination of views of affected state and local elected officials in one state with those of another state when proposed federal financial assistance has an impact on interstate metropolitan urban centers or other interstate areas; and
7. Supports state and local governments by discouraging the reauthorization or creation of any planning organization which is federally funded, which has a limited purpose, and which is not adequately representative of, or accountable to, state or local elected officials.

§ 79.5 What is the Secretary's obligation with respect to Federal interagency coordination?
The Secretary, to the maximum extent practicable, consults with and seeks advice from all other substantially affected federal departments and agencies in an effort to assure full coordination between such agencies and the Department regarding programs and activities covered under these regulations.

§ 79.6 What procedures apply to the selection of programs and activities under these regulations?
A state may select any program or activity published in the Federal Register for intergovernmental review under these regulations. Each state, before selecting programs and activities, shall consult with local elected officials. If changes in its selections must be made, a State may notify the Secretary at any time; but for each change, the state shall submit an assurance that the state has consulted with local elected officials regarding the change.

§ 79.7 How does the Secretary communicate with State and local officials concerning the Department's programs and activities?
The Secretary provides notice to directly affected state, area-wide, regional, and local entities in a state of proposed federal financial assistance if the state has not adopted a process under the Order, or the assistance involves a program or activity not selected for the state process.

§ 79.8 How does the Secretary provide States an opportunity to comment on proposed Federal financial assistance?
The Secretary generally gives State processes or directly affected officials and entities:

1. At least 30 days to comment on proposed Federal financial assistance in the form of noncompeting continuation awards; and
2. At least 60 days to comment on such assistance other than noncompeting continuation awards.

The Secretary establishes a date for mailing or hand-delivering comments using one of the following procedures:

1. If the comments relate to continuation award applications, the Secretary notifies each applicant and each State Single Point of Contact (SPOC) of the date by which SPOC comments should be submitted; and
2. If the comments relate to applications for new grants, the Secretary establishes the date in a notice published in the Federal Register.

§ 79.9 How does the Secretary receive and respond to comments?
The Secretary follows the procedure in §79.10 if:

1. A state office or official is designated to act as a single point of contact between a state process and all federal agencies; and
2. That office or official transmits a State process recommendation, and identifies it as such, for a program selected under §79.6.

The single point of contact is not obligated to transmit comments from state, areawide, regional, or local officials and entities if there is no state process recommendation. If a state has not established a process, or is unable to submit a state process recommendation, state, areawide, regional, and local officials and entities may submit comments to the Department.

§ 79.10 How does the Secretary make efforts to accommodate intergovernmental concerns?
If a state process provides a state process recommendation to ED through its single point of contact, the Secretary either:

1. Accepts the recommendation;
2. Reaches a mutually agreeable solution with the state process; or
3. Provides the point of contact with a written explanation of the decision in such form as the Secretary deems appropriate.

The Secretary may also supplement the written explanation by providing the explanation to the single point of contact by telephone, other telecommunication, or other means.

§ 79.11 What are the Secretary's obligations in interstate situations?

The Secretary is responsible for:

1. Identifying proposed federal financial assistance that has an impact on interstate areas;
2. Notifying appropriate officials and entities in states which have adopted a process and which select the Department's program or activity.
3. Making efforts to identify and notify the affected state, areawide, regional, and local officials and entities in those states that have not adopted a process under the Order or do not select the Department's program or activity;
4. Responding under §79.10 if the Secretary receives a recommendation from a designated areawide agency transmitted by a single point of contact, in cases in which the review, coordination, and communication with the Department have been delegated.

§ 79.12 How may a State simplify, consolidate, or substitute federally required State plans?

Simplify - that a state may develop its own format, choose its own submission date, and select the planning period for a state plan.

Consolidate - that a state may meet statutory and regulatory requirements by combining two or more plans into one document and that the state can select the format, submission date, and planning period for the consolidated plan.

Substitute - that a state may use a plan or other document that it has developed for its own purposes to meet Federal requirements.

If not inconsistent with law, a state may decide to try to simplify, consolidate, or substitute federally required state plans without prior approval by the Secretary. The Secretary reviews each state plan that a state has simplified, consolidated, or substituted and accepts the plan only if its contents meet federal requirements.

PART 80—UNIFORM ADMINISTRATIVE REQUIREMENTS FOR GRANTS AND COOPERATIVE AGREEMENTS TO STATE AND LOCAL GOVERNMENTS

Subpart A—General

§ 80.1 Purpose and scope of this part.

This part establishes uniform administrative rules for Federal grants and cooperative agreements and subawards to State, local, and Indian tribal governments.

§ 80.2 Scope of subpart.

This subpart contains general rules pertaining to this part and procedures for control of exceptions from this part.

§ 80.3 Definitions used in this part.

- *Accrued expenditures* - the charges incurred by the grantee during a given period requiring the provision of funds for:
  1. Goods and other tangible property received;
  2. Services performed by employees, contractors, subgrantees, subcontractors, and other payees; and
  3. Other amounts becoming owed under programs for which no current services or performance is required, such as annuities, insurance claims, and other benefit payments.
- *Accrued income* - the sum of:
  1. Earnings during a given period from services performed by the grantee and goods and other tangible property delivered to purchasers, and
  2. Amounts becoming owed to the grantee for which no current services or performance is required by the grantee.
- *Acquisition cost of an item of purchased equipment* - the net invoice unit price of the property including the cost of modifications, attachments, accessories, or auxiliary apparatus necessary to make the property usable for the purpose for which it was acquired. Other charges such as the cost of installation, transportation, taxes, duty or protective in-transit insurance, shall be included or excluded in accordance with the grantee's regular accounting practices.
- *Administrative requirements* - those matters common to grants in general, such as financial management, frequency of reports, and record retention. These are distinguished from programmatic requirements, which concern matters treated only on a program-by-program or grant-by-grant basis, such as activities that can be supported by grants under a particular program.
- *Awarding agency* - with respect to a grant, the Federal agency; with respect to a subgrant, the party that awarded the subgrant.
- *Cash contributions* - the grantee's cash outlay, including the outlay of money contributed to the grantee or subgrantee by other public agencies and institutions, and private organizations and individuals. When authorized by Federal legislation, Federal funds received from other assistance agreements may be considered as grantee or subgrantee cash contributions.
- *Contract* (except as used in the definitions for grant and subgrant in this section and except where qualified by Federal regulation) - a procurement contract under a grant or subgrant, and procurement subcontract under a contract.
- *Cost sharing or matching* - the value of the third party in-kind contributions and the portion of the costs of a federally assisted project or program not borne by the Federal Government.
- *Cost-type contract* - a contract or subcontract under a grant in which the contractor or subcontractor is paid on the basis of the costs it incurs, with or without a fee.
- *Equipment* - tangible, nonexpendable, personal property having a useful life of more than one year and an acquisition cost of $5,000 or more per unit. A grantee may use its own definition of equip-

ment provided that such definition would at least include all equipment defined above.

- *Expenditure report –*
  1. For nonconstruction grants, the SF–269 "Financial Status Report" (or other equivalent report);
  2. For construction grants, the SF–271 "Outlay Report and Request for Reimbursement" (or other equivalent report).
- *Federally recognized Indian tribal government* - the governing body or a governmental agency of any Indian tribe, band, nation, organized group, or community (including any Native village as defined in Section 3 of the Alaska Native Claims Settlement Act) certified by the Secretary of the Interior as eligible for the special programs/services provided by the Bureau of Indian Affairs.
- *Government* - a State or local government or a federally recognized Indian tribal government.
- *Grant* - an award of financial assistance, including cooperative agreements, in the form of money, or property in lieu of money, by the Federal Government to an eligible grantee. The term does not include technical assistance which provides services instead of money, or other assistance in the form of revenue sharing, loans, loan guarantees, interest subsidies, insurance, or direct appropriations. Also, the term does not include assistance, such as a fellowship or other lump sum award, which the grantee is not required to account for.
- *Grantee* - the entity to which a grant is awarded and which is accountable for the use of the funds provided. The grantee is the entire legal entity even if only a particular component of the entity is designated in the grant award document.
- *Local government* - a county, municipality, city, town, township, local public authority (including any public and Indian housing agency under the United States Housing Act of 1937) school district, special district, intrastate district, council of governments (whether or not incorporated as a nonprofit corporation under state law), any other regional or interstate government entity, or any agency or instrumentality of a local government.
- *Obligations* - the amounts of orders placed, contracts and subgrants awarded, goods and services received, and similar transactions during a given period that require payment by the grantee during the same or a future period.
- *OMB* - the United States Office of Management and Budget.
- *Outlays (expenditures)* - charges made to the project or program. They may be reported on a cash or accrual basis. For reports prepared on a cash basis, outlays are the sum of actual cash disbursement for direct charges for goods and services, the amount of indirect expense incurred, the value of in-kind contributions applied, and the amount of cash advances and payments made to contractors and subgrantees. For reports prepared on an accrued expenditure basis, outlays are the sum of actual cash disbursements, the amount of indirect expense incurred, the value of in-kind contributions applied, and the new increase (or decrease) in the amounts owed by the grantee for goods and other property received, for services performed by employees, contractors, subgrantees, subcontractors, and other payees, and other amounts becoming owed under programs for which no current services or performance are required, such as annuities, insurance claims, and other benefit payments.
- *Percentage of completion method* - a system under which payments are made for construction work according to the percentage of completion of the work, rather than to the grantee's cost incurred.
- *Prior approval* - documentation evidencing consent prior to incurring specific cost.
- *Real property* - land, including land improvements, structures and appurtenances thereto, excluding movable machinery and equipment.
- *Share* - when referring to the awarding agency's portion of real property, equipment or supplies, means the same percentage as the awarding agency's portion of the acquiring party's total costs under the grant to which the acquisition costs under the grant to which the acquisition cost of the property was charged. Only costs are to be counted—not the value of third-party in-kind contributions.
- *State* - any of the several States of the U.S, the District of Columbia, the Commonwealth of Puerto

Rico, any territory or possession of the United States, or any agency or instrumentality of a State exclusive of local governments. The term does not include any public and Indian housing agency under United States Housing Act of 1937. Note: the definition of State in this section is used for the purpose of determining the scope of Part 80 regulations. Some program regulations contain different definitions for State based on program statute eligibility requirements.

- *Subgrant* - an award of financial assistance in the form of money, or property in lieu of money, made under a grant by a grantee to an eligible subgrantee. The term includes financial assistance when provided by contractual legal agreement, but does not include procurement purchases, nor does it include any form of assistance which is excluded from the definition of grant in this part.
- Subgrantee - the government or other legal entity to which a subgrant is awarded and which is accountable to the grantee for the use of the funds provided.
- *Supplies* - all tangible personal property other than equipment as defined in this part.
- *Suspension* - depending on the context, either:
    1. Temporary withdrawal of the authority to obligate grant funds pending corrective action by the grantee or a decision to terminate the grant, or
    2. An action taken by a suspending official in accordance with agency regulations implementing E.O. 12549 to immediately exclude a person from participating in grant transactions for a period, pending completion of an investigation and such legal or debarment proceedings as may ensue.
- *Termination* - permanent withdrawal of the authority to obligate previously-awarded grant funds before that authority would otherwise expire. It also means the voluntary relinquishment of that authority by the grantee or subgrantee. Termination does not include:
    1. Withdrawal of funds awarded on the basis of the grantee's underestimate of the unobligated balance in a prior period;
    2. Withdrawal of the unobligated balance as of the expiration of a grant;
    3. Refusal to extend a grant or award additional funds, to make a competing or noncompeting continuation, renewal, extension, or supplemental award; or
    4. Voiding of a grant upon determination that the award was obtained fraudulently, or was otherwise illegal or invalid from inception.
- *Terms of a grant or subgrant* - all requirements of the grant or subgrant, whether in statute, regulations, or the award document.
- *Third party in-kind contributions* - property or services which benefit a federally assisted project or program and which are contributed by non-Federal third parties without charge to the grantee, or a cost-type contractor under the grant agreement.
- *Unliquidated obligations* - for reports prepared on a cash basis mean the amount of obligations incurred by the grantee that has not been paid. For reports prepared on an accrued expenditure basis, they represent the amount of obligations incurred by the grantee for which an outlay has not been recorded.
- *Unobligated balance* - the portion of the funds authorized by the Federal agency that has not been obligated by the grantee and is determined by deducting the cumulative obligations from the cumulative funds authorized.

§ 80.4 Applicability.

General. Subparts A through D of this part apply to all grants and subgrants to governments, except where inconsistent with Federal statutes or with regulations authorized in accordance with the exception provision of §80.6, or:

1. Grants and subgrants to State and local IHEs or State and local hospitals;
2. The block grants authorized by the Omnibus Budget Reconciliation Act of 1981;
3. Entitlement grants authorized to carry out programs of the Social Security Act;

4. Entitlement grants authorized under programs of The National School Lunch Act;
5. Entitlement grants authorized under programs of The Child Nutrition Act of 1966;
6. Entitlement grants for State Administrative expenses under The Food Stamp Act of 1977;
7. Some grants for experimental, pilot, or demonstration project supported by this section;
8. Some grant funds awarded under the Immigration and Nationality Act and the Refugee Education Assistance Act of 1980, for cash and medical assistance, supplemental security income benefits to refugees and entrants, and the administrative costs of providing the assistance and benefits;
9. Grants to local education agencies under portions of the Impact Aid program; and
10. Payments under the Veterans Administration's State Home Per Diem Program.

Entitlement programs. Entitlement programs enumerated above in §80.4(a) (3-8) are subject to Subpart E.

§ 80.5 Effect on other issuances.
All other grants administration provisions of codified program regulations, program manuals, handbooks and other non-regulatory materials which are inconsistent with this part are superseded, except to the extent they are required by statute, or authorized in accordance with the exception provision in §80.6.

§ 80.6 Additions and exceptions.
For classes of grants and grantees subject to this part, Federal agencies may not impose additional administrative requirements except in codified regulations published in the Federal Register. Exceptions for classes of grants or grantees may be authorized only by the Secretary after consultation with OMB, and such exceptions may be authorized on a case-by-case basis.

Subpart B—Pre-Award Requirements

§ 80.10 Forms for applying for grants.
Scope. This section prescribes forms and instructions to be used by governmental organizations (except hospitals and IHEs operated by a government) in applying for grants. This section is not applicable, however, to formula grant programs which do not require applicants to apply for funds on a project basis. This section applies only to applications to Federal agencies for grants, and is not required to be applied by grantees in dealing with applicants for subgrants. However, grantees are encouraged to avoid more detailed or burdensome application requirements for subgrants.

Authorized forms and instructions for governmental organizations. In applying for grants, applicants shall only use standard application forms or those prescribed by the granting agency with the approval of OMB under the Paperwork Reduction Act of 1980. Applicants are not required to submit more than one original and two copies of preapplications or applications. Applicants must follow all applicable instructions that bear OMB clearance numbers. When a grantee applies for additional funding (such as a continuation or supplemental award) or amends a previously submitted application, only the affected pages need be submitted. Previously submitted pages with information that is still current need not be resubmitted.

§ 80.11 State plans.
Scope. Statutes for some programs require States to submit plans before receiving grants. Under regulations implementing E.O. 12372, "Intergovernmental Review of Federal Programs," States are allowed to simplify, consolidate, and substitute plans.

Requirements. A State need meet only Federal administrative or programmatic requirements for a plan that are in statutes or codified regulations.

Assurances. In each plan, the State will include an assurance that it shall comply with all applicable Federal statutes and regulations in effect with respect to the periods for which it receives grant funding. For this assurance and other assurances required in the plan, the State may:

1. Cite by number the statutory or regulatory provisions requiring the assurances and affirm that it gives the assurances required by those provisions;
2. Repeat the assurance language in the statutes or regulations; or
3. Develop its own language to the extent permitted by law.

Amendments. A State will amend a plan whenever necessary to reflect:

1. New or revised Federal statutes or regulations; or
2. A material change in any State law, organization, policy, or State agency operation.

§ 80.12 Special grant or subgrant conditions for "high-risk" grantees.

A grantee or subgrantee may be considered "high risk" if an awarding agency determines that a grantee or subgrantee:

1. Has a history of unsatisfactory performance;
2. Is not financially stable;
3. Has a management system which does not meet the management standards set forth in this part;
4. Has not conformed to terms and conditions of previous awards; and/or
5. Is otherwise not responsible; and if the awarding agency determines that an award will be made, special conditions and/or restrictions shall correspond to the high risk condition and shall be included in the award.

Special conditions or restrictions may include:

1. Payment on a reimbursement basis;
2. Withholding authority to proceed to the next phase until receipt of evidence of acceptable performance within a given funding period;
3. Requiring additional, more detailed financial reports;
4. Additional project monitoring;
5. Requiring the grante or subgrantee to obtain technical or management assistance; or
6. Establishing additional prior approvals.

If an awarding agency decides to impose such conditions, the awarding official will notify the grantee or subgrantee as early as possible, in writing, of:

1. The nature of the special conditions/restrictions;
2. The reason(s) for imposing them;
3. The corrective actions which must be taken before they will be removed and the time allowed for completing the corrective actions and
4. The method of requesting reconsideration of the conditions/restrictions imposed.

Subpart C—Post-Award Requirements

Financial Administration

§ 80.20 Standards for financial management systems.

A State must expand and account for grant funds in accordance laws and procedures for expending and accounting for its own funds. Fiscal control and accounting procedures of the State, as well as its subgrantees and cost-type contractors, must be sufficient to permit:

1. Preparation of reports required by this part and the statutes authorizing the grant; and

2. The tracing of funds adequate to establish that funds have not been used in violation of the restrictions and prohibitions of applicable statutes.

The financial management systems of other grantees and subgrantees must meet the following standards:

1. *Financial reporting.* Accurate and complete disclosure of the financial results of activities must be made in accordance with the financial reporting requirements of the grant or subgrant.
2. *Accounting records.* Grantees and subgrantees must maintain records which adequately identify the source and application of funds provided for financially-assisted activities. These records must contain information pertaining to grant or subgrant awards and authorizations, obligations, unobligated balances, assets, liabilities, outlays or expenditures, and income.
3. *Internal control.* Effective control and accountability must be maintained for all grant and subgrant cash, real and personal property, and assets. Grantees and subgrantees must adequately safeguard all such property and must assure that it is used solely for authorized purposes.
4. *Budget control.* Actual expenditures or outlays must be compared with budgeted amounts for each grant or subgrant. Financial information must be related to performance or productivity data, including the development of unit cost information whenever appropriate or specifically required in the grant or subgrant agreement. If unit cost data are required, estimates based on available documentation will be accepted whenever possible.
5. *Allowable cost.* Applicable OMB cost principles, agency regulations, and the terms of grant and subgrant agreements will be followed in determining the reasonableness and allocability of costs.
6. *Source documentation.* Accounting records must be supported by such source documentation as cancelled checks, paid bills, payrolls, time records, contract and subgrant award documents, etc.
7. *Cash management.* Procedures for minimizing the time elapsing between the transfer of funds from the U.S. Treasury and disbursement by grantees and subgrantees must be followed whenever advance payment procedures are used. Grantees must establish reasonable procedures to ensure the receipt of reports on subgrantees' cash balances and cash disbursements in sufficient time to enable them to prepare complete and accurate cash transactions reports to the awarding agency. When advances are made by letter-of-credit or electronic transfer of funds methods, the grantee must make drawdowns as close as possible to the time of making disbursements. Grantees must monitor cash drawdowns by their subgrantees to assure that they conform substantially to the same standards of timing and amount as apply to advances to the grantees.

§ 80.21 Payment.

Scope. This section prescribes the basic standard and methods under which a Federal agency will make payments to grantees, and grantees will make payments to subgrantees and contractors.

Basic standard. Methods and procedures for payment shall minimize the time between the transfer of funds and disbursement by grantees or subgrantees (in accordance with Treasury regulations at 31 CFR Part 205).

Advances. Grantees and subgrantees shall be paid in advance, provided they maintain or demonstrate the willingness and ability to maintain procedures to minimize the time elapsing between the transfer of the funds and their disbursement by the grantee or subgrantee.

Reimbursement. Reimbursement shall be the preferred method when the requirements of Advances (above) are not met. Grantees and subgrantees may also be paid by reimbursement for any construction grant.

Working capital advances. If a grantee cannot meet the criteria for advance payments described in Advances (above), and the Federal agency has determined that reimbursement is not feasible, the awarding agency may provide cash or a working capital advance basis.

Effect of program income, refunds, and audit recoveries on payment. Grantees and subgrantees shall disburse repayments to and interest earned on a revolving fund before requesting additional cash payments for the same activity. Except as previously stated, grantees and subgrantees shall disburse program income, rebates, refunds, contract settlements, audit recoveries and interest earned on such funds before requesting additional cash payments.

Withholding payments. Unless otherwise required by Federal statute, awarding agencies shall not withhold payments for proper charges incurred by grantees or subgrantees unless the grantee or subgrantee has failed to comply with grant award conditions, or is indebted to the U.S. Cash withheld for failure to comply with grant award condition, but without suspension of the grant, shall be released to the grantee upon subsequent compliance. A Federal agency shall not make payment to grantees for amounts that are withheld by grantees or subgrantees from payment to contractors to assure satisfactory completion of work. Payments shall be made by the Federal agency when the grantees or subgrantees actually disburse the withheld funds to the contractors or to escrow accounts established to assure satisfactory completion of work.

Cash depositories. Grantees and subgrantees are encouraged to use a bank which is owned at least 50% by minority group members. A list of minority owned banks can be obtained from the Minority Business Development Agency, Department of Commerce, Washington, DC 20230. Grantees or subgrantees shall maintain a separate bank account when required by Federal-State agreement.

Interest earned on advances. Except for interest earned on advances of funds exempt under the Intergovernmental Cooperation Act and the Indian Self-Determination Act, grantees and subgrantees shall, at least quarterly, remit interest earned on advances to the Federal agency. Grantees or subgrantees may keep interest up to $100 per year for administrative expenses.

<u>§ 80.22 Allowable costs.</u>

Limitation on use of funds. Grant funds may be used only for:

1. Allowable costs of the grantees, subgrantees and cost-type contractors, including allowable costs in the form of payments to fixed-price contractors; and
2. Reasonable fees or profit to cost-type contractors but not any fee or profit (or other increment above allowable costs) to the grantee or subgrantee.

The below table outlines the Federal principles to be used in determining allowable costs for each type of grantee:

For the costs of a—	Use the principles in
State, local or Indian tribal government	OMB A–87.
Private nonprofit organization other than an institution of higher education, hospital, or organization named in OMB A–122 as not subject to that circular	OMB A–122.
Educational institutions	OMB A–21.
For-profit organization other than a hospital and an organization named in OBM A–122 as not subject to that circular	48 CFR Part 31.

<u>§ 80.23 Period of availability of funds.</u>

General. Where a funding period is specified, a grantee may charge to the award only costs resulting from obligations of the funding period unless carryover of unobligated balances is permitted, in which case the carryover balances may be charged for costs resulting from obligations of the subsequent funding period.

Liquidation of obligations. A grantee must liquidate all obligations incurred under the award not later than 90 days after the end of the funding period (or as specified in a program regulation) to coincide with the submission of the annual Financial Status Report (SF–269). The Federal agency may extend this deadline at the request of the grantee.

§ 80.24 Matching or cost sharing.
Basic rule: Costs and contributions acceptable. With the qualifications and exceptions listed below, a matching or cost sharing requirement may be satisfied by either or both of the following:

1. Allowable costs incurred by the grantee, subgrantee or a cost-type contractor under the assistance agreement (this includes allowable costs borne by non-Federal grants or by others cash donations from non-Federal third parties); and/or
2. The value of third party in-kind contributions applicable to the period to which the cost sharing or matching requirements applies.

Qualifications and exceptions: Costs borne by other Federal grant agreements. Except as provided by Federal statute, a cost sharing or matching requirement may not be met by costs borne by another Federal grant. This prohibition does not apply to income earned by a grantee under another Federal grant.

Qualifications and exceptions: Cost or contributions counted towards other Federal costs-sharing requirements. Neither costs nor the values of third party in-kind contributions may count towards a cost sharing or matching requirement of a grant if the costs are to be counted towards satisfying a cost sharing or matching requirement of another Federal award.

Qualifications and exceptions: Records. Costs and third party in-kind contributions counting towards satisfying a cost sharing or matching requirement must be verifiable from the records of grantees, showing show how the value placed on third party in-kind contributions was derived.

Qualifications and exceptions: Special standards for third party in-kind contributions. (i) Third party in-kind contributions count towards satisfying a cost sharing or matching requirement only where, if the party receiving the contributions were to pay for them, the payments would be allowable costs.

Valuation of donated services: Volunteer services. Unpaid services provided to a grantee or subgrantee by individuals will be valued at rates consistent with those ordinarily paid for similar work in the grantee's organization or with those paid by other employers for similar work in the same labor market. In either case, a reasonable amount for fringe benefits may be included in the valuation.

Valuation of donated services: Employees of other organizations. When an employer other than a grantee furnishes free of charge the services of an employee in the employee's normal line of work, the services will be valued at the employee's regular rate of pay exclusive of the employee's fringe benefits and overhead costs.

Valuation of third party donated supplies and loaned equipment or space. If a third party donates supplies, the contribution will be valued at the market value of the supplies at the time of donation. If a third party donates the use of equipment or space in a building but retains title, the contribution will be valued at the fair rental rate of the equipment or space.

Valuation of third party donated equipment, buildings, and land. If a third party donates equipment, buildings, or land, and title passes to a grantee or subgrantee, the treatment of the donated property will depend upon the purpose of the grant or subgrant (see full section for details).

Valuation of grantee or subgrantee donated real property for construction/acquisition. If a grantee or subgrantee donates real property for a construction or facilities acquisition project, the current market value of that property may be counted as cost sharing or matching. If any part of the donated property was acquired with Federal funds, only the non-federal share of the property may be counted as cost sharing or matching.

§ 80.25 Program income.

General. Grantees are encouraged to earn income to defray program costs. Program income includes income from fees for services performed, from the use or rental of real or personal property acquired with grant funds, from the sale of commodities or items fabricated under a grant agreement, and from payments of principal and interest on loans made with grant funds. Except as otherwise provided, program income does not include interest on grant funds, rebates, credits, discounts, refunds, etc. and interest earned on any of them.

Definition of program income. Program income means gross income received by a grantee directly generated by a grant supported activity, or earned only as a result of the grant agreement during the grant period.

Cost of generating program income. If authorized, costs incident to the generation of program income may be deducted from gross income to determine program income.

Governmental revenues. Taxes, special assessments, levies, fines, and other such revenues raised by a grantee or subgrantee are not program income unless the revenues are specifically identified in the grant agreement or ED regulations as program income.

Royalties. Income from royalties and license fees for copyrighted material, patents, and inventions developed by a grantee or subgrantee is program income only if the revenues are specifically identified in the grant agreement or Federal agency regulations as program income.

Property. Proceeds from the sale of real property or equipment will be handled in accordance with the requirements of §§80.31 and 80.32.

Use of program income. Program income shall be deducted from outlays which may be both Federal and non-Federal as described below, unless ED regulations or the grant agreement specify another alternative (or a combination of alternatives). Alternatives may include:

1. *Deduction.* Ordinarily program income shall be deducted from total allowable costs to determine the net allowable costs. Program income shall be used for current costs unless the Federal agency authorizes otherwise. Program income which the grantee did not anticipate at the time of the award shall be used to reduce the Federal agency and grantee contributions rather than to increase the funds committed to the project.
2. *Addition.* When authorized, program income may be added to the funds committed to the grant agreement by the Federal agency and the grantee. The program income shall be used for the purposes and under the conditions of the grant agreement.
3. *Cost sharing or matching.* When authorized, program income may be used to meet the cost sharing or matching requirement of the grant agreement. The amount of the Federal grant award remains the same.

Income after the award period. There are no Federal requirements governing the disposition of program income earned after the end of the award period (i.e., until the ending date of the final financial report, unless the terms of the agreement or the Federal agency regulations provide otherwise.

§ 80.26 Non-Federal audit.

Basic Rule. Grantees and subgrantees are responsible for obtaining audits in accordance with the Single Audit Act Amendments of 1996 and OMB A–133. Audits shall be made by an independent auditor in accordance with generally accepted government auditing standards covering financial audits.

Auditor selection. In arranging for audit services, §80.36 shall be followed.

Subgrantees. State or local governments, as defined for purposes of the Single Audit Act Amendments of 1996, that provide Federal awards to a subgrantee which expends $300,000 or more (or other amount as specified by OMB) in Federal awards in a fiscal year shall:

1. Determine whether State or local subgrantees have met the audit requirements of the Act, and whether subgrantees covered by OMB A–110 have met the audit requirements of the Act. Commercial contractors (private for-profit and private and governmental organizations) providing goods and services to State and local governments are not required to have a single audit performed. State and local governments should use their own procedures to ensure contractor compliance with laws and regulations affecting the expenditures of Federal funds;
2. Determine whether the subgrantee spent Federal assistance funds provided in accordance with applicable laws and regulations. This may be accomplished by reviewing an audit of the subgrantee made in accordance with the Act, OMB A–133, or through other means (e.g., program reviews) if the subgrantee has not had such an audit;
3. Ensure that appropriate corrective action is taken within six months after receipt of the audit report in instance of noncompliance with Federal laws and regulations;
4. Consider whether subgrantee audits necessitate adjustment of the grantee's own records; and
5. Require subgrantees to permit independent auditors to access records and financial statements.

Changes, Property, and Subawards

§ 80.30 Changes.

General. Grantees and subgrantees are permitted to rebudget within the approved direct cost budget to meet unanticipated requirements and may make limited program changes to the approved project. However, unless waived by the awarding agency, certain types of post-award changes in budgets and projects shall require the prior written approval of the awarding agency.

Relation to cost principles. The applicable cost principles (see §80.22) contain requirements for prior approval of certain types of costs.

Budget changes:

1. *Non-construction projects.* Except as stated in other regulations or an award document, grantees or subgrantees shall obtain prior approval whenever any of the following changes is anticipated under a non-construction award:
    a. Any revision which would result in the need for additional funding;
    b. Unless waived by the awarding agency, cumulative transfers among direct cost categories, or among separately budgeted programs, projects, functions, or activities which exceed or are expected to exceed 10% of the current total approved budget, whenever the awarding agency's share exceeds $100,000; or
    c. Transfer of funds allotted for training allowances (i.e., from direct payments to trainees to other expense categories).
2. *Construction projects.* Grantees and subgrantees shall obtain prior written approval for any budget revision which would result in the need for additional funds.

3. *Combined construction and non-construction projects.* When a grant or subgrant provides funding for both construction and non-construction activities, the grantee or subgrantee must obtain prior written approval from the awarding agency before making any fund or budget transfer from non-construction to construction or vice versa.

Programmatic changes. Grantees or subgrantees must obtain the prior approval of the awarding agency whenever any of the following actions is anticipated:

1. Any revision of the scope or objectives of the project (regardless of whether there is an associated budget revision requiring prior approval);
2. Need to extend the period of availability of funds;
3. Changes in key persons in cases where specified in an application or a grant award. In research projects, a change in the project director or principal investigator shall always require approval unless waived by the awarding agency; or
4. Under non-construction projects, contracting out, subgranting (if authorized by law) or otherwise obtaining the services of a third party to perform activities which are central to the purposes of the award. This approval requirement is in addition to the approval requirements of §80.36 but does not apply to the procurement of equipment, supplies, and general support services.

Additional prior approval requirements. The awarding agency may not require prior approval for any budget revision which is not described above in Budget Changes.

Requesting prior approval.

1. A request for prior approval of any budget revision will be in the same budget format the grantee used in its application and shall be accompanied by a narrative justification for the proposed revision.
2. A prior approval request under the applicable Federal cost principles may be made by letter.
3. A request by a subgrantee for prior approval will be addressed in writing to the grantee. The grantee will promptly review such request and shall approve or disapprove the request in writing. A grantee will not approve any budget or project revision which is inconsistent with the purpose or terms and conditions of the Federal grant to the grantee. If the revision, requested by the subgrantee would result in a change to the grantee's approved project which requires Federal prior approval, the grantee will obtain the Federal agency's approval before approving the subgrantee's request.

§ 80.31 Real property.

Title. Subject to the conditions set forth in this section, title to real property acquired under a grant or subgrant will vest upon acquisition in the grantee or subgrantee respectively.

Use. Except as provided by Federal statutes, real property will be used for the originally authorized purposes as long as needed for that purposes, and the grantee or subgrantee shall not dispose of or encumber its title or other interests.

Disposition. When real property is no longer needed for the authorized purpose, the grantee or subgrantee will request disposition instructions from the awarding agency. The instructions will provide for one of the following alternatives:

1. *Retention of title.* Retain title after compensating the awarding agency. The amount paid to the awarding agency will be computed by applying the awarding agency's percentage of participation in the cost of the original purchase to the fair market value of the property.
2. *Sale of property.* Sell the property and compensate the awarding agency. The amount due to the

awarding agency will be calculated by applying the awarding agency's percentage of participation in the cost of the original purchase to the proceeds of the sale after deduction of any actual and reasonable selling and fixing-up expenses. If the grant is still active, the net proceeds from sale may be offset against the original cost of the property. When a grantee or subgrantee is directed to sell property, sales procedures shall be followed that provide for competition to the extent practicable and result in the highest possible return.

3. *Transfer of title.* Transfer title to the awarding agency or a third-party designated/approved by the awarding agency. Awardees shall be paid an amount calculated by applying the percentage of participation in purchasing the real property to the fair market property value.

The provisions of Disposition do not apply to disaster assistance under 20 U.S.C. 241–1(b)–(c) and the construction provisions of the Impact Aid Program, 20 U.S.C. 631–647.

§ 80.32 Equipment.

Title. Subject to the obligations and conditions set forth in this section, title to equipment acquired under a grant or subgrant will vest upon acquisition in the grantee or subgrantee respectively.

States. A State will use, manage, and dispose of equipment acquired under a grant by the State in accordance with State laws and procedures.

Use. Equipment shall be used by the grantee or subgrantee in the program or project for which it was acquired as long as needed, whether or not the project or program continues to be supported by Federal funds. When no longer needed for the original program or project, the equipment may be used in other activities currently or previously supported by a Federal agency. The grantee or subgrantee shall also make equipment available for use on other projects or programs currently or previously supported by the Federal Government, providing such use will not interfere with the work on the project for which it was originally acquired. First preference for other use shall be given to other programs or projects supported by the awarding agency. User fees should be considered if appropriate, but any awardee must not use equipment acquired with grant funds to provide services for a fee to compete unfairly with private companies that provide equivalent services.

Management requirements. Procedures for managing equipment (including replacement equipment), whether acquired in whole or in part with grant funds, until disposition takes place will, as a minimum, meet the following requirements:

1. Property records must be maintained that include a description of the property, a serial number or other identification number, the source of property, who holds title, the acquisition date, and cost of the property, percentage of Federal participation in the cost of the property, the location, use and condition of the property, and any ultimate disposition data including the date of disposal and sale price of the property.
2. A physical inventory of the property must be taken and the results reconciled with the property records at least once every two years.
3. A control system must be developed to ensure adequate safeguards to prevent loss, damage, or theft of the property. Any loss, damage, or theft shall be investigated.
4. Adequate maintenance procedures must be developed to keep the property in good condition.
5. If the grantee or subgrantee is authorized or required to sell the property, proper sales procedures must be established to ensure the highest possible return.

Disposition. When original or replacement equipment acquired under a grant or subgrant is no longer needed for the original project or program or for other activities currently or previously supported by a Federal agency, disposition of the equipment will be made as follows:

1. Items of equipment with a current per-unit fair market value of less than $5,000 may be retained, sold or otherwise disposed of with no further obligation to the awarding agency.
2. Items of equipment with a current per unit fair market value in excess of $5,000 may be retained or sold and the awarding agency shall have a right to an amount calculated by multiplying the current market value or proceeds from sale by the awarding agency's share of the equipment.
3. In cases where a grantee or subgrantee fails to take appropriate disposition actions, the awarding agency may direct the grantee or subgrantee to take excess and disposition actions.

Federal equipment. In the event a grantee or subgrantee is provided federally-owned equipment:

1. Title will remain vested in the Federal Government.
2. Grantees or subgrantees will manage the equipment in accordance with Federal agency rules and procedures, and submit an annual inventory listing.
3. When the equipment is no longer needed, the grantee or subgrantee will request disposition instructions from the Federal agency.

Right to transfer title. The Federal awarding agency may reserve the right to transfer title to the Federal Government or a third part named by the awarding agency when such a third party is otherwise eligible under existing statutes. Such transfers shall be subject to the following standards:

1. The property shall be identified in the grant or otherwise made known to the grantee in writing.
2. The Federal awarding agency shall issue disposition instruction within 120 calendar days after the end of the Federal support of the project for which it was acquired. If the Federal awarding agency fails to issue disposition instructions within the 120 calendar-day period the grantee shall follow §80.32(e).
3. When title to equipment is transferred, the grantee shall be paid an amount calculated by applying the percentage of participation in the purchase to the current fair market value of the property.

§ 80.33 Supplies.

Title to supplies acquired under a grant or subgrant will vest, upon acquisition, in the grantee or subgrantee respectively. If there is a residual inventory of unused supplies exceeding $5,000 in total aggregate fair market value upon termination or completion of the award (and if the supplies are not needed for any other federally sponsored programs), the grantee or subgrantee shall compensate the awarding agency for its share at the time of disposition.

§ 80.34 Copyrights.

The Federal awarding agency reserves a royalty-free, nonexclusive, and irrevocable license to reproduce, publish or otherwise use, and to authorize others to use, for Federal Government purposes:

1. The copyright in any work developed under a grant, subgrant, or contract under a grant or subgrant; and
2. Any rights of copyright to which a grantee, subgrantee or a contractor purchases ownership with grant support.

§ 80.35 Subawards to debarred and suspended parties.

Grantees and subgrantees must not make any award or permit any award to any party which is debarred, suspended, excluded from, or ineligible for participation in Federal programs under E.O. 12549.

§ 80.36 Procurement.

States. When procuring property and services under a grant, a State will follow the same policies and procedures it uses for procurements from its non-Federal funds. The State will ensure that every purchase order or other contract includes any clauses required by Federal statutes and E.O.s and their implementing regulations.

Procurement standards.

1. Grantees and subgrantees will use their own procurement procedures which reflect applicable State and local laws and regulations, provided that the procurements conform to applicable Federal law and the standards identified in this section.
2. Grantees and subgrantees will maintain a contract administration system which ensures that contractors perform in accordance with the terms, conditions, and specifications of their contracts or purchase orders.
3. Grantees and subgrantees will maintain a written code of standards of conduct governing the performance of their employees engaged in the award and administration of contracts. No employee, officer or agent of the grantee or subgrantee shall participate in selection, or in the award or administration of a contract supported by Federal funds if a conflict of interest, real or apparent, would be involved. Such a conflict would arise when the employee, officer or agent; any member of his immediate family; his or her partner; or an organization which employs (or is about to employ) any of the above has a financial or other interest in the firm selected for award. The awarding agency may in regulation provide additional prohibitions relative to real, apparent, or potential conflicts of interest.
4. Grantee and subgrantee procedures will provide for a review of proposed procurements to avoid purchase of unnecessary or duplicative items. Consideration should be given to consolidating or breaking out procurements to obtain a more economical purchase. Where appropriate, an analysis will be made of lease versus purchase alternatives, and any other appropriate analysis to determine the most economical approach.
5. To foster greater efficiency, grantees and subgrantees are encouraged to enter into State and local intergovernmental agreements for procurement or use of common goods and services.
6. Grantees and subgrantees are encouraged to use Federal excess and surplus property in lieu of purchasing new equipment and property whenever it is feasible and reduces project costs.
7. Grantees and subgrantees are encouraged to use value engineering clauses in contracts for construction projects of sufficient size to offer reasonable opportunities for cost reductions.
8. Grantees and subgrantees will make awards only to responsible contractors possessing the ability to perform successfully under the terms and conditions of a proposed procurement.
9. Grantees and subgrantees will maintain records sufficient to detail the significant history of a procurement. These records will include, but are not necessarily limited to the following: rationale for the method of procurement, selection of contract type, contractor selection or rejection, and the basis for the contract price.
10. Grantees and subgrantees will use time and material type contracts only after a determination that no other contract is suitable, and if the contract includes a ceiling price that the contractor exceeds at its own risk.
11. Grantees and subgrantees alone will be responsible, in accordance with good administrative practice and sound business judgment, for the settlement of all contractual and administrative issues arising out of procurements. These standards do not relieve the grantee or subgrantee of any contractual responsibilities under its contracts. Violations of law will be referred to the local, State, or Federal authority having proper jurisdiction.
12. Grantees and subgrantees will have protest procedures to handle and resolve disputes relating to their procurements and shall in all instances disclose information regarding the protest to the awarding agency.

Competition.

1. All procurement transactions will be conducted in a manner providing full and open competition consistent with the standards of §80.36.
2. Grantees and subgrantees will conduct procurements in a manner that prohibits the use of statuto-

rily or administratively imposed in-State or local geographical preferences in the evaluation of bids or proposals, except in those cases where applicable Federal statutes expressly mandate or encourage geographic preference.

3. Grantees will have written selection procedures for procurement transactions.
4. Grantees and subgrantees will ensure that all prequalified lists of persons, firms, or products which are used in acquiring goods and services are current and include enough qualified sources to ensure maximum open and free competition.

Methods of procurement to be followed.

1. Procurement by small purchase procedures. Small purchase procedures are those relatively simple and informal procurement methods for securing services, supplies, or other property that do not cost more than the simplified acquisition threshold fixed at 41 U.S.C. 403(11) (currently set at $100,000). If small purchase procedures are used, price or rate quotations shall be obtained from an adequate number of qualified sources.
2. Procurement by sealed bids (formal advertising). Bids are publicly solicited and a firm-fixed-price contract (lump sum or unit price) is awarded to the responsible bidder whose bid, conforming with all the material terms and conditions of the invitation for bids, is the lowest in price. The sealed bid method is the preferred method for procuring construction, if the conditions in §80.36(d)(2)(i) of the full Federal section apply.
3. Procurement by competitive proposals. The technique of competitive proposals is normally conducted with more than one source submitting an offer, and either a fixed-price or cost-reimbursement type contract is awarded. It is generally used when conditions are not appropriate for the use of sealed bids.
4. Procurement by noncompetitive proposals is procurement through solicitation of a proposal from only one source, or after solicitation of a number of sources, competition is determined inadequate.

Contracting with small and minority firms, women's business enterprise and labor surplus area firms. The grantee and subgrantee will take all necessary affirmative steps to assure that minority firms, women's business enterprises, and labor surplus area firms are used when possible.

Contract cost and price.

1. Grantees and subgrantees must perform a cost or price analysis in connection with every procurement action including contract modifications.
2. Grantees and subgrantees will negotiate profit as a separate element of the price for each contract where there is no price competition and in all cases where cost analysis is performed.
3. Costs or prices based on estimated costs for contracts under grants will be allowable only to the extent that costs incurred or cost estimates included in negotiated prices are consistent with Federal cost principles (see §80.22).
4. The cost plus a percentage of cost and percentage of construction cost methods of contracting shall not be used.

Awarding agency review.

1. Grantees and subgrantees must make available, upon request of the awarding agency, technical specifications on proposed procurements where the awarding agency believes such review is needed to ensure that the item and/or service specified is the one being proposed for purchase.
2. Grantees and subgrantees must on request make available for awarding agency pre-award review procurement documents, such as requests for proposals or invitations for bids, independent cost estimates, etc. in circumstances outlined by the full Federal section.

Bonding requirements. For construction or facility improvement contracts or subcontracts exceeding the simplified acquisition threshold, the awarding agency may accept the bonding policy and requirements of the grantee or subgrantee provided the awarding agency has made a determination that the awarding agency's interest is adequately protected.

Contract provisions. A grantee's and subgrantee's contracts must contain provisions as stated in the full Federal section. Federal agencies are permitted to require changes, remedies, changed conditions, access and records retention, suspension of work, and other clauses approved by the Office of Federal Procurement Policy.

1. Administrative, contractual, or legal remedies in instances where contractors violate or breach contract terms, and provide for such sanctions and penalties as may be appropriate for contracts more than the simplified acquisition threshold.
2. Termination for cause and for convenience by the grantee or subgrantee including the manner by which it will be effected and the basis for settlement. (All contracts in excess of $10,000)
3. Compliance with E.O. 11246 (Equal Employment Opportunity) for all construction contracts awarded in excess of $10,000 by grantees and their contractors or subgrantees.
4. Compliance with the Copeland "Anti-Kickback" Act for contracts and subgrants for construction or repair.
5. Compliance with the Davis-Bacon Act for construction contracts in excess of $2000 awarded by grantees and subgrantees when required by Federal grant program legislation.
6. Compliance with sections 103 and 107 of the Contract Work Hours and Safety Standards Act for construction contracts awarded by grantees and subgrantees in excess of $2000, and in excess of $2500 for other contracts which involve the employment of mechanics or laborers.
7. Notice of awarding agency requirements and regulations pertaining to reporting.
8. Notice of awarding agency requirements and regulations pertaining to patent rights with respect to any discovery or invention developed in the course of or under such contract.
9. Awarding agency requirements and regulations pertaining to copyrights and rights in data.
10. Access by the grantee, the subgrantee, the Federal grantor agency, the Comptroller General of the United States, or any of their duly authorized representatives to any books, documents, papers, and records of the contractor which are directly pertinent to that specific contract for the purpose of making audit, examination, excerpts, and transcriptions.
11. Retention of all required records for three years after grantees or subgrantees make final payments and all other pending matters are closed.
12. Compliance with all applicable standards, orders, or requirements issued under section 306 of the Clean Air Act, Clean Water Act, E.O. 11738, and EPA regulations in 40 CFR Part 15 for Contracts, subcontracts, and subgrants of amounts in excess of $100,000.
13. Mandatory standards and policies relating to energy efficiency contained in the state energy conservation plan issued in compliance with the Energy Policy and Conservation Act.

Contracting with faith-based organizations. A faith-based organization is eligible to contract with awardees, including States, on the same basis as any other private organization, with respect to contracts for which such other organizations are eligible. In the selection of goods and services providers, grantees and subgrantees (including States) shall not discriminate for or against a private organization on the basis of the organization's religious character or affiliation. A private organization that engages in inherently religious activities, such as religious worship, instruction, or proselytization, must offer those services separately in time or location from any programs or services supported by a contract, and participation in any such inherently religious activities by beneficiaries of the programs supported by the contract must be voluntary, unless the organization is selected as a result of the genuine and independent private choices of individual beneficiaries of the program and provided the organization otherwise satisfies the requirements of the program.

§ 80.37 Subgrants.

States. States shall follow state law and procedures when awarding and administering subgrants (whether on a cost reimbursement or fixed amount basis) of financial assistance to local and Indian tribal governments. States shall:

1. Ensure that every subgrant includes any clauses required by Federal statute and E.O.s and their implementing regulations;
2. Ensure that subgrantees are aware of requirements imposed by Federal statute and regulation;
3. Ensure that a provision for compliance with §80.42 is placed in every cost reimbursement subgrant; and
4. Conform any advances of grant funds to subgrantees substantially to the same standards of timing and amount that apply to cash advances by Federal agencies.

All other grantees. All other grantees shall follow the provisions of this part which are applicable to awarding agencies when awarding and administering subgrants (whether on a cost reimbursement or fixed amount basis) of financial assistance to local and Indian tribal governments. Grantees shall:

1. Ensure that every subgrant includes a provision for compliance with this part;
2. Ensure that every subgrant includes any clauses required by Federal statute and E.O.s and their implementing regulations; and
3. Ensure that subgrantees are aware of requirements imposed by Federal statutes and regulations.

Exceptions. By their own terms, certain provisions of this part do not apply to the award and administration of subgrants. These include Section 80.10, Section 80.11; Section 80.50, and the letter-of-credit procedures specified in Treasury Regulations at 31 CFR Part 205, cited in §80.21.

Reports, Records Retention, and Enforcement

§ 80.40 Monitoring and reporting program performance.

Monitoring by grantees. Grantees are responsible for managing the day-to-day operations of grant and subgrant supported activities. Grantees must monitor these activities to assure compliance with applicable Federal requirements and that performance goals are being achieved. Grantee monitoring must cover each program, function or activity.

Non-construction performance reports. If the Federal agency decides that performance information from subsequent applications is insufficient, it may require the grantee to submit a performance report only upon expiration or termination of grant support. Unless waived by the Federal agency, this report will be due on the same date as the final Financial Status Report.

1. Grantees shall submit annual performance reports unless the awarding agency requires quarterly or semi-annual reports. However, performance reports will not be required more frequently than quarterly. Annual reports shall be due 90 days after the grant year, quarterly or semi-annual reports shall be due 30 days after the reporting period. The final performance report will be due 90 days after the expiration or termination of grant support. If a justified request is submitted by a grantee, ED may extend the due date for any performance report. Additionally, requirements for unnecessary performance reports may be waived by ED.
2. Performance reports will contain a comparison of actual accomplishments to the objectives established for the period, reasons for slippage if established objectives were not met, analysis and explanation of cost overruns or high unit costs.
3. Grantees will submit no more than one original and two copies of performance reports.
4. Grantees will adhere to the standards in this section in prescribing performance reporting requirements for subgrantees.

Construction performance reports. Federal agencies rely upon on-site technical inspections and certified percentage-of-completion data to monitor progress under construction grants.

Significant developments. Events may occur between the scheduled performance reporting dates which impact the grant or subgrant supported activity. In such cases, the grantee must inform ED as soon as the following types of conditions become known:

1. Problems, delays, or adverse conditions which will materially impair the ability to meet the objective of the award; and
2. Favorable developments which enable meeting time schedules and objectives sooner or at less cost than anticipated or producing more beneficial results than originally planned.

Site visits. Federal agencies may make site visits as warranted by program needs.

Waivers, extensions. Federal agencies may waive any performance report required by this part if not needed. The grantee may waive any performance report from a subgrantee when not needed.

§ 80.41 Financial reporting.
General.

1. Except as provided in 2) and 5) below, grantees will use only the forms specified in this section, and such supplementary or forms as may be authorized by OMB, for submitting financial reports to Federal agencies or requesting advances or reimbursements when letters of credit are not used.
2. Grantees need not apply the forms prescribed in this section in dealing with their subgrantees; however, grantees shall not impose more burdensome requirements on subgrantees.
3. Grantees shall follow all applicable standard and supplemental Federal agency instructions approved by OMB to the extend required under the Paperwork Reduction Act of 1980 for use in connection with forms specified in following paragraphs of this section. Federal agencies may issue substantive supplementary instructions only with the approval of OMB, but may instruct grantees to disregard any line item that ED finds unnecessary for decision-making purposes.
4. Grantees will not be required to submit more than one original and two copies of forms required under this part.
5. Federal agencies may provide computer outputs to grantees to expedite or contribute to the accuracy of reporting. Federal agencies may accept the required information from grantees in machine usable format or computer printouts instead of prescribed forms.
6. Federal agencies may waive any report required by this section if not needed.
7. Federal agencies may extend the due date of any financial report upon receiving a justified request from a grantee.

Financial Status Report.

1. *Form.* Grantees will use SF269 or 269A (Financial Status Report) to report the status of funds for all non-construction grants, and for construction grants when required in accordance with criteria listed in the full Federal section.
2. *Accounting basis.* Each grantee will report program outlays and program income on a cash or accrual basis as prescribed by the awarding agency. If the Federal agency requires accrual information and the grantee's accounting records are not normally kept on the accrual basis, the grantee shall not be required to convert its accounting system but shall develop such accrual information through and analysis of the documentation on hand.
3. *Frequency.* The Federal agency may prescribe the frequency of the report for each project or program; however, the report will not be required more frequently than quarterly. If the Federal agency

does not specify the frequency of the report, it will be submitted annually. A final report will be required upon expiration or termination of grant support.

4. *Due date.* When reports are required on a quarterly or semiannual basis, they will be due 30 days after the reporting period. When required on an annual basis, they will be due 90 days after the grant year. Final reports will be due 90 days after the expiration or termination of grant support.

Federal Cash Transactions Report.

1. *Form.* For grants paid by letter or credit, Treasury check advances or electronic transfer of funds, the grantee will submit the SF272 (Federal Cash Transactions Report) and SF272A (unless the terms of the award exempt the grantee from this requirement). These reports will be used by ED to monitor cash advanced to grantees and to obtain disbursement or outlay information for each grant from grantees. The format of the report may be adapted as appropriate when reporting is to be accomplished with the assistance of automatic data processing equipment provided that the information to be submitted is not changed in substance.
2. *Forecasts of Federal cash requirements.* Forecasts of Federal cash requirements may be required in the "Remarks" section of the report.
3. *Cash in hands of subgrantees.* When considered necessary by ED, grantees may be required to report the amount of cash advances in excess of three days' needs in the hands of their subgrantees or contractors and to provide short narrative explanations of actions taken by the grantee to reduce the excess balances.
4. *Frequency and due date.* Grantees must submit the report no later than 15 working days following the end of each quarter. Where an advance either by letter of credit or electronic transfer of funds is authorized at an annualized rate of $1 million or more, the Federal agency may require the report to be submitted within 15 working days following the end of each month.

Request for advance or reimbursement.

1. *Advance payments.* Requests for Treasury check advance payments will be submitted on SF-270 (Request for Advance or Reimbursement).
2. *Reimbursements.* Requests for reimbursement under non-construction grants will also be submitted on SF-270.
3. The frequency for submitting payment requests is treated in second paragraph, number 3.

Outlay report and request for reimbursement for construction programs.

1. *Grants that support construction activities paid by reimbursement method.* Requests for reimbursement under construction grants will be submitted on SF271 (Outlay Report and Request for Reimbursement for Construction Programs). Federal agencies may prescribe the Request for Advance or Reimbursement form instead of this form. The frequency for submitting reimbursement requests is treated in this section in paragraph two, number three.
2. *Grants that support construction activities paid by letter of credit, electronic funds transfer or Treasury check advance.* When a construction grant is paid by letter of credit, electronic funds transfer or Treasury check advances, the grantee will report its outlays to the Federal agency using SF-271 (Outlay Report and Request for Reimbursement for Construction Programs). The Federal agency will provide any necessary special instruction. However, frequency and due date shall be governed by numbers three and four of the second paragraph above. When a construction grant is paid by Treasury check advances based on periodic requests from the grantee, advances will be requested, generally, on the SF-270.
3. *Accounting basis.* The accounting basis for the Outlay Report and Request for Reimbursement for Construction Programs shall be governed by the second paragraph of this section, number two.

§ 80.42 Retention and access requirements for records.

Applicability. This section applies to all financial and programmatic records, supporting documents, statistical records, and other records of grantees or subgrantees which are:

1. Required to be maintained by the terms of this part, program regulations or the grant agreement; or
2. Otherwise reasonably considered as pertinent to program regulations or the grant agreement. This section does not apply to records maintained by contractors or subcontractors.

Length of retention period. Except as otherwise provided, records must be retained for three years from the starting date specified in the starting date of retention period (below). If any litigation, claim, negotiation, or audit involving the records has been started before the expiration of the three-year period, the records must be retained the action is resolved, or until the end of the regular three-year period, whichever is later. When the records are transferred to or maintained by the Federal agency, the three-year retention requirement is not applicable to the grantee or subgrantee.

Starting date of retention period. In general, when grant support is continued or renewed at annual or other intervals, the retention period for the records of each funding period starts on the day the grantee or subgrantee submits to the awarding agency a single or last expenditure report for that period. However, if grant support is continued or renewed quarterly, the retention period for each year's records starts on the day the grantee submits its expenditure report for the last quarter of the Federal fiscal year. In all other cases, the retention period starts on the day the grantee submits its final expenditure report. If an expenditure report has been waived, the retention period starts on the day the report would have been due.

1. *Real property and equipment records.* The retention period for real property and equipment records starts from the date of the disposition, replacement, or transfer at the direction of the awarding agency.
2. *Records for income transactions after grant or subgrant support.* In some cases grantees must report income after the period of grant support. Where there is such a requirement, the retention period for the records pertaining to the earning of the income starts from the end of the grantee's fiscal year in which the income is earned.
3. *Indirect cost rate proposals, cost allocations plans, etc.* This paragraph applies to indirect cost rate computations or proposals, cost allocation plans, and any similar accounting computations of the rate at which a particular group of costs is chargeable (such as computer usage chargeback rates or composite fringe benefit rates).

Substitution of microfilm. Copies made by microfilming, photocopying, or similar methods may be substituted for the original records.

Access. The Secretary and Comptroller General of the U.S., or any of their duly authorized representatives, have the right of access to any books, documents, papers, or other records of recipients that are pertinent to the award, in order to make audits, examinations, excerpts, transcripts, and copies of documents.

Restrictions on public access. The Freedom of Information Act (5 U.S.C. 552) does not apply to records. Unless required by Federal, State, or local law, grantees and subgrantees are not required to permit public access to their records.

§ 80.43 Enforcement.

Remedies for noncompliance. If a grantee or subgrantee fails to comply with any term of an award, the awarding agency may take one or more of the following actions, as appropriate in the circumstances:

1. Temporarily withhold cash payments pending correction of the deficiency by the grantee or subgrantee or more severe enforcement action by the awarding agency;

2. Disallow (that is, deny both use of funds and matching credit for) all or part of the cost of the activity or action not in compliance;
3. Wholly or partly suspend or terminate the current award for the grantee's or subgrantee's program; or
4. Withhold further awards for the program.

Hearings, appeals. In taking an enforcement action, the awarding agency will provide the grantee or subgrantee an opportunity for a hearing, appeal, or other administrative proceeding to which they are entitled under any statute or regulation applicable to the action involved.

Effects of suspension and termination. Costs resulting from obligations incurred by the grantee or subgrantee during a suspension or after termination of an award are not allowable unless the awarding agency expressly authorizes them. Other grantee or subgrantee costs during suspension or after termination which are necessary and not reasonably avoidable are allowable if:

1. The costs result from obligations which were properly incurred by the grantee or subgrantee before the effective date of suspension or termination, are not in anticipation of it, and, in the case of a termination, are non-cancellable; and
2. The costs would be allowable if the award were not suspended or expired normally at the end of the funding period in which the termination takes effect.

Relationship to debarment and suspension. The enforcement remedies identified in this section, including suspension and termination, do not preclude grantee or subgrantee from being subject to "Debarment and Suspension" under E.O. 12549.

§ 80.44 Termination for convenience.

Except as provided in §80.43, awards may be terminated in whole or in part only as follows:

1. By the awarding agency with the consent of the grantee or subgrantee, in which case the two parties shall agree upon termination conditions; or
2. By the grantee or subgrantee upon written notification to the awarding agency, setting forth the reasons and conditions for such termination.

Subpart D—After-the-Grant Requirements

§ 80.50 Closeout.

General. The Federal agency will close out the award when it determines that all applicable administrative actions and required work of the grant has been completed.

Reports. Within 90 days after the expiration or termination of the grant, the grantee must submit all financial, performance, and other reports required as a condition of the grant. Upon request by the grantee, Federal agencies may extend this timeframe. These may include but are not limited to:

1. Final performance or progress report.
2. Financial Status Report (SF 269) or Outlay Report and Request for Reimbursement for Construction Programs (SF–271) (as applicable).
3. Final request for payment (SF–270) (if applicable).
4. Invention disclosure (if applicable).

Federally-owned property report. In accordance with §80.32(f), a grantee must submit an inventory of all federally owned property (as distinct from property acquired with grant funds) for which it is accountable and request disposition instructions from the Federal agency of property no longer needed.

Cost adjustment. The Federal agency will, within 90 days after receipt of reports in paragraph (b) of this section, make upward or downward adjustments to the allowable costs.

Cash adjustments. The Federal agency will make prompt payment to grantees for allowable reimbursable costs. Grantees must immediately refund any balance of unobligated (unencumbered) cash advanced that is not authorized to be retained for use on other grants.

§ 80.51 Later disallowances and adjustments.

The closeout of a grant does not affect:

1. The Federal agency's right to disallow costs and recover funds on the basis of a later audit or other review;
2. The grantee's obligation to return any funds due as a result of later refunds, corrections, or other transactions;
3. Records retention as required in §80.42;
4. Property management requirements in §§80.31 and 80.32; and
5. Audit requirements in §80.26.

§ 80.52 Collection of amounts due.

Funds paid to a recipient in excess of the amount to which the recipient is determined to be entitled under the terms of the award constitute a debt to the Government. If not paid within a reasonable period after the demand for payment, the Secretary may reduce the debt by making an administrative offset against other requests for reimbursements or withholding advance payments due to the recipient. Except as otherwise provided by law, the Secretary charges interest on overdue debts in accordance with 4 CFR Chapter II—Federal Claims Collection Standards.

PART 81—GENERAL EDUCATION PROVISIONS ACT—ENFORCEMENT

Subpart A—General Provisions

§ 81.1 Purpose.
The regulations in this part govern the enforcement of legal requirements under applicable programs administered by the ED and implement Part E of the General Education Provisions Act (GEPA).

§ 81.2 Definitions.
The following definitions apply to the terms used in this part:

- *Administrative Law Judge (ALJ)* - a judge appointed by the Secretary in accordance with section 451 (b) and (c) of GEPA.
- *Applicable program* - any program for which the Secretary of Education has administrative responsibility, except a program authorized by:
    1. The Higher Education Act of 1965, as amended;
    2. The Act of September 30, 1950 (Pub. L. 874, 81st Congress), as amended; or
    3. The Act of September 23, 1950 (Pub. L. 815, 81st Congress), as amended.
- *Department* and *ED* - the United States Department of Education.
- *Disallowance decision* - the decision of an authorized ED official that a recipient must return funds because it made an expenditure of funds that was not allowable or otherwise failed to discharge its obligation to account properly for funds.
- *Party* means either of the following:
    1. A recipient that appeals a decision;
    2. An authorized ED official who issues a decision that is appealed.
- *Recipient* - the recipient of a grant or cooperative agreement under an applicable program.
- *Secretary* - the Secretary of the ED or an official acting under a delegation of authority.

§ 81.3 Jurisdiction of the Office of Administrative Law Judges.
The Office of Administrative Law Judges (established under Part E of GEPA and whose regulations are at 34 CFR Part 81) has the jurisdiction to conduct:

1. Recovery of Funds hearings under section 452 of GEPA;
2. Withholding Hearings under section 455 of GEPA;
3. Cease and Desist hearings under section 456 of GEPA; and any other proceeding designated by the Secretary under section 451 of GEPA.

§ 81.4 Membership and assignment to cases.
The Secretary appoints Administrative Law Judges (ALJ) as members of the OALJ. A chief judge will be responsible for the administration of the OALJ and will assign an ALJ to each case or class of cases within the jurisdiction of the OALJ.

§ 81.5 Authority and responsibility of an Administrative Law Judge.
An ALJ assigned to a case conducts a hearing on the record, and regulates the course of the proceedings and the conduct of the parties to ensure a fair, expeditious, and economical resolution of the case in accordance with applicable law.

§ 81.6 Hearing on the record.
A hearing on the record is a process for the orderly presentation of evidence and arguments by the parties. Except as otherwise provided, an ALJ conducts a hearing on the basis of briefs and other written submissions unless he or she determines:

1. That an evidentiary hearing is needed to resolve a material factual issue in dispute; or
2. That oral argument is needed to clarify the issues in the case.

§ 81.7 Non-party participation.
A person or organization, other than a party, that wishes to participate in a case shall file an application to participate with the ALJ assigned to the case. The application must identify:
1. The case in which participation is sought;
2. How the applicant's interest relates to the case;
3. How the applicant's participation would aid in the disposition of the case; and
4. How the applicant seeks to participate.

§ 81.8 Representation.
A party to, or other participant in, a case may be represented by counsel.

§ 81.9 Location of proceedings.
Any in-person conference, hearing, argument, telephone conference call, or other proceeding at which the parties are required to appear in person is held in the Washington, DC area unless the ALJ determines that the convenience and necessity of the parties or their representatives requires that it be held elsewhere.

§ 81.10 Ex parte communications.
A party to, or other participant in, a case may not communicate with an ALJ on any fact in issue in the case or on any matter relevant to the merits of the case unless the parties are given notice and an opportunity to participate.

§ 81.11 Motions.
To obtain an order or a ruling from an ALJ, a party shall make a motion to the ALJ (generally in writing). If a party files a motion, the party shall serve a copy of the motion on the other party on the filing date by hand-delivery or by mail. If agreed upon by the parties, service of the motion may be made upon the other party by facsimile transmission. Except for a request for an extension of time, the ALJ may not grant a party's written motion without the consent of the other party unless the other party has had at least 21 days from the date of service of the motion to respond. However, the ALJ may deny a motion without awaiting a response.

§ 81.12 Filing requirements.
Any written submission to an ALJ or the OALJ under this part must be filed by hand-delivery, mail, or by fax. Note: a party filing by fax is responsible for confirming that a complete and legible copy of the document was received by ED, and must also file a hand-delivered or mailed copy. Any written submission to an ALJ or the OALJ must be accompanied by a statement certifying the date that the filed material was filed and served on the other party.

§ 81.13 Mediation.
Voluntary mediation is available for proceedings that are pending before the OALJ. A party may request mediation by filing a motion with the ALJ assigned to the case, and the OALJ arranges for an independent mediator (agreed by both parties) if the parties to the case agree to mediation.

§ 81.14 Settlement negotiations.
If the parties to a case file a joint motion requesting a stay of the proceedings for settlement negotiations, or for approval of a settlement agreement, the ALJ may grant a stay of the proceedings upon a finding of good cause. Parties may not disclose the contents of settlement negotiations to the ALJ. If the parties enter into a settlement agreement and file a joint motion to dismiss the case, the ALJ grants the motion.

§ 81.15 Evidence.

The Federal Rules of Evidence do not apply to proceedings under this part. However, the ALJ accepts only evidence that is relevant, material, not unduly repetitious, and not inadmissible under §81.13 or §81.14. The ALJ may take official notice of facts that are generally known or capable of accurate and ready determination by resort to sources whose accuracy cannot reasonably be questioned.

§ 81.16 Discovery.

The parties to a case are encouraged to exchange relevant documents and information voluntarily. The ALJ, at a party's request, may order compulsory discovery if he or she determines that:

1. The order is necessary to secure a fair, expeditious, and economical resolution of the case;
2. The discovery requested is likely to elicit relevant information with respect to an issue in the case;
3. The discovery request was not made primarily for the purposes of delay or harassment; and
4. The order would serve the ends of justice.

If a compulsory discovery is permissible, the ALJ may order a party to do one or more of the following:

1. Make relevant documents available for inspection and copying by the party making the request.
2. Answer written interrogatories that inquire into relevant matters.
3. Have depositions taken.

§ 81.17 Privileges.

The privilege of a person or governmental organization not to produce documents or provide information in a proceeding under this part is governed by the principles of common law as interpreted by U.S. courts.

§ 81.18 The record.

The ALJ arranges for any evidentiary hearing or oral argument to be recorded and transcribed and makes the transcript available to the parties at a cost not to exceed the actual cost of duplication. The record of a hearing consists of all papers filed in the proceeding, admitted documentary evidence, the transcript of any evidentiary hearing or oral argument, and any materials issued by the ALJ.

§ 81.19 Costs and fees of parties.

The Equal Access to Justice Act, 5 U.S.C. 504, applies by its terms to proceedings under this part. Regulations under that statute are in 34 CFR Part 21.

§ 81.20 Interlocutory appeals to the Secretary from rulings of an ALJ.

A petition for interlocutory review of an interim ruling must include the following:

1. A statement of the facts necessary to an understanding of the issue on which review is sought.
2. A statement of the issue.
3. A statement of the reasons showing that the ruling complained of involves a controlling question of substantive or procedural law and why immediate review of the ruling will materially advance the disposition of the case, or why subsequent review will be an inadequate remedy.

A petition may not exceed 10 double-spaced pages and must be accompanied by a copy of the ruling and any findings and opinions relating to the ruling. The petition must be filed with the Office of Hearings and Appeals, which forwards it to the Office of the Secretary. A copy must be provided to the ALJ at the time the petition is filed, and a copy of a petition or any certification must be served upon the parties by certified mail, return receipt requested. The petition or certification must reflect that service.

Subpart B—Hearings for Recovery of Funds

§ 81.30 Basis for recovery of funds.

Subject to §81.31, an authorized ED official requires a recipient to return funds to the Department if the recipient:

1. Made an unallowable expenditure of funds under a grant or cooperative agreement; or
2. Otherwise failed to discharge its obligation to account properly for funds under a grant or cooperative agreement.

§ 81.31 Measure of recovery.

A recipient that made an unallowable expenditure or otherwise failed to discharge its obligation to account properly for funds shall return an amount that:

1. Meets the standards for proportionality in §81.32;
2. In the case of a state or lea, excludes any amount attributable to mitigating circumstances under the standards in §81.23; and
3. Excludes any amount expended in a manner not authorized by law more than five years before the recipient received the notice of a disallowance decision under §81.34.

§ 81.32 Proportionality.

A recipient that made an unallowable expenditure or failed to properly account for funds shall return an amount proportional to the extent of harm its violation caused to an identifiable Federal interest associated with the program under which it received the grant or cooperative agreement. An identifiable Federal interest of this section includes, but is not limited to, the following:

1. Serving only eligible beneficiaries.
2. Providing only authorized services or benefits.
3. Complying with expenditure requirements and conditions, such as set-aside, excess cost, maintenance of effort, comparability, supplement-not-supplant, and matching requirements.
4. Preserving the integrity of planning, application, recordkeeping, and reporting requirements.
5. Maintaining accountability for the use of funds.

§ 81.33 Mitigating circumstances.

A recipient that is a State or LEA that has made an unallowable expenditure or failed to properly account for funds is not required to return any amount that is attributable to the mitigating circumstances described in paragraph (b), (c), or (d) of the full Federal section. Mitigating circumstances exist if it would be unjust to compel the recovery of funds because the recipient's violation was caused by erroneous written guidance from ED, failure by ED to provide timely guidance, or compliance with a judicial decree from a court of competent jurisdiction. To prove mitigating circumstances under this paragraph, the recipient shall prove that mitigating circumstances.

§ 81.34 Notice of a disallowance decision.

If an authorized ED official decides that a recipient must return funds under §81.30, the official gives written notice of a disallowance decision by certified mail, return receipt requested, or other means that ensure proof of receipt. The notice must inform the recipient that it may obtain a review of the disallowance decision by the OALJ and request mediation under §81.13. The notice must also describe the time available to apply for a review of the disallowance decision and the procedure for filing an application for review.

§ 81.35 Reduction of claims.

The Secretary or an authorized ED official as appropriate may, after the issuance of a disallowance decision, reduce the amount of a claim established under this subpart by:

1. Redetermining the claim on the basis of the proper application of the law, including the standards for the measure of recovery under §81.31, to the facts;
2. Compromising the claim under the Federal Claims Collection Standards in 4 CFR Part 103; or
3. Compromising the claim under §81.36, if applicable.

§ 81.36 Compromise of claims under General Education Provisions Act.
ED may compromise a claim established under this subpart without following the procedures in 4 CFR 103 if the amount does not exceed $200,000 or the difference between the amount of the claim and the amount agreed to be returned does not exceed $200,000. Not less than 45 days before compromising a claim under this section, ED publishes a notice in the Federal Register stating the intention to compromise the claim and that interested persons may comment on the proposed compromise.

§ 81.37 Application for review of a disallowance decision.
If a recipient wishes to obtain review of a disallowance decision, they shall file a written application for review with the Office of Administrative Law Judges, c/o Docket Clerk, Office of Hearings and Appeals, and serve a copy on the applicable Departmental official who made the disallowance decision. This shall be filed for review not later than 60 days after the date it receives the notice of a disallowance decision. An application for review must contain:

1. A copy of the disallowance decision of which review is sought;
2. A statement certifying the date the recipient received the notice of that decision;
3. A short and plain statement of the disputed issues of law and fact, the recipient's position with respect to these issues, and the disallowed funds the recipient contends need not be returned; and
4. A statement of the facts and the reasons that support the recipient's position.

§ 81.38 Consideration of an application for review.
The ALJ assigned to the case under §81.4 considers an application for review of a disallowance decision. The ALJ decides whether the notice of a disallowance decision meets the requirements of §81.34, as provided by Section 451(e) of GEPA. If the notice does not meet those requirements, the ALJ:

1. Returns the notice, as expeditiously as possible, to the authorized Departmental official who made the disallowance decision;
2. Gives the official the reasons why the notice does not meet the requirements of §81.34; and
3. Informs the recipient of the ALJ's decision by certified mail, return receipt requested.

§ 81.39 Submission of evidence.
The ALJ schedules the submission of the evidence to occur within 90 days of the OALJ's receipt of an acceptable application for review. The ALJ may waive the 90-day requirement for good cause.

§ 81.40 Burden of proof.
If the OALJ accepts jurisdiction of a case under §81.38, the recipient shall present its case first and have the burden of proving that the recipient is not required to return the amount of funds that the disallowance decision requires to be returned because:

1. An expenditure identified in the disallowance decision as unallowable was allowable;
2. The recipient discharged its obligation to account properly for the funds;
3. The amount required to be returned does not meet the standards for proportionality in §81.32;
4. The amount required to be returned includes an amount attributable to mitigating circumstances under the standards in §81.33; or
5. The amount required to be returned includes an amount expended in a manner not authorized by law more than five years before the recipient received the notice of the disallowance decision.

§ 81.41 Initial decision.
The ALJ makes an initial decision based on the record that includes the ALJ's findings of fact, conclusions of law, and reasoning on all material issues. The initial decision is transmitted to the Secretary, and to the parties (by certified mail, return receipt requested), by the OALJ.

§ 81.42 Petition for review of initial decision.
If a party seeks to obtain the Secretary's review of the initial decision of an ALJ, the party shall file a petition for review with the Office of Hearings and Appeals, which immediately forwards the petition to the Office of the Secretary. A party shall file a petition no later than 30 days after it receives the initial decision. Any written submission to the Secretary under this section must be accompanied by a statement certifying the date that the filed material was served on the other party. A petition for review of an initial decision must contain the identity of the initial decision for which review is sought and a statement of the reasons asserted by the party for affirming, modifying, setting aside, or remanding the initial decision in whole or in part. The filing date for written submissions under this section is the date the document is hand delivered, mailed, or faxed.

§ 81.43 Review by the Secretary.
The Secretary's review of an initial decision is based on the record of the case, the initial decision, and any proper submissions of the parties or other participants in the case. During this review, there shall not be any ex parte contact between the Secretary and individuals representing ED or the recipient. The Secretary may affirm, modify, set aside, or remand the ALJ's initial decision to take further evidence, and the ALJ may make new or modified findings of fact and may modify the initial decision based on new evidence. These new findings of fact are likewise conclusive if supported by substantial evidence.

§ 81.44 Final decision of the Department.
The ALJ's initial decision becomes the final decision of the Department 60 days after the recipient receives the ALJ's decision unless the Secretary modifies, sets aside, or remands the decision during the 60-day period.

§ 81.45 Collection of claims.
Pursuant to 34 CFR Part 30, a claim established under this subpart may be collected:

1. 30 days after a recipient receives notice of a disallowance decision if the recipient fails to file an acceptable application for review under §81.37; or
2. On the date of the final ED decision under §81.44 if the recipient obtains review of a disallowance decision.

Appendix to Part 81—Illustrations of Proportionality
Ineligible beneficiaries. A State uses 15% of its grant to meet the special educational needs of children who were migratory, but who have not migrated for more than five years as a program statute requires for eligibility to participate in the program. Result: Recovery of 15% of the grant—all program funds spent for the benefit of ineligible children.

Ineligible beneficiaries. A Federal program designed to meet the special educational needs of gifted and talented children requires that at least 80% of the children served in any project must be identified as gifted or talented. A local educational agency (LEA) conducts a project in which 76 students are gifted or talented and 24 are not. The project was designed and implemented to meet the special educational needs of gifted and talented students. Result: The LEA must return 5% of the project costs. The LEA provided authorized services for a project in which the 76 target students had to constitute at least 80% of the total. Thus, the maximum number of non-target students permitted was 19. Project costs relating to the remaining five students must be returned.

Unauthorized activities. An LEA uses 10% of its grant under a Federal program that authorizes activities only to meet the special educational needs of educationally deprived children to pay for health services that are available to all children in the LEA. All the children who use the Federally funded health services happen to be educationally deprived, and thus eligible to receive program services. Result: Recovery of 10% of the grant—all program funds spent for the health services. Although the children were eligible to receive program services, the health services were unrelated to a special educational need and, therefore, not authorized by law.

Set-aside requirement. A State uses 22% of its grant for one fiscal year under a Federal adult education program to provide programs of equivalency to a certificate of graduation from a secondary school. The adult education program statute restricts those programs to no more than 20% of the State's grant. Result: 2% of the State's grant must be returned. Although all 22% of the funds supported adult education, the State had no authority to spend more than 20% on secondary school equivalency programs.

Set-aside requirement. A State uses 8% of its basic State grant under a Federal vocational education program to pay for the excess cost of vocational education services and activities for handicapped individuals. The program statute requires a State to use 10% of its basic State grant for this purpose. Result: The State must return 2% of its basic State grant, regardless of how it was used. Because the State was required to spend that 2% on services and activities for handicapped individuals and did not do so, it diverted those funds from their intended purposes, and the Federal interest was harmed to that extent.

Excess cost requirement. An LEA uses funds reserved for the disadvantaged under a Federal vocational education program to pay for the cost of the same vocational education services it provides to non-disadvantaged individuals. Program statute requires that funds reserved for the disadvantaged must be used to pay for the additional costs of vocational education services that are not provided to other individuals and that are required for disadvantaged individuals to participate in vocational education. Result: All the funds spent on the disadvantaged must be returned. Although the funds were spent to serve the disadvantaged, the funds were available to pay for only the supplemental or additional costs of providing services to the disadvantaged.

Supplanting prohibition. An LEA uses funds under a Federal drug education program to provide drug abuse prevention counseling to students in the 8th grade. The LEA is required to provide that same counseling under State law. Funds under the Federal program statute are subject to a supplement-not-supplant requirement. Result: All the funds used to provide the required counseling to the 8th grade students must be returned. The Federal funds did not increase the total amount of spending for program purposes because the counseling would have been provided with non-Federal funds if the Federal funds were not available.

Matching requirement. A State receives an allotment of $90,000 for fiscal year 1988 under a Federal adult education program. It spends its full allotment and $8,000 from its own resources for adult education. Under the Federal statute, the Federal share of expenditures for the State's program is 90%. Result: The State must return the unmatched Federal funds, or $18,000. Expenditure of a $90,000 Federal allotment required $10,000 in matching State expenditures, $2,000 more than the State's actual expenditures. At a ratio of one State dollar for every nine Federal dollars, $18,000 in Federal funds were unmatched.

Harmless violation. Under a Federal program, a grantee is required to establish a 15-member advisory council of affected teachers, school administrators, parents, and students to assist in program design, monitoring, and evaluation. Although the law requires at least three student members of the council, a grantee's council contains only two. The project is carried out, and no damage to the project attributable to the lack of a third student member can be identified. Result: No financial recovery is required, although the grantee must take other appropriate steps to come into compliance with the law. The grantee's violation has not measurably harmed a Federal interest associated with the program.

PART 82—NEW RESTRICTIONS ON LOBBYING

Subpart A—General

§ 82.100 Conditions on use of funds.

No appropriated funds may be expended by the recipient of a Federal contract, grant, loan, or cooperative agreement to pay any person for influencing or attempting to influence an officer or employee of any agency, a Member of Congress, an officer or employee of Congress, or an employee of a Member of Congress in connection with any of the following covered Federal actions: the awarding of any Federal contract, the making of any Federal grant, the making of any Federal loan, the entering into of any cooperative agreement, and the extension, continuation, renewal, amendment, or modification of any Federal contract, grant, loan, or cooperative agreement. See Appendix A and B to this part.

§ 82.105 Definitions for purposes of this part.

- *Agency*, as defined in 5 U.S.C. 552(f), includes Federal executive departments and agencies as well as independent regulatory commissions and Government corporations, as defined in 31 U.S.C. 9101(1).
- *Covered Federal action* - any of the following Federal actions:
  1. The awarding of any Federal contract;
  2. The making of any Federal grant;
  3. The making of any Federal loan;
  4. The entering into of any cooperative agreement; and,
  5. The extension, continuation, renewal, amendment, or modification of any Federal contract, grant, loan, or cooperative agreement.
- *Federal contract* - an acquisition contract awarded by an agency, including those subject to the Federal Acquisition Regulation (FAR), and any other acquisition contract for real or personal property or services not subject to the FAR.
- *Federal cooperative agreement* - a cooperative agreement entered into by an agency.
- *Federal grant* - an award of financial assistance in the form of money, or property in lieu of money, by the Federal Government or a direct appropriation made by law to any person. The term does not include technical assistance which provides services instead of money, or other assistance in the form of revenue sharing, loans, loan guarantees, loan insurance, interest subsidies, insurance, or direct United States cash assistance to an individual.
- *Federal loan* - a loan made by an agency (not including loan guarantee or loan insurance).
- *Indian tribe* and *tribal organization* have the meaning provided in section 4 of the Indian Self-Determination and Education Assistance Act (25 U.S.C. 450B). Alaskan Natives are included under the definitions of Indian tribes in that Act.
- *Influencing or attempting to influence* - making, with the intent to influence, any communication to or appearance before an officer or employee or any agency, a Member of Congress, an officer or employee of Congress, or an employee of a Member of Congress in connection with any covered Federal action.
- *Loan guarantee, loan insurance* - an agency's guarantee or insurance of a loan made by a person.
- *Local government* - a unit of government in a State and, if chartered, established, or otherwise recognized by a State for the performance of a governmental duty, including a local public authority, a special district, an intrastate district, a council of governments, a sponsor group representative organization, and any other instrumentality of a local government.
- *Officer or employee of an agency* - includes the following individuals employed by an agency:
  1. An individual who is appointed to a position in the Government under Title 5, U.S. Code, including a position under a temporary appointment;

2. A member of the uniformed services as defined in Section 101(3), Title 37, U.S. Code;
3. A special Government employee as defined in Section 202, Title 18, U.S. Code; and,
4. An individual who is a member of a Federal advisory committee, as defined by the Federal Advisory Committee Act, Title 5, U.S. Code Appendix 2.

- *Person* - an individual, corporation, company, association, authority, firm, partnership, society, State, and local government, regardless of whether such entity is operated for profit or not for profit. This term excludes an Indian tribe, tribal organization, or any other Indian organization with respect to expenditures specifically permitted by other Federal law.
- *Reasonable compensation* - with respect to a regularly employed officer or employee of any person, compensation consistent with the normal compensation for such officer or employee for work that is not furnished to, by, or in cooperation with the Government.
- *Reasonable payment* - with respect to professionals and other technical services, a payment in an amount consistent with the amount normally paid for such services in the private sector.
- *Recipient* - all contractors, subcontractors at any tier, and subgrantees at any tier of the recipient of funds received in connection with a Federal contract, grant, loan, or cooperative agreement. The term excludes an Indian tribe, tribal organization, or any other Indian organization with respect to expenditures specifically permitted by other Federal law.
- *Regularly employed* - with respect to an officer or employee of a person requesting or receiving a Federal contract, grant, loan, or cooperative agreement or a commitment providing for the United States to insure or guarantee a loan, an officer or employee who is employed by such person for at least 130 working days within one year immediately preceding the date of the submission that initiates agency consideration of such person for receipt of such contract, grant, loan, cooperative agreement, loan insurance commitment, or loan guarantee commitment. An officer or employee who is employed by such person for less than 130 working days within one year immediately preceding the date of the submission that initiates agency consideration of such person shall be considered to be regularly employed as soon as he or she is employed by such person for 130 working days.
- *State* - a State of the United States, the District of Columbia, the Commonwealth of Puerto Rico, a territory or possession of the United States, an agency or instrumentality of a State, and a multi-State, regional, or interstate entity having governmental duties and powers.

§ 82.110 Certification and disclosure.

With each submission. Each person shall file a certification and disclosure form with a submission for:

1. An award of a Federal contract, grant, or cooperative agreement exceeding $100,000; or
2. An award of a Federal loan or a commitment providing for the U.S. to insure or guarantee a loan exceeding $150,000.

Upon receipt. Each person shall file a certification and disclosure form upon receipt by such person of the following (unless the person previously filed a certification and disclosure form upon submission):

1. A Federal contract, grant, or cooperative agreement exceeding $100,000; or
2. A Federal loan or a commitment providing the U.S. to insure or guarantee a loan exceeding $150,000.

Annually. Each person shall file a disclosure form at the end of each calendar quarter in which there occurs any event that requires disclosure or materially affects the accuracy of the information contained in any form previously filed at submission or upon receipt. An event that materially affects the accuracy of the information reported includes:

1. A cumulative increase of $25,000 or more in the amount paid or expected to be paid for influencing or attempting to influence a covered Federal action; or
2. A change in the person(s) or individual(s) influencing or attempting to influence a covered Federal action; or,

3. A change in the officer(s), employee(s), or Member(s) contacted to influence or attempt to influence a covered Federal action.

Higher tier. Any person shall file a certification and disclosure form to the next tier above if they have requested or received the following:

1. A subcontract exceeding $100,000 at any tier under a Federal contract;
2. A subgrant, contract, or subcontract exceeding $100,000 at any tier under a Federal grant;
3. A contract or subcontract exceeding $100,000 at any tier under a Federal loan exceeding $150,000; or,
4. A contract or subcontract exceeding $100,000 at any tier under a Federal cooperative agreement.

Subpart B—Activities by Own Employees

§ 82.200 Agency and legislative liaison.

The prohibition on the use of appropriated funds (see §82.100) does not apply in the case of a payment of reasonable compensation made to an officer or employee of a person requesting or receiving a Federal contract, grant, loan, or cooperative agreement if the payment is for agency and legislative liaison activities not directly related to a covered Federal action. Providing any information specifically requested by an agency or Congress is allowable at any time.

§ 82.205 Professional and technical services.

The prohibition on the use of appropriated funds (see §82.100) does not apply in the case of a payment of reasonable compensation made to an officer or employee of a person requesting or receiving a Federal contract, grant, loan, or cooperative agreement or an extension, continuation, renewal, amendment, or modification of a Federal contract, grant, loan, or cooperative agreement if payment is for professional or technical services rendered directly in the preparation, submission, or negotiation of any bid, proposal, or application for that Federal contract, grant, loan, or cooperative agreement or for meeting requirements imposed by or pursuant to law as a condition for receiving that Federal contract, grant, loan, or cooperative agreement. "Professional and technical services" are limited to advice and analysis directly applying any professional or technical discipline.

§ 82.210 Reporting.

No reporting is required with respect to payments of reasonable compensation made to regularly employed officers or employees of a person.

Subpart C—Activities by Other Than Own Employees

§ 82.300 Professional and technical services.

The prohibition on the use of appropriated funds (see §82.100) does not apply in the case of any reasonable payment to a person, other than an officer or employee of a person requesting or receiving a covered Federal action, if the payment is for professional or technical services rendered directly in the preparation, submission, or negotiation of any bid, proposal, or application for that Federal contract, grant, loan, or cooperative agreement or for meeting requirements imposed by or pursuant to law as a condition for receiving that Federal contract, grant, loan, or cooperative agreement. The reporting requirements regarding filing a disclosure form by each person shall not apply with respect to professional or technical services rendered directly in the preparation, submission, or negotiation of any commitment providing for the United States to insure or guarantee a loan. "Professional and technical services" are limited to advice and analysis directly applying any professional or technical discipline.

Subpart D—Penalties and Enforcement

§ 82.400 Penalties.
Any person who makes a prohibited expenditure or fails to file (or amend) the disclosure form (see Appendix B) shall be subject to a civil penalty of not less than $10,000 and not more than $100,000 for each such expenditure or failure. First offenders shall be subject to a civil penalty of $10,000, absent aggravating circumstances. Second and subsequent offenses shall be subject to an appropriate civil penalty between $10,000 and $100,000, as determined by the agency head or his or her designee.

§ 82.405 Penalty procedures.
Agencies shall impose and collect civil penalties pursuant to the provisions of the Program Fraud and Civil Remedies Act, 31 U.S.C. sections 3803 (except Subsection (c)), 3804, 3805, 3806, 3807, 3808, and 3812, insofar as these provisions are not inconsistent with the requirements herein.

§ 82.410 Enforcement.
The head of each agency shall take such actions as are necessary to ensure that the provisions herein are vigorously implemented and enforced in that agency.

Subpart E—Exemptions

§ 82.500 Secretary of Defense.
The Secretary of Defense may exempt, on a case-by-case basis, a covered Federal action from the prohibition whenever the Secretary determines, in writing, that an exemption is in the national interest.

Subpart F—Agency Reports

§ 82.600 Semi-annual compilation.
The head of each agency shall collect and compile the disclosure reports (see Appendix B) and, on May 31 and November 30 of each year, submit to the Secretary of the Senate and the Clerk of the House of Representatives a report containing a compilation of the information contained in the disclosure reports received during the six-month period ending on March 31 or September 30, respectively, of that year. The report, including the compilation, shall be available for public inspection 30 days after receipt by the Secretary and the Clerk.

§ 82.605 Inspector General report.
The Inspector General (or other official) of each agency shall annually prepare and submit to Congress an evaluation of the compliance of that agency with, and the effectiveness of, the requirements herein. The evaluation may include any recommended changes that may be necessary to strengthen or improve the requirements. The annual report shall be submitted at the same time the agency submits its annual budget justifications to Congress.

Appendix A to Part 82—Certification Regarding Lobbying
Certification for Contracts, Grants, Loans, and Cooperative Agreements. The undersigned certifies, to the best of his or her knowledge and belief, that:

1. No Federal appropriated funds have been paid or will be paid, by or on behalf of the undersigned, to any person for influencing or attempting to influence an officer or employee of an agency, a Member of Congress, an officer or employee of Congress, or an employee of a Member of Congress in connection with the awarding of any Federal contract, the making of any Federal grant, the making of any Federal loan, the entering into of any cooperative agreement, and the extension, continuation, renewal, amendment, or modification of any Federal contract, grant, loan, or cooperative agreement.

2. If any funds other than Federal appropriated funds have been paid or will be paid to any person for influencing or attempting to influence an officer or employee of any agency, a Member of Congress, an officer or employee of Congress, or an employee of a Member of Congress in connection with this Federal contract, grant, loan, or cooperative agreement, the undersigned shall complete and submit Standard Form-LLL, "Disclosure Form to Report Lobbying," in accordance with its instructions.
3. The undersigned shall require that the language of this certification be included in the award documents for all subawards at all tiers (including subcontracts, subgrants, and contracts under grants, loans, and cooperative agreements) and that all subrecipients shall certify and disclose accordingly.

Statement for Loan Guarantees and Loan Insurance. The undersigned shall complete and submit Standard Form-LLL (Disclosure Form to Report Lobbying) identifying if any funds have been paid or will be paid to any person for influencing or attempting to influence an officer or employee of any agency, a Member of Congress, an officer or employee of Congress, or an employee of a Member of Congress in connection with this commitment providing for the U.S. to insure or guarantee a loan.

Appendix B to Part 82—Disclosure Form To Report Lobbying

The Disclosure of Lobbying Activities form can be found at the following links:

- http://ecfr.gpoaccess.gov/graphics/pdfs/ec21oc91.056.pdf
- http://ecfr.gpoaccess.gov/graphics/pdfs/ec21oc91.057.pdf
- http://ecfr.gpoaccess.gov/graphics/pdfs/ec21oc91.058.pdf

PART 84—GOVERNMENT-WIDE REQUIREMENTS FOR DRUG-FREE WORKPLACE (FINANCIAL ASSISTANCE)

Subpart A—Purpose and Coverage

§ 84.100 What does this part do?
This part carries out the portion of the Drug-Free Workplace Act of 1988 (41 U.S.C. 701 et seq., as amended) that applies to grants. It also applies the provisions of the Act to cooperative agreements and other financial assistance awards, as a matter of Federal Government policy.

§ 84.105 Does this part apply to me?
Portions of this part apply to you if you are either a recipient of an assistance award from ED or an ED awarding official. The following table shows the subparts that apply:

If you are . . .	see Subparts . . .
A recipient who is not an individual	A, B and E.
A recipient who is an individual	A, C and E.
A(n) ED awarding official	A, D and E.

§ 84.110 Are any of my Federal assistance awards exempt from this part?
This part does not apply to any award that the ED determines would be inconsistent with the international obligations of the U.S. or the laws of a foreign government.

§ 84.115 Does this part affect the Federal contracts that I receive?
It will affect future contract awards indirectly if you are debarred or suspended for a violation of the requirements of this part, as described in §84.510(c). This part does not apply directly to procurement contracts. The portion of the Drug-Free Workplace Act of 1988 that applies to Federal procurement contracts is carried out through the Federal Acquisition Regulation in chapter 1 of Title 48 of the Code of Federal Regulations (the drug-free workplace coverage currently is in 48 CFR Part 23, Subpart 23.5).

Subpart B—Requirements for Recipients Other Than Individuals

§ 84.200 What must I do to comply with this part?
If you are a recipient other than an individual, you must:

1. Make a good faith effort, on a continuing basis, to maintain a drug-free workplace; and
2. Identify all known workplaces under your federal awards (see §84.230).

§ 84.205 What must I include in my drug-free workplace statement?
You must publish a statement that:

1. Tells your employees that the unlawful manufacture, distribution, dispensing, possession, or use of a controlled substance is prohibited in your workplace;
2. Specifies the actions that you will take against employees for violating that prohibition; and
3. Lets each employee know that, as a condition of employment under any award, he or she will abide by the terms of the statement and must notify you in writing if he or she is convicted for a violation of a criminal drug statute occurring in the workplace and must do so no more than five calendar days after the conviction.

§ 84.210 To whom must I distribute my drug-free workplace statement?

A copy of the statement described in §84.205 must be given to each employee who will be engaged in the performance of any Federal award.

§ 84.215 What must I include in my drug-free awareness program?

You must establish an ongoing drug-free awareness program to inform employees about:

1. The dangers of drug abuse in the workplace;
2. Your policy of maintaining a drug-free workplace;
3. Any available drug counseling, rehabilitation, and employee assistance programs; and
4. The penalties that you may impose upon them for drug abuse violations occurring in the workplace.

§ 84.220 By when must I publish my drug-free workplace statement and establish my drug-free awareness program?

If you are a new recipient that does not already have a policy statement as described in §84.205 and an ongoing awareness program as described in §84.215, you must publish the statement and establish the program by the time given in the following table:

If...	then you...
The performance period of the award is less than 30 days	must have the policy statement and program in place as soon as possible, but before the date on which performance is expected to be completed.
The performance period of the award is 30 days or more	must have the policy statement and program in place within 30 days after award.
You believe there are extraordinary circumstances requiring more than 30 days to publish the policy statement and establish the awareness program	may ask ED to give you more time to do so. The amount of additional time to be given is at the discretion of the awarding official.

§ 84.225 What actions must I take concerning employees who are convicted of drug violations in the workplace?

If an employee is convicted of a drug violation in the workplace, you must notify Federal agencies if an employee who is engaged in the performance of an award informs you about a conviction or you otherwise learn of the conviction. This notification must:

1. Be in writing;
2. Include the employee's position title;
3. Include the identification number(s) of each affected award;
4. Be sent within 10 calendar days after you learn of the conviction; and
5. Be sent to every federal agency on whose award the convicted employee was working.

In addition, within 30 calendar days of learning about an employee's conviction, you must either:

1. Take appropriate personnel action against the employee, up to and including termination, consistent with the requirements of the Rehabilitation Act of 1973 (29 U.S.C. 794); or
2. Require the employee to participate satisfactorily in a drug abuse assistance or rehabilitation program approved by a Federal, State or local health, law enforcement, or other appropriate agency.

§ 84.230 How and when must I identify workplaces?

You must identify all known workplaces under each ED award either:

1. To the ED official making the award (either during the application process or upon award); or
2. In documents that kept on file in your office(s) during the performance of the award.

Failure to do so is a violation of your drug-free workplace requirements. You may identify the workplaces. If any identified workplaces changes during the performance of the award, the ED awarding official must be notified.

Subpart C—Requirements for Recipients Who Are Individuals

§ 84.300 What must I do to comply with this part if I am an individual recipient?

As a condition of receiving a(n) ED award, if you are an individual recipient, you must agree that:

1. You will not engage in the unlawful manufacture, distribution, dispensing, possession, or use of a controlled substance in conducting any activity related to the award; and
2. If you are convicted of a criminal drug offense resulting from a violation occurring during the conduct of any award activity, you will report the conviction in writing, within 10 calendar days of the conviction, and to the ED awarding official for each award currently being managed.

Subpart D—Responsibilities of ED Awarding Officials

§ 84.400 What are my responsibilities as a(n) ED awarding official?

As a(n) ED awarding official, you must obtain each recipient's agreement, as a condition of the award, to comply with the requirements in:

1. Subpart B of this part, if the recipient is not an individual; or
2. Subpart C of this part, if the recipient is an individual.

Subpart E—Violations of this Part and Consequences

§ 84.500 How are violations of this part determined for recipients other than individuals?

A recipient other than an individual is in violation of the requirements of this part if the ED Deciding Official determines, in writing, that:

1. The recipient has violated the requirements of Subpart B of this part; or
2. The number of convictions of the recipient's employees for violating criminal drug statutes in the workplace is large enough to indicate that the recipient has failed to make a good faith effort to provide a drug-free workplace.

§ 84.505 How are violations of this part determined for recipients who are individuals?

An individual recipient is in violation of the requirements of this part if the ED Deciding Official determines, in writing, that:

1. The recipient has violated the requirements of Subpart C of this part; or
2. The recipient is convicted of a criminal drug offense resulting from a violation occurring during the conduct of any award activity.

§ 84.510 What actions will the Federal Government take against a recipient determined to have violated this part?

If a recipient is determined to have violated this part, as described in §84.500 or §84.505, the ED may take one or more of the following actions:

1. Suspension of payments under the award;
2. Suspension or termination of the award; and
3. Suspension or debarment of the recipient under 34 cfr part 85, for a period not to exceed five years.

§ 84.515 Are there any exceptions to those actions?

The ED Deciding Official may waive with respect to a particular award, in writing, a suspension of payments under an award, suspension or termination of an award, or suspension or debarment of a recipient if the ED Deciding Official determines that such a waiver would be in the public interest. This exception authority cannot be delegated to any other official.

Subpart F—Definitions

§ 84.605 Award.

Award means an award of financial assistance by the ED or other Federal agency directly to a recipient. The term award includes:

1. A Federal grant or cooperative agreement, in the form of money or property in lieu of money.
2. A block grant or a grant in an entitlement program, whether or not the grant is exempted from coverage under the Government-wide rule 34 CFR Part 85 that implements OMB A–102 (for availability, see 5 CFR 1310.3) and specifies uniform administrative requirements.

The term award does not include:

1. Technical assistance that provides services instead of money.
2. Loans.
3. Loan guarantees.
4. Interest subsidies.
5. Insurance.
6. Direct appropriations.
7. Veterans' benefits to individuals (i.e., any benefit to veterans, their families, or survivors by virtue of the service of a veteran in the Armed Forces of the United States).

§ 84.610 Controlled substance.

Controlled substance means a controlled substance in Schedules I through V of the Controlled Substances Act (21 U.S.C. 812), and as further defined by regulation at 21 CFR 1308.11 through 1308.15.

§ 84.615 Conviction.

Conviction means a finding of guilt (including a plea of nolo contendere) or imposition of sentence, or both, by any judicial body charged with the responsibility to determine violations of the Federal or State criminal drug statutes.

§ 84.620 Cooperative agreement.

Cooperative agreement means an award of financial assistance that, consistent with 31 U.S.C. 6305, is used to enter into the same kind of relationship as a grant (see definition of grant in §84.650), except that substantial involvement is expected between the Federal agency and the recipient when carrying out the activity contemplated by the award. The term does not include cooperative research and development agreements as defined in 15 U.S.C. 3710a.

§ 84.625 Criminal drug statute.

Criminal drug statute means a Federal or non-Federal criminal statute involving the manufacture, distribution, dispensing, use, or possession of any controlled substance.

§ 84.630 Debarment.

Debarment means an action taken by a Federal agency to prohibit a recipient from participating in Federal Government procurement contracts and covered non-procurement transactions.

§ 84.635 Drug-free workplace.
Drug-free workplace means a site for the performance of work done in connection with a specific award at which employees of the recipient are prohibited from engaging in the unlawful manufacture, distribution, dispensing, possession, or use of a controlled substance.

§ 84.640 Employee.
Employee means the employee of a recipient directly engaged in the performance of work under the award, including:

1. All direct charge employees;
2. All indirect charge employees, unless their impact or involvement in the performance of work under the award is insignificant to the performance of the award; and
3. Temporary personnel and consultants who are directly engaged in the performance of work under the award and who are on the recipient's payroll.

This definition does not include workers not on the payroll of the recipient (e.g., volunteers, even if used to meet a matching requirement; consultants or independent contractors not on the payroll; or employees of subrecipients or subcontractors in covered workplaces).

§ 84.645 Federal agency or agency.
Federal agency or agency means any U.S. executive department, military department, government corporation, government controlled corporation, any other establishment in the executive branch (including the Executive Office of the President), or any independent regulatory agency.

§ 84.650 Grant.
Grant means an award of financial assistance that, consistent with 31 U.S.C. 6304, is used to enter into a relationship:

1. The principal purpose of which is to transfer a thing of value to the recipient to carry out a public purpose of support or stimulation authorized by a law of the United States, rather than to acquire property or services for the Federal Government's direct benefit or use; and
2. In which substantial involvement is not expected between the Federal agency and the recipient when carrying out the activity contemplated by the award.

§ 84.655 Individual.
Individual means a natural person.

§ 84.660 Recipient.
Recipient means any individual, corporation, partnership, association, unit of government (except a Federal agency) or legal entity, however organized, that receives an award directly from a Federal agency.

§ 84.665 State.
State means any of the States of the United States, the District of Columbia, the Commonwealth of Puerto Rico, or any territory or possession of the United States.

§ 84.670 Suspension.
Suspension means an action taken by a Federal agency that immediately prohibits a recipient from participating in Federal Government procurement contracts and covered non-procurement transactions for a temporary period, pending completion of an investigation and any judicial or administrative proceedings that may ensue.

PART 85—GOVERNMENT-WIDE DEBARMENT AND SUSPENSION (NON-PROCUREMENT)

§ 85.25 How is this part organized?

This part is divided into 10 subparts, each containing information related to a broad topic or specific audience with special responsibilities, as shown in the following table:

In Subpart	You will find provisions related to
A	general information about this rule.
B	types of ED transactions that are covered by the Government-wide non-procurement suspension and debarment system.
C	the responsibilities of persons who participate in covered transactions.
D	the responsibilities of ED officials who are authorized to enter into covered transactions.
E	the responsibilities of Federal agencies for the Excluded Parties List System (Disseminated by the General Services Administration).
F	general principles governing suspension, debarment, voluntary exclusion and settlement.
G	suspension actions.
H	debarment actions.
I	definitions of terms used in this part.

The following table shows which subparts may be of special interest to you, depending on who you are:

If you are . . .	See Subpart(s) . . .
a participant or principal in a non-procurement transaction	A, B, C, and I.
a respondent in a suspension action	A, B, F, G and I.
a respondent in a debarment action	A, B, F, H and I.
a suspending official	A, B, D, E, F, G and I.
a debarring official	A, B, D, E, F, H and I.
a(n) ED official authorized to enter into a covered transaction	A, B, D, E and I.

§ 85.50 How is this part written?

This part uses a "plain language" format to make it easier for the general public to use. The section headings and text, often in the form of questions and answers, must be read together. Pronouns, such as "I" and "you," change from subpart to subpart depending on the audience being addressed. The pronoun "we" is always ED.

§ 85.75 Do terms in this part have special meanings?

This part uses terms throughout the text that have special meaning. Those terms are defined in Subpart I of this part. For example, three important terms are:

- *Exclusion* or *excluded* refers to discretionary actions taken by a suspending or debarring official under this part or the Federal Acquisition Regulation (48 CFR Part 9, Subpart 9.4);
- *Disqualification* or *disqualified* refers to prohibitions under specific statutes, E.O.s (other than E.O. 12549 and E.O. 12689), or other authorities.
- *Ineligibility* or *ineligible*, which generally refers to a person who is excluded or disqualified.

Subpart A—General

§ 85.100 What does this part do?

This part adopts a government-wide system of debarment and suspension for ED non-procurement activities. It also provides for reciprocal exclusion of persons who have been excluded under the Federal Acquisition Regulation, and provides for the consolidated listing of all persons who are excluded or disqualified by statute, E.O., or other legal authority.

§ 85.105 Does this part apply to me?

Portions of this part (see table at §85.25) apply to you if you are a(n):

1. Person who has been, is, or may reasonably be expected to be, a participant or principal in a covered transaction;
2. Respondent (a person against whom the ED has initiated a debarment or suspension action);
3. ED debarring or suspending official; or
4. ED official who is authorized to enter into covered transactions with non-Federal parties.

§ 85.110 What is the purpose of the non-procurement debarment and suspension system?

To protect the public interest, the Federal Government ensures the integrity of Federal programs by conducting business only with responsible persons.

§ 85.115 How does an exclusion restrict a person's involvement in covered transactions?

With the exceptions stated in §§85.120, 85.315, and 85.420, a person who is excluded by ED or any other Federal agency may not:

1. Be a participant in a(n) ED transaction that is a covered transaction under subpart B of this part;
2. Be a participant in a transaction of any other Federal agency that is a covered transaction under that agency's regulation for debarment and suspension; or
3. Act as a principal of a person participating in one of those covered transactions.

§ 85.120 May we grant an exception to let an excluded person participate in a covered transaction?

The ED Deciding Official may grant an exception permitting an excluded person to participate in a particular covered transaction. If an exception is granted, it must be in writing and state the reason(s) for deviating from the government-wide policy in E.O. 12549. An exception granted by one agency for an excluded person does not extend to the covered transactions of another agency.

§ 85.125 Does an exclusion under the non-procurement system affect a person's eligibility for Federal procurement contracts?

If any Federal agency excludes a person under its non-procurement common rule on or after August 25, 1995, the excluded person is also ineligible to participate in Federal procurement transactions under the FAR. Therefore, an exclusion under this part has reciprocal effect in Federal procurement transactions.

§ 85.130 Does exclusion under the Federal procurement system affect a person's eligibility to participate in non-procurement transactions?

If any Federal agency excludes a person under the FAR on or after August 25, 1995, the excluded person is also ineligible to participate in non-procurement covered transactions under this part. Therefore, an exclusion under the FAR has reciprocal effect in Federal non-procurement transactions.

§ 85.135 May ED exclude a person who is not currently participating in a non-procurement transaction?

Given a cause that justifies an exclusion under this part, we may exclude any person who has been involved, is currently involved, or may reasonably be expected to be involved in a covered transaction.

§ 85.140 How do I know if a person is excluded?
Check the Excluded Parties List System (EPLS) to determine whether a person is excluded. The General Services Administration (GSA) maintains the EPLS and makes it available, as detailed in Subpart E of this part.

§ 85.145 Does this part address persons who are disqualified, as well as those who are excluded from non-procurement transactions?
Except if provided for in Subpart J of this part, this part addresses disqualified persons (only to provide for their inclusion in the EPLS, and state responsibilities of Federal agencies and participants to check for disqualified persons before entering into covered transactions). This part does not specify the:

1. ED transactions for which a disqualified person is ineligible. Those transactions vary on a case-by-case basis, because they depend on the language of the specific statute, E.O., or regulation that caused the disqualification;
2. Entities to which the disqualification applies; or
3. Process that the agency uses to disqualify a person.

Subpart B—Covered Transactions

§ 85.200 What is a covered transaction?
A covered transaction is a non-procurement or procurement transaction that is subject to the prohibitions of this part. It may be a transaction at:

1. The primary tier, between a Federal agency and a person; or
2. A lower tier, between a participant in a covered transaction and another person.

§ 85.205 Why is it important if a particular transaction is a covered transaction?
Participant. As a participant in the transaction, you have the responsibilities laid out in Subpart C of this part. Those include responsibilities to the person or Federal agency at the next higher tier from whom you received the transaction, if any. They also include responsibilities if you subsequently enter into other covered transactions with persons at the next lower tier.

Federal official. As a Federal official who enters into a primary tier transaction, you have the responsibilities laid out in Subpart D of this part.

Excluded person. As an excluded person, you may not be a participant or principal in the transaction unless:

1. The person who entered into the transaction with you allows you to continue your involvement in a transaction that predates your exclusion; or
2. The ED deciding official allows you to be involved in the transaction.

§ 85.210 Which non-procurement transactions are covered transactions?
All non-procurement transactions, as defined in §85.970, are covered transactions unless listed in §85.215.

§ 85.215 Which non-procurement transactions are not covered transactions?
The following types of non-procurement transactions are not covered transactions:

1. A direct award to a foreign government (including foreign government agencies) or public international organization.
2. A benefit to an individual as a personal entitlement without regard to the individual's present responsibility (but benefits received in an individual's business capacity are not excepted).
3. Federal employment.
4. A transaction that needed by ED to respond to a recognized emergency or disaster.
5. A permit, license, certificate, or similar instrument issued as a means to regulate public health,

safety, or the environment, unless the ED specifically designates it to be a covered transaction.
6. An incidental benefit that results from ordinary governmental operations.
7. Any other transaction if the application of an exclusion to the transaction is prohibited by law.

§ 85.220 Are any procurement contracts included as covered transactions?
Covered transactions under this part do not include any procurement contracts awarded directly by a Federal agency; however, they do include some procurement contracts awarded by non-Federal participants in non-procurement covered transactions. Specifically, a contract for goods or services is a covered transaction if any of the following applies:

1. The contract is awarded by a participant in a non-procurement transaction that is covered under §85.210, and the amount of the contract is expected to equal or exceed $25,000.
2. The contract requires the consent of a(n) ED official. In that case, the contract, regardless of the amount, always is a covered transaction, and it does not matter who awarded it.
3. The contract is for federally-required audit services.

§ 85.225 How do I know if a transaction in which I may participate is a covered transaction?
You will know a covered transaction because the agency regulations governing the transaction, the appropriate agency official, or participant at the next higher tier who enters into the transaction with you will tell you that you must comply with applicable portions of this part.

Subpart C—Responsibilities of Participants Regarding Transactions

Doing Business With Other Persons

§ 85.300 What must I do before I enter into a covered transaction with another person at the next lower tier?
When you enter into a covered transaction with another person at the next lower tier, you must verify that the person with whom you intend to do business is not excluded or disqualified. You do this by checking the EPLS, collecting certifications from persons if allowed by this rule, or adding a clause or condition to the covered transaction with that person.

§ 85.305 May I enter into a covered transaction with an excluded or disqualified person?
You as a participant may not enter into a covered transaction with an excluded person, unless ED grants an exception under §85.120. Furthermore, you may not enter into any transaction with a person who is disqualified from that transaction, unless you have obtained an exception under the disqualifying statute, E.O., or regulation.

§ 85.310 What must I do if a Federal agency excludes a person with whom I am already doing business in a covered transaction?
You as a participant may continue covered transactions with an excluded person if the transactions were in existence when the agency excluded the person. However, you are not required to continue the transactions. You may not renew or extend covered transactions (other than no-cost time extensions) with any excluded person unless ED grants an exception under §85.120. If you are a Title IV HEA participant, you may not continue a transaction with an excluded person after the effective date of the exclusion unless permitted by 34 CFR 668.26, 682.702, or 668.94, as applicable.

§ 85.315 May I use the services of an excluded person as a principal under a covered transaction?
You as a participant may continue to use the services of an excluded person as a principal under a covered transaction if you were using the services of that person in the transaction before the person was excluded. However, you are not required to continue using that person's services as a principal. You may not begin to

use the services of an excluded person as a principal under a covered transaction unless the ED grants an exception under §85.120. If you are a Title IV HEA participant, you may not:

1. Renew or extend the term of any contract or agreement for the services of an excluded person as a principal with respect to a Title IV HEA transaction; and
2. Continue to use the services of that excluded person as a principal under this kind of an agreement or arrangement more than 90 days after you learn of the exclusion or after the close of the Federal fiscal year in which the exclusion takes effect, whichever is later.

§ 85.320 Must I verify that principals of my covered transactions are eligible to participate?

Yes, you as a participant are responsible for determining whether any of your principals of your covered transactions are excluded or disqualified from the transaction. You may decide the method and frequency by which you do so. You may, but you are not required to, check the EPLS.

§ 85.325 What happens if I do business with an excluded person in a covered transaction?

If as a participant you knowingly do business with an excluded person, we may disallow costs, terminate the transaction, issue a stop work order, debar or suspend you, or take other appropriate remedies.

§ 85.330 What requirements must I pass down to persons at lower tiers with whom I intend to do business?

Before entering into a covered transaction with a participant at the next lower tier, you must require that participant to:

1. Comply with this subpart as a condition of participation in the transaction; and
2. Pass the requirement to comply with this subpart to each person with whom the participant enters into a covered transaction at the next lower tier.

Disclosing Information—Primary Tier Participants

§ 85.335 What information must I provide before entering into a covered transaction with the ED?

Before you enter into a covered transaction at the primary tier, you as the participant must notify the ED office that is entering into the transaction with you, if you know that you or any of the principals for that covered transaction:

1. Are presently excluded or disqualified;
2. Have been convicted within the preceding three years of any of the offenses listed in §85.800(a) or had a civil judgment rendered against you for one of those offenses within that time period;
3. Are presently indicted for or otherwise criminally or civilly charged by a governmental entity (Federal, State or local) with commission of any of the offenses listed in §85.800(a); or
4. Have had one or more public transactions (Federal, State, or local) terminated within the preceding three years for cause or default.

§ 85.340 If I disclose unfavorable information required under §85.335, will I be prevented from participating in the transaction?

As a primary tier participant, your disclosure of unfavorable information about yourself or a principal under §85.335 will not necessarily cause us to deny your participation in the covered transaction. We consider the information when we determine whether to enter into the covered transaction. We also will consider any additional information that you elect to submit with the disclosed information.

§ 85.345 What happens if I fail to disclose information required under §85.335?

If we later determine that you failed to disclose information under §85.335 that you knew at the time you entered into the covered transaction, we may terminate the transaction for material failure to comply with the terms of the transaction, or pursue any other available remedies, including suspension and debarment.

§ 85.350 What must I do if I learn of information required under §85.335 after entering into a covered transaction with the ED?
At any time after you enter into a covered transaction, you must give immediate written notice to the ED office with which you entered into the transaction if you learn either that you failed to disclose information earlier (as required by §85.335) or due to changed circumstances, you or any of the principals for the transaction now meet any of the criteria in §85.335.

Disclosing Information—Lower Tier Participants

§ 85.355 What information must I provide to a higher tier participant before entering into a covered transaction with that participant?
Before you enter into a covered transaction with a person at the next higher tier, you must notify that person if you know that you or any of the principals are presently excluded or disqualified.

§ 85.360 What happens if I fail to disclose the information required under §85.355?
If we later determine that you failed to tell the person at the higher tier that you were excluded or disqualified at the time you entered into the covered transaction with that person, we may pursue any available remedies, including suspension and debarment.

§ 85.365 What must I do if I learn of information required under §85.355 after entering into a covered transaction with a higher tier participant?
At any time after you enter into a lower tier covered transaction with a person at a higher tier, you must provide immediate written notice to that person if you learn either that you failed to disclose information earlier (as required by §85.355), or due to changed circumstances, you or any of the principals for the transaction now meet any of the criteria in §85.355.

Subpart D—Responsibilities of ED Officials Regarding Transactions

§ 85.400 May I enter into a transaction with an excluded or disqualified person?
You as an agency official may not enter into a covered transaction with an excluded person unless you obtain an exception under §85.120. Furthermore, you may not enter into any transaction with a person who is disqualified from that transaction, unless you obtain a waiver or exception under the statute, E.O., or regulation that is the basis for the person's disqualification.

§ 85.405 May I enter into a covered transaction with a participant if a principal of the transaction is excluded?
As an agency official, you may not enter into a covered transaction with a participant if you know that a principal of the transaction is excluded, unless you obtain an exception under §85.120.

§ 85.410 May I approve a participant's use of the services of an excluded person?
After entering into a covered transaction with a participant, you as an agency official may not approve a participant's use of an excluded person as a principal under that transaction, unless you obtain an exception under §85.120.

§ 85.415 What must I do if a Federal agency excludes the participant or a principal after I enter into a covered transaction?
You as an agency official may continue covered transactions with an excluded person, or under which an excluded person is a principal, if the transactions were in existence when the person was excluded. You are

not required to continue the transactions, however, and you may consider termination. You may not renew or extend covered transactions (other than no-cost time extensions) with any excluded person, or under which an excluded person is a principal, unless you obtain an exception under §85.120.

Title IV, HEA transactions. If you are a Title IV, HEA participant, you may not:

1. Renew or extend the term of any contract or agreement for the services of an excluded person as a principal with respect to a title IV, HEA transaction; and
2. Continue to use the services of that excluded person as a principal under this kind of an agreement or arrangement more than 90 days after you learn of the exclusion or after the close of the Federal fiscal year in which the exclusion takes effect, whichever is later.

§ 85.420 May I approve a transaction with an excluded or disqualified person at a lower tier?

If a transaction at a lower tier is subject to your approval, you may not approve:

1. A covered transaction with a person who is currently excluded, unless you obtain an exception under §85.120; or
2. A transaction with a person who is disqualified from that transaction, unless you obtain a waiver or exception under the statute, e.o., or regulation that is the basis for the person's disqualification.

§ 85.425 When do I check to see if a person is excluded or disqualified?

As an agency official, you must check to see if a person is excluded or disqualified before you:

1. Enter into a primary tier covered transaction;
2. Approve a principal in a primary tier covered transaction;
3. Approve a lower tier participant if agency approval of the lower tier participant is required; or
4. Approve a principal in connection with a lower tier transaction if agency approval of the principal is required.

§ 85.430 How do I check to see if a person is excluded or disqualified?

You check to see if a person is excluded or disqualified in two ways:

1. You as an agency official must check the EPLS when you take any action listed in §85.425; and
2. You must review information that a participant gives you about its status or the status of the principals of a transaction.

§ 85.435 What must I require of a primary tier participant?

You as an agency official must require each participant in a primary tier covered transaction to:

1. Comply with Subpart C of this part as a condition of participation in the transaction; and
2. Communicate the requirement to comply with Subpart C of this part to persons at the next lower tier with whom the primary tier participant enters into covered transactions.

§ 85.440 What method do I use to communicate those requirements to participants?

To communicate those requirements, you must include a term or condition in the transaction requiring each participant's compliance with Subpart C of this part and requiring the participant to include a similar term or condition in lower-tier covered transactions.

§ 85.445 What action may I take if a primary tier participant knowingly does business with an excluded or disqualified person?

If a participant knowingly does business with an excluded or disqualified person, you as an agency official may refer the matter for suspension and debarment consideration. You may also disallow costs, annul or terminate the transaction, issue a stop work order, or take any other appropriate remedy.

§ 85.450 What action may I take if a primary tier participant fails to disclose the information required under §85.335?

If you as an agency official determine that a participant failed to disclose information, as required by §85.335, at the time it entered into a covered transaction with you, you may:

1. Terminate the transaction for material failure to comply with the terms and conditions of the transaction; or
2. Pursue any other available remedies, including suspension and debarment.

§ 85.455 What may I do if a lower tier participant fails to disclose the information required under §85.355 to the next higher tier?

If you determine that a lower tier participant failed to disclose information (as required by §85.355) at the time it entered into a covered transaction with higher tier participant, you may pursue any remedies available to you, including the initiation of a suspension or debarment action.

Subpart E—Excluded Parties List System

§ 85.500 What is the purpose of the Excluded Parties List System (EPLS)?

The EPLS is a widely available source of the most current information about persons who are excluded or disqualified from covered transactions.

§ 85.505 Who uses the EPLS?

Agency officials use EPLS to determine whether to enter into a transaction with a person, as required under §85.430. Participants and any other general public individual or agency may also use the EPLS to determine if:

1. Principals of their transactions are excluded or disqualified, as required under §85.320; or
2. Persons with whom they are entering into covered transactions at the next lower tier are excluded or disqualified.

§ 85.510 Who maintains the EPLS?

In accordance with OMB guidelines, the General Services Administration (GSA) maintains the EPLS. When a Federal agency takes action to exclude a person under the non-procurement or procurement debarment and suspension system, the agency enters information about excluded person(s) into the EPLS.

§ 85.515 What specific information is in the EPLS?

At a minimum, the EPLS indicates:

1. The full name (where available) and address of each excluded or disqualified person, in alphabetical order, with cross references if more than one name is involved in a single action;
2. The type of action;
3. The cause for the action;
4. The scope of the action;
5. Any termination date for the action;
6. The agency and name and telephone number of the agency point of contact for the action; and
7. The Dun and Bradstreet Number (DUNS), or other similar code approved by the GSA, of the excluded or disqualified person, if available.
8. The social security number of appropriate individuals, if permitted under law.

§ 85.520 Who places the information into the EPLS?

Federal officials who take actions to exclude persons under this part (or officials who are responsible for identifying disqualified persons) must enter the following information about those persons into the EPLS:

1. Information required by §85.515(a);

2. The taxpayer identification number of the excluded or disqualified person, including the social security number for an individual if the number is available and may be disclosed under law;
3. Information about an excluded or disqualified person after taking an exclusion action, modifying or rescinding an exclusion action, finding that a person is disqualified, or finding that there has been a change in the status of a person who is listed as disqualified.

§ 85.525 Whom do I ask if I have questions about a person in the EPLS?
If you have questions about a person in the EPLS, ask the point of contact for the Federal agency that placed the person's name into the EPLS. You may find the agency point of contact from the EPLS.

§ 85.530 Where can I find the EPLS?
You may access the EPLS through the Internet, currently at http://epls.arnet.gov.

Subpart F—General Principles Relating to Suspension and Debarment Actions

§ 85.600 How do suspension and debarment actions start?
When we receive information from any source concerning a cause for suspension or debarment, we will promptly report and investigate it. We refer the question of whether to suspend or debar you to our suspending or debarring official for consideration, if appropriate.

§ 85.605 How does suspension differ from debarment?
Suspension differs from debarment in that:

A suspending official . . .	A debarring official . . .
Imposes suspension as a temporary status of ineligibility for procurement and non-procurement transactions, pending completion of an investigation or legal proceedings	Imposes debarment for a specified period as a final determination that a person is not presently responsible.
Must: 1) have adequate evidence that there may be a cause for debarment of a person; and 2) conclude that immediate action is necessary to protect the Federal interest	Must conclude (based on a preponderance of the evidence) that the person has engaged in conduct that warrants debarment.
Usually imposes the suspension first, and then notifies the suspended person (giving them an opportunity to contest the suspension and have it lifted	Imposes debarment after giving the respondent notice and an opportunity to contest the proposed debarment.

§ 85.610 What procedures does the ED use in suspension and debarment actions?
In deciding whether to suspend or debar you, we handle the actions as informally as practicable, consistent with principles of fundamental fairness. For suspension actions, we use the procedures in this subpart and Subpart G of this part. For debarment actions, we use the procedures in this subpart and Subpart H of this part.

§ 85.611 What procedures do we use for a suspension or debarment action involving a title IV, HEA transaction?
Suspension. If we suspend a Title IV, HEA participant under E.O. 12549, we use the following procedures to ensure that the suspension prevents participation in Title IV, HEA transactions:

1. The notification procedures in §85.715.
2. Instead of the procedures in §85.720 through §85.760, the procedures in 34 CFR Part 668, Subpart G or 34 CFR Part 682, Subpart D or G as applicable.
3. The suspending official and, on appeal, the Secretary determines whether there is sufficient cause for suspension as explained in §85.700.

Debarrment. If we debar a Title IV, HEA participant under E.O. 12549, we use the following procedures to ensure that the debarment also precludes participation in Title IV, HEA transactions:

1. The notification procedures in §85.805 and §85.870.
2. Instead of the procedures in §85.810 through §85.885, the procedures in 34 CFR Part 668, Subpart G or 34 CFR Part 682, Subpart D or G, as applicable.
3. On appeal from a decision debarring a Title IV, HEA participant, we issue a final decision after receipt of any written materials from the parties.
4. The debarring official and, on appeal, the Secretary determines whether there is sufficient cause for debarment as explained in §85.800.

§ 85.612 When does an exclusion by another agency affect the ability of the excluded person to participate in a title IV, HEA transaction?

In general, if a Title IV, HEA participant is debarred or suspended by another agency under E.O. 12549 or under the Federal Acquisition Regulation, that party is not eligible to enter into Title IV, HEA transactions for the duration of the debarment or suspension.

§ 85.615 How does the ED notify a person of a suspension or debarment action?

The suspending or debarring official sends a written notice to the last known street address, facsimile number, or e-mail address of:

1. You or your identified counsel; or
2. Your agent for service of process, or any of your partners, officers, directors, owners, or joint venturers.

§ 85.620 Do Federal agencies coordinate suspension and debarment actions?

Yes, when more than one Federal agency has an interest in a suspension or debarment, the agencies may consider designating one agency as the lead agency for making the decision. Agencies are encouraged to establish methods and procedures for coordinating their suspension and debarment actions.

§ 85.625 What is the scope of a suspension or debarment?

Your suspension or debarment affects all of your divisions and other organizational elements from all covered transactions (unless the suspension or debarment is limited by its terms to specifically identified individuals, divisions, or to specific transactions). Any affiliate of a participant may be included in a suspension or debarment action if the suspending or debarring official formally names the affiliate in the notice and gives the affiliate an opportunity to contest the action.

§ 85.630 May the ED impute conduct of one person to another?

For purposes of actions taken under this rule, we may impute conduct as follows:

1. Conduct imputed from an individual to an organization. We may impute the fraudulent, criminal, or other improper conduct of any officer, director, shareholder, partner, employee, or other individual associated with an organization, to that organization when the improper conduct occurred in connection with the individual's performance of duties for or on behalf of that organization, or with the organization's knowledge, approval or acquiescence.
2. Conduct imputed from an organization to an individual, or between individuals. We may impute the fraudulent, criminal, or other improper conduct of any organization to an individual, or from one individual to another individual, if the individual to whom the improper conduct is imputed either participated in, had knowledge of, or reason to know of the improper conduct.
3. Conduct imputed from one organization to another organization. We may impute the fraudulent, criminal, or other improper conduct of one organization to another when the improper conduct occurred in connection with a partnership, joint venture, joint application, or similar arrangement, or when the organization to whom the improper conduct is imputed has the power to direct, manage,

control, or influence the activities of the organization responsible for the improper conduct.

§ 85.635 May the ED settle a debarment or suspension action?
Yes, we may settle a debarment or suspension action at any time, in the best interest of the Government.

§ 85.640 May a settlement include a voluntary exclusion?
Yes, if we enter into a settlement with you in which you agree to be excluded, it is called a voluntary exclusion and has government-wide effect.

§ 85.645 Do other Federal agencies know if the ED agrees to a voluntary exclusion?
Yes, ED enters information regarding a voluntary exclusion into the EPLS. Any agency or person may contact ED to find out the details of a voluntary exclusion.

Subpart G—Suspension

§ 85.700 When may the suspending official issue a suspension?
Suspension is a serious action. Using applicable procedures, the suspending official may impose suspension only when that official determines that:

1. There exists an indictment for, or other adequate evidence to suspect, an offense listed under §85.800(a); or
2. There exists adequate evidence to suspect any other cause for debarment listed under §85.800(b) through (d).

Suspension may also be imposed when immediate action is necessary to protect the public interest.

§ 85.705 What does the suspending official consider in issuing a suspension?
The suspending official considers how much information is available, how credible it is given the circumstances, whether or not important allegations are corroborated, and what inferences can reasonably be drawn as a result. During this assessment, the suspending official may examine the basic documents, including grants, cooperative agreements, loan authorizations, contracts, and other relevant documents (including such findings as civil judgments and convictions).

§ 85.710 When does a suspension take effect?
A suspension is effective when the suspending official signs the decision to suspend.

§ 85.711 When does a suspension affect title IV, HEA transactions?
A suspension under §85.611(a) takes effect immediately if the Secretary takes an emergency action under 34 CFR Part 668 (Subpart G) or 34 CFR Part 682 (Subpart D or G) at the same time the suspension is issued. If an emergency action is not taken, a suspension takes effect 20 days after procedures are complete. If the respondent appeals the suspension to the Secretary before the expiration of the 20 days, the suspension takes effect when the respondent receives the Secretary's decision.

§ 85.715 What notice does the suspending official give me if I am suspended?
After deciding to suspend you, the suspending official sends you a Notice of Suspension advising you:

1. That you have been suspended;
2. That your suspension is based on an indictment, conviction, or other adequate evidence;
3. Of any other irregularities sufficient to put you on notice without disclosing Federal evidence;
4. Of the cause(s) upon which we relied under §85.700 for imposing suspension;
5. That your suspension is for a temporary period pending the completion of an investigation or re-

sulting legal or debarment proceedings;
6. Of the applicable provisions of this subpart, Subpart F of this part, and any other ED procedures governing suspension decision making; and
7. Of the government-wide effect of your suspension from procurement and non-procurement programs and activities.

§ 85.720 How may I contest a suspension?

If you as a respondent wish to contest a suspension, you must provide the suspending official with information in opposition to the suspension. You may do this orally or in writing, but any information provided orally must also be submitted in writing for the official record.

§ 85.725 How much time do I have to contest a suspension?

As a respondent you or your representative must either send (or make arrangements to appear and present) the information and argument to the suspending official within 30 days after you receive a Notice of Suspension. The notice is considered when received by you:

1. When delivered, if we mail the notice to the last known street address, or five days after we send it if the letter is undeliverable;
2. When sent, if we send the notice by facsimile or five days after we send it if the facsimile is undeliverable; or
3. When delivered, if we send the notice by e-mail or five days after we send it if the e-mail is undeliverable.

§ 85.730 What information must I provide to the suspending official if I contest a suspension?

In addition to any information and argument in opposition, as a respondent your submission to the suspending official must identify:

1. Specific facts that contradict the statements contained in the Notice of Suspension. A general denial is insufficient to raise a genuine dispute over facts material to the suspension;
2. All existing, proposed, or prior exclusions under regulations implementing E.O. 12549 and all similar actions taken by Federal, state, or local agencies, including administrative agreements that affect only those agencies;
3. All criminal and civil proceedings not included in the Notice of Suspension that grew out of facts relevant to the cause(s) stated in the notice; and
4. All of your affiliates.

If you fail to disclose this information, or provide false information, the ED may seek further criminal, civil or administrative action against you, as appropriate.

§ 85.735 Under what conditions do I get an additional opportunity to challenge the facts on which the suspension is based?

You will not have an additional opportunity to challenge facts if a suspending official determines that:

1. Your suspension is based upon an indictment, conviction, civil judgment, or other finding by a Federal, State, or local body for which an opportunity to contest the facts was provided;
2. Your presentation contains only general denials to data contained in the suspension notice;
3. The issues raised in your presentation in opposition to the suspension are not factual in nature, or are not material to the suspending official's initial decision to suspend, or the official's decision whether to continue the suspension; or
4. On the basis of advice from the Department of Justice, an office of the U.S. Attorney, a State Attorney General's office, or a State or local prosecutor's office, that substantial interests of the government in pending or contemplated legal proceedings based on the same facts as the suspension would be prejudiced by conducting fact-finding.

You will have an opportunity to challenge the facts if the suspending official determines that such conditions do not exist and your presentation in opposition raises a genuine dispute over facts material to the suspension. If you have an opportunity to challenge disputed material facts under this section, the suspending official or designee must conduct additional proceedings to resolve those facts.

§ 85.740 Are suspension proceedings formal?

Suspension proceedings are conducted in a fair and informal manner. The suspending official may use flexible procedures to allow you to present matters in opposition. In so doing, the suspending official is not required to follow formal rules of evidence or procedure in creating an official record upon which the official will base a final suspension decision.

§ 85.745 How is fact-finding conducted?

If fact-finding is conducted:

1. You may present witnesses and other evidence, and confront any witness presented; and
2. The fact-finder must prepare written findings of fact for the record. A transcribed record of fact-finding proceedings must be made, unless you as a respondent and ED agree to waive it in advance. If you want a copy of the transcribed record, you may purchase it.

§ 85.750 What does the suspending official consider in deciding whether to continue or terminate my suspension?

The suspending official bases the decision on all information contained in the official record, which includes:

1. All information in support of the suspending official's initial decision to suspend you;
2. Any further information and argument presented in support of, or opposition to, the suspension; and
3. Any transcribed record of fact-finding proceedings.

§ 85.755 When will I know whether the suspension is continued or terminated?

The suspending official must make a written decision whether to continue, modify, or terminate your suspension within 45 days of closing the official record. The official record closes upon the suspending official's receipt of final submissions, information and findings of fact, if any. The suspending official may extend that period for good cause.

§ 85.760 How long may my suspension last?

If legal or debarment proceedings are initiated at the time of (or during) your suspension, the suspension may continue until the conclusion of the proceedings. If proceedings are not initiated, a suspension may not exceed 12 months. The suspending official may extend the 12 month limit for an additional 6 months if an office of a U.S. Assistant Attorney General, U.S. Attorney, or other responsible prosecuting official requests an extension in writing. In no event may a suspension exceed 18 months.

Subpart H—Debarment

§ 85.800 What are the causes for debarment?

A person may be debarred for reasons which may include some of the following:

1. Conviction of or civil judgment for commission of fraud or a criminal offense in connection with obtaining, attempting to obtain, or performing a public or private agreement or transaction;
2. Violation of Federal or State antitrust statutes, including those proscribing price fixing between competitors, allocation of customers between competitors, and bid rigging;
3. Commission of embezzlement, theft, forgery, bribery, falsification or destruction of records, making false statements, tax evasion, receiving stolen property, making false claims, or obstruction of justice; or

4. Commission of any other offense indicating a lack of business integrity or business honesty that seriously and directly affects your present responsibility;
5. Violation of the terms of a public agreement or transaction so serious as to affect the integrity of an agency program;
6. Knowingly doing business with an ineligible person;
7. Failure to pay a single substantial debt, or a number of outstanding debts owed to any Federal agency;
8. Violation of the provisions of the Drug-Free Workplace Act of 1988 (41 U.S.C. 701).

§ 85.805 What notice does the debarring official give me if I am proposed for debarment?

After consideration of the causes in §85.800 of this subpart, if the debarring official proposes to debar you, the official sends you a Notice of Proposed Debarment advising you:

1. That the debarring official is considering debarring you;
2. Of the reasons for proposing to debar you in terms sufficient to put you on notice of the conduct or transactions upon which the proposed debarment is based;
3. Of the cause(s) under §85.800 on which the official proposed your debarment;
4. Of the applicable provisions and any other ED procedures governing debarment; and
5. Of the government-wide effect of a debarment from procurement and non-procurement programs and activities.

§ 85.810 When does a debarment take effect?

A debarment is not effective until the debarring official issues a decision. The debarring official does not issue a decision until the respondent has had an opportunity to contest the proposed debarment.

§ 85.811 When does a debarment affect title IV, HEA transactions?

A debarment under §85.611(b) takes effect 30 days after those procedures are complete. If the respondent appeals the debarment to the Secretary before the expiration of the 30 days, the debarment takes effect when the respondent receives the Secretary's decision.

§ 85.815 How may I contest a proposed debarment?

If you as a respondent wish to contest a proposed debarment, you or your representative must provide the debarring official with information in opposition to the proposed debarment. You may do this orally or in writing (but any information provided orally must also be submitted in writing for the official record).

§ 85.820 How much time do I have to contest a proposed debarment?

As a respondent you or your representative must either send, or make arrangements to appear and present, the information and argument to the debarring official within 30 days after you receive the Notice of Proposed Debarment. ED considers the Notice of Proposed Debarment to be received by you:

1. When delivered, if we mail the notice to the last known street address, or five days after we send it if the letter is undeliverable;
2. When sent, if we send the notice by facsimile or five days after we send it if the facsimile is undeliverable; or
3. When delivered, if we send the notice by e-mail or five days after we send it if the e-mail is undeliverable.

§ 85.825 What information must I provide to the debarring official if I contest a proposed debarment?

In addition to any information in opposition, your submission to the debarring official must identify:

1. Specific facts that contradict the statements contained in the Notice of Proposed Debarment.
2. All existing, proposed, or prior exclusions under regulations implementing E.O. 12549 and all simi-

lar actions taken by Federal, State, or local agencies, including administrative agreements that affect only those agencies;

3. All criminal and civil proceedings not included in the Notice of Proposed Debarment that grew out of facts relevant to the cause(s) stated in the notice; and
4. All of your affiliates.

If you fail to disclose this information or provide false information, an appropriate criminal, civil or administrative action may be taken.

§ 85.830 Under what conditions do I get an additional opportunity to challenge the facts on which a proposed debarment is based?

You as a respondent will not have an additional opportunity to challenge the facts if the debarring official determines that:

1. Your debarment is based upon a conviction or civil judgment;
2. Your presentation in opposition contains only general denials to information contained in the notice of proposed debarment; or
3. The issues raised in your presentation in opposition to the proposed debarment are not factual in nature or are not material to the debarring official's decision whether to debar.

§ 85.835 Are debarment proceedings formal?

Debarment proceedings are conducted in a fair and informal manner. The debarring official may use flexible procedures to allow a respondent to present matters in opposition. In so doing, the official is not required to follow formal rules of evidence or procedure in creating an official record upon which the decision to debar will be based. The respondent must submit any documentary evidence that the debarring official is to consider.

§ 85.840 How is fact-finding conducted?

If fact-finding is conducted, you may present witnesses and other evidence, and confront any witness presented. The fact-finder must prepare written findings of fact for the record. A transcribed record of the proceedings must be made, unless waived by both the respondent and ED in advance. You may purchase a copy of the transcribed record.

§ 85.845 What does the debarring official consider in deciding whether to debar me?

The debarring official may debar you for any of the causes in §85.800. However, the official need not debar you even if a cause for debarment exists, and he or she may reject any resultant findings, in whole or in part, after specifically determining them to be arbitrary, capricious, or clearly erroneous. The official may consider the seriousness of your acts or omissions and the factors set forth at §85.860.

§ 85.850 What is the standard of proof in a debarment action?

In any debarment action, ED must establish the cause for debarment by a preponderance of the evidence. If the proposed debarment is based upon a conviction or civil judgment, the standard of proof is met.

§ 85.855 Who has the burden of proof in a debarment action?

ED has the burden to prove that a cause for debarment exists. Once a cause for debarment is established, the recipient (as a respondent) has the burden of demonstrating to the satisfaction of the debarring official that the recipient is presently responsible and that debarment is not necessary.

§ 85.860 What factors may influence the debarring official's decision?

The debarring official may consider the following mitigating and aggravating factors in determining whether to debar you and the length of your debarment period:

1. The actual or potential harm or impact that results (or may result) from the wrongdoing.
2. The frequency of incidents and/or duration of the wrongdoing.
3. Whether there is a pattern or prior history of wrongdoing.
4. Whether you are or have been excluded or disqualified by an agency of the Federal Government or have not been allowed to participate in State or local contracts or assistance agreements on a basis of conduct similar to one or more of the causes for debarment specified in this part.
5. Whether you have entered into an administrative agreement with a Federal agency or a State or local government that is not government-wide but is based on conduct similar to one or more of the causes for debarment specified in this part.
6. Whether and to what extent you planned, initiated, or carried out the wrongdoing.
7. Whether you have accepted responsibility for the wrongdoing and recognize the seriousness of the misconduct that led to the cause for debarment.
8. Whether you have paid or agreed to pay all criminal, civil and administrative liabilities for the improper activity, including any investigative or administrative costs incurred by the government, and have made or agreed to make full restitution.
9. Whether you have cooperated fully with government agencies during the investigation and any court or administrative action. In determining the extent of cooperation, the debarring official may consider when the cooperation began and whether you disclosed all pertinent information known to you.
10. Whether the wrongdoing was pervasive within your organization.
11. The kind of positions held by the individuals involved in the wrongdoing.
12. Whether your organization took appropriate corrective action or remedial measures, such as establishing ethics training and implementing programs to prevent recurrence.
13. Whether your principals tolerated the offense.
14. Whether you brought the activity cited as a basis for the debarment to the attention of the appropriate government agency in a timely manner.
15. Whether you have fully investigated the circumstances surrounding the cause for debarment and, if so, made the result of the investigation available to the debarring official.
16. Whether you had effective standards of conduct and internal control systems in place at the time the questioned conduct occurred.
17. Whether you have taken appropriate disciplinary action against the individuals responsible for the activity which constitutes the cause for debarment.
18. Whether you have had adequate time to eliminate the circumstances within your organization that led to the cause for the debarment

§ 85.865 How long may my debarment last?

The period of debarment will be based on the seriousness of the cause(s) upon which your debarment is based. Generally, debarment should not exceed three years (or five years if a violation is made under the Drug-Free Workplace Act of 1988). If a suspension has preceded your debarment, the debarring official must consider the time you were suspended.

§ 85.870 When do I know if the debarring official debars me?

The debarring official must make a written decision whether to debar within 45 days of closing the official record. The debarring official sends you written notice of his or her decision. The debarment notice will:

1. Refer to the Notice of Proposed Debarment;
2. Specify reasons for your debarment;
3. State the period of your debarment, including the effective dates; and
4. Advise you that your debarment is effective for covered transactions and contracts subject to the Federal Acquisition Regulation.

§ 85.875 May I ask the debarring official to reconsider a decision to debar me?
Yes, as a debarred person you may ask the debarring official to reconsider the debarment decision or to reduce the time period or scope of the debarment. However, you must put your request in writing and support it with documentation.

§ 85.880 What factors may influence the debarring official during reconsideration?
The debarring official may reduce or terminate your debarment based on:
1. Newly discovered material evidence;
2. A reversal of the conviction or civil judgment upon which your debarment was based;
3. A bona fide change in ownership or management;
4. Elimination of other causes for which the debarment was imposed; or
5. Other reasons the debarring official finds appropriate.

§ 85.885 May the debarring official extend a debarment?
Yes, the debarring official may extend a debarment for an additional period, if that official determines that an extension is necessary to protect the public interest. The official may not extend a debarment solely on the basis of the facts and circumstances upon which the initial debarment action was based.

Subpart I—Definitions

§ 85.900 Adequate evidence.
Adequate evidence means information sufficient to support the reasonable belief that a particular act or omission has occurred.

§ 85.905 Affiliate.
Persons are affiliates of each other if, directly or indirectly, either one controls or has the power to control the other or a third person controls or has the power to control both. ED metrics to determine control include, but are not limited to:
1. Interlocking management or ownership;
2. Identity of interests among family members;
3. Shared facilities and equipment;
4. Common use of employees; or
5. A business entity which has been organized following the exclusion of a person which has the same or similar management, ownership, or principal employees as the excluded person.

§ 85.910 Agency.
Agency means any U.S. executive department, military department, defense agency, or any other agency of the executive branch. Other agencies of the Federal government are not considered "agencies" for the purposes of this part unless they issue regulations adopting the government-wide debarment and suspension system under E.O.s 12549 and 12689.

§ 85.915 Agent or representative.
Agent or representative means any person who acts on behalf of, or who is authorized to commit, a participant in a covered transaction.

§ 85.920 Civil judgment.
Civil judgment means the disposition of a civil action by any court of competent jurisdiction, whether by verdict, decision, settlement, stipulation, other disposition which creates a civil liability for the complained of wrongful acts, or a final determination of liability under the Program Fraud Civil Remedies Act of 1988.

§ 85.925 Conviction.
Conviction means:

1. A judgment or any other determination of guilt of a criminal offense by any court of competent jurisdiction, whether entered upon a verdict or plea, including a plea of nolo contendere; or
2. Any other resolution that is the functional equivalent of a judgment, including probation before judgment and deferred prosecution.

§ 85.930 Debarment.
Debarment means an action taken by a debarring official under Subpart H of this part to exclude a person from participating in covered transactions and transactions covered under the Federal Acquisition Regulation (48 CFR Chapter 1). A person so excluded is debarred.

§ 85.935 Debarring official.
Debarring official means an agency official who is authorized to impose debarment. A debarring official is either the agency head or an official designated by the agency head.

§ 85.940 Disqualified.
Disqualified means that a person is prohibited from participating in specified Federal procurement or non-procurement transactions as required under a statute, E.O. (other than E.O.s 12549 and 12689) or other authority. Examples of disqualifications include persons prohibited under:

1. The Davis-Bacon Act (40 U.S.C. 276(a));
2. The Equal Employment Opportunity Acts and E.O.s; or
3. The Clean Air Act (42 U.S.C. 7606), Clean Water Act (33 U.S.C. 1368) and E.O. 11738.

§ 85.942 ED Deciding Official.
The ED Deciding Official is an officer who has delegated authority under the procedures of the ED to decide whether to affirm a suspension or enter a debarment.

§ 85.945 Excluded or exclusion.
Excluded or exclusion means:

1. That a person or commodity is prohibited from being a participant in covered transactions, whether the person has been suspended; voluntarily excluded, debarred, or proposed for debarment under 48 CFR Part 9, Subpart 9.4; or
2. The act of excluding a person.

§ 85.950 Excluded Parties List System
Excluded Parties List System (EPLS) means the list maintained and disseminated by the General Services Administration (GSA) containing the names and other information about persons who are ineligible.

§ 85.952 HEA.
HEA means the Higher Education Act of 1965, as amended.

§ 85.955 Indictment.
Indictment means an indictment for a criminal offense. A presentment, information, or other filing by a competent authority charging a criminal offense shall be given the same effect as an indictment.

§ 85.960 Ineligible or ineligibility.
Ineligible or ineligibility means that a person or commodity is prohibited from covered transactions because of an exclusion or disqualification.

§ 85.965 Legal proceedings.

Legal proceedings means any criminal proceeding or civil judicial proceeding (including a proceeding under the Program Fraud Civil Remedies Act) to which the Government, State, local government, or quasi-governmental authority is a party. The term also includes appeals from those proceedings.

§ 85.970 Non-procurement transaction.

Non-procurement transaction means any transaction, regardless of type (except procurement contracts). These include, but are not limited to the following:

1. Grants.
2. Cooperative agreements.
3. Scholarships.
4. Fellowships.
5. Contracts of assistance.
6. Loans.
7. Loan guarantees.
8. Subsidies.
9. Insurances.
10. Payments for specified uses.
11. Donation agreements.

§ 85.975 Notice.

Notice means a written communication served in person, sent by certified mail or its equivalent, or sent electronically by e-mail or facsimile.

§ 85.980 Participant.

Participant means any person who submits a proposal for or who enters into a covered transaction, including an agent or representative of a participant.

§ 85.985 Person.

Person means any individual, corporation, partnership, association, unit of government, or legal entity, however organized.

§ 85.990 Preponderance of the evidence.

Preponderance of the evidence means proof by information that, compared with information opposing it, leads to the conclusion that the fact at issue is more probably true than not.

§ 85.995 Principal.

Principal means:

1. An officer, director, owner, partner, principal investigator, or other person within a participant with management or supervisory responsibilities related to a covered transaction; or
2. A consultant or other person, whether or not employed by the participant or paid with federal funds, who is in a position to handle federal funds, control the use of those funds, or influence the development or outcome of an activity required to perform the covered transaction.

§ 85.1000 Respondent.

Respondent means a person against whom an agency has initiated a debarment or suspension action.

§ 85.1005 State.
State means:
1. Any of the states of the United States;
2. The District of Columbia;
3. The Commonwealth of Puerto Rico;
4. Any territory or possession of the U.S.; or
5. Any agency or instrumentality of a state.

§ 85.1010 Suspending official.
Suspending official means an agency official who is authorized to impose suspension. The suspending official is either the agency head or an official designated by the agency head.

§ 85.1015 Suspension.
Suspension is an action taken by a suspending official under Subpart G of this part that immediately prohibits a person from participating in covered transactions and transactions covered under the Federal Acquisition Regulation for a temporary period, pending completion of an agency investigation and any judicial or administrative proceedings that may ensue. A person so excluded is suspended.

§ 85.1016 Title IV, HEA participant.
A Title IV, HEA participant is:
1. An institution described in 34 CFR 600.4, 600.5, or 600.6 that provides postsecondary education; or
2. A lender, third-party servicer, or guaranty agency, as those terms are defined in 34 CFR 668.2 or 682.200.

§ 85.1017 Title IV, HEA program.
A Title IV, HEA program includes any program listed in 34 CFR 668.1(c).

§ 85.1018 Title IV, HEA transaction.
A Title IV, HEA transaction includes:
1. A disbursement or delivery of funds provided under a Title IV, HEA program to a student or borrower;
2. A certification by an educational institution of eligibility for a loan under a title IV, HEA program;
3. Guaranteeing a loan made under a title IV, HEA program; and
4. The acquisition or exercise of any servicing responsibility for a grant, loan, or work study assistance under a title IV, HEA program.

§ 85.1020 Voluntary exclusion or voluntarily excluded.
- Voluntary exclusion - a person's agreement to be excluded under the terms of a settlement between the person and one or more agencies. This must have government-wide effect.
- Voluntarily excluded - the status of a person who has agreed to a voluntary exclusion.

Appendix to Part 85—Covered Transactions

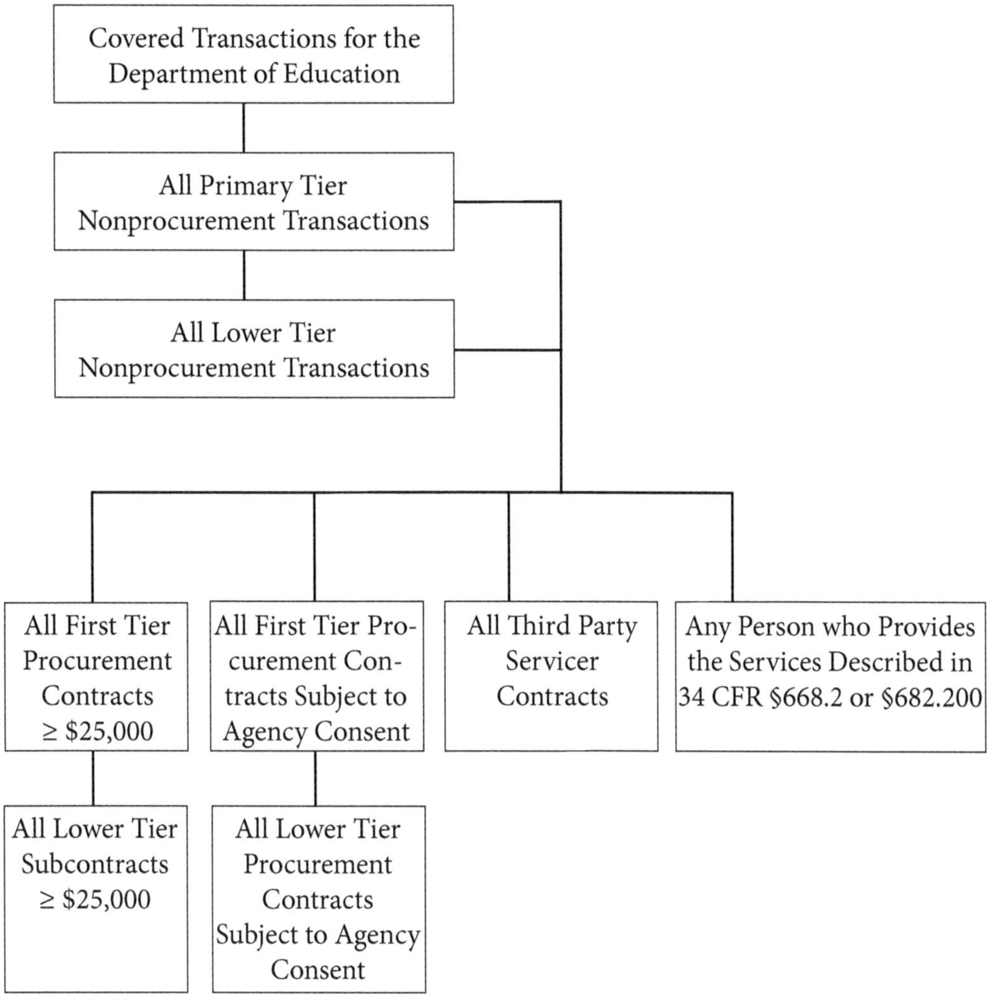

PART 86—DRUG AND ALCOHOL ABUSE PREVENTION

Subpart A—General

§ 86.1 What is the purpose of the Drug and Alcohol Abuse Prevention regulations?

The purpose of the Drug and Alcohol Abuse Prevention regulations is to implement Section 22 of the Drug-Free Schools and Communities Act Amendments of 1989, which added section 1213 to the Higher Education Act. These amendments require that, as a condition of receiving funds or any other form of financial assistance under any Federal program, an institution of higher education (IHE) must certify that it has adopted and implemented a drug prevention program as described in this part.

§ 86.2 What Federal programs are covered by this part?

The Federal programs covered by this part include:

1. All programs administered by the ED under which an IHE may receive funds or any other form of Federal financial assistance; and
2. All programs administered by any other Federal agency under which an IHE may receive Federal financial assistance.

§ 86.3 What actions shall an IHE take to comply with the requirements of this part?

An IHE shall implement a drug prevention program as described in §86.100 to prevent the unlawful possession, use, or distribution of illicit drugs and alcohol by all students and employees on school premises or as part of any of its activities.

§ 86.4 What are the procedures for submitting a drug prevention program certification?

An IHE shall submit to the Secretary the drug prevention program certification required by §86.3(b).

§ 86.5 What are the consequences if an IHE fails to submit a drug prevention program certification?

An IHE that fails to submit a drug prevention program certification is not eligible to receive funds or any other form of financial assistance under any Federal program. The effect of loss of eligibility to receive funds or any other form of Federal financial assistance is determined by the statute and regulations governing the Federal programs under which an IHE receives or desires to receive assistance.

§ 86.6 When must an IHE submit a drug prevention program certification?

The Secretary may allow an IHE until not later than April 1, 1991, to submit the drug prevention program certification, only if the IHE establishes that it has a need, other than administrative convenience, for more time to adopt and implement its drug prevention program. An IHE that wants to receive an extension of time to submit its drug prevention program certification shall submit a written justification to the Secretary that:

1. Describes each part of its drug prevention program, whether in effect or planned;
2. Provides a schedule to complete and implement its drug prevention program; and
3. Explains why it has a need, other than administrative convenience, for more time to adopt and implement its drug prevention program.

§ 86.7 What definitions apply to this part?

- *Department* and *ED* - the U.S. Department of Education.
- *EDGAR* - the Education Department General Administrative Regulations.
- *Secretary* - the Secretary of the Department of Education or an official or employee of the Department acting for the Secretary under a delegation of authority.
- *Compliance agreement* - an agreement between the Secretary and an IHE that is not in full compliance

with its drug prevention program certification. The agreement specifies steps the IHE will take to comply fully with its drug prevention program certification, and provides a schedule for the accomplishment of those steps. A compliance agreement does not excuse or remedy past violations of this part.

- *Institution of higher education* means:
    1. An institution of higher education, as defined in 34 CFR 600.4;
    2. A proprietary institution of higher education, as defined in 34 CFR 600.5;
    3. A postsecondary vocational institution, as defined in 34 CFR 600.6; and
    4. A vocational school, as defined in 34 CFR 600.7.

Subpart B—Institutions of Higher Education

§ 86.100 What must the IHE's drug prevention program include?

The IHE's drug prevention program must, at a minimum, include two elements. First, the IHE must review its program, biennially, to:

1. Determine its effectiveness and implement changes to the program if they are needed; and
2. Ensure that the disciplinary sanctions are consistently enforced.

Second, the distribute in writing, annually, to each employee, and to each student who is taking one or more classes for any type of academic credit except for continuing education units, regardless of the length of the student's program of study, of:

1. Standards of conduct that clearly prohibit, at a minimum, the unlawful possession, use, or distribution of illicit drugs and alcohol by students and employees on its property or as part of any of its activities;
2. A description of the applicable legal sanctions under local, State, or Federal law for the unlawful possession or distribution of illicit drugs and alcohol;
3. A description of the health risks associated with the use of illicit drugs and the abuse of alcohol;
4. A description of any drug or alcohol counseling, treatment, or rehabilitation or re-entry programs that are available to employees or students; and
5. A clear statement that the IHE will impose disciplinary sanctions on students and employees (consistent with local, State, and Federal law), and a description of those sanctions, up to and including expulsion or termination of employment and referral for prosecution, for violations of the standards of conduct required by paragraph (a)(1) of the full Federal section.

§ 86.101 What review of IHE drug prevention programs does the Secretary conduct?

The Secretary annually reviews a representative sample of IHE drug prevention programs.

§ 86.102 What is required of an IHE that the Secretary selects for annual review?

If the Secretary selects an IHE for review under §86.101, the IHE shall provide the Secretary access to personnel, records, documents and any other necessary information requested by the Secretary to review the IHE's adoption and implementation of its drug prevention program.

§ 86.103 What records and information must an IHE make available to the Secretary and the public concerning its drug prevention program?

Each IHE that provides the drug prevention program certification required by §86.3(b) shall, upon request, make available to the Secretary and the public a copy of each item required by §86.100(a) as well as the results of the biennial review required by §86.100(b). An IHE shall retain records related to the IHE's compliance with the drug prevention program certification for three years after the fiscal year in which the record was created. If any litigation, claim, negotiation, audit, review, or other action involving the records has been started before expiration of the three-year period, the IHE shall retain the records until completion of the action and resolution of all issues that arise from it, or until the end of the regular three-year period, whichever is later.

Subpart C [Reserved]

Subpart D—Responses and Sanctions Issued or Imposed by the Secretary for Violations by an IHE

§ 86.300 What constitutes a violation of this part by an IHE?

An IHE violates this part by:

1. Receiving any form of Federal financial assistance after becoming ineligible to receive that assistance because of failure to submit a certification in accordance with §86.3(b); or
2. Violating its certification.

Violation of a certification includes failure of an IHE to adopt or implement its drug prevention program, or consistently enforce its disciplinary sanctions for violations by students and employees of the standards of conduct adopted by an IHE under §86.100(a)(1).

§ 86.301 What actions may the Secretary take if an IHE violates this part?

If an IHE violates its certification, the Secretary may issue a response to the IHE. A response may include, but is not limited to:

1. Provision of information and technical assistance; and
2. Formulation of a compliance agreement designed to bring the ihe into full compliance with this part as soon as feasible.

If an IHE receives any form of Federal financial assistance without having submitted a certification or violates its certification, the Secretary may impose one or more sanctions on the IHE, including:

1. Repayment of any or all forms of Federal financial assistance received by the IHE when it was in violation of this part; and
2. Possible termination of any or all forms of Federal financial assistance.

§ 86.302 What are the procedures used by the Secretary for providing information or technical assistance?

The Secretary provides information or technical assistance to an IHE in writing, through site visits, or by other means. The IHE shall inform the Secretary of any corrective action it has taken within a period specified by the Secretary.

§ 86.303 What are the procedures used by the Secretary for issuing a response other than the formulation of a compliance agreement or the provision of information or technical assistance?

If the Secretary intends to issue a response other than the formulation of a compliance agreement or the provision of information or technical assistance, the IHE is notified in writing of:

1. The Secretary's determination that there are grounds to issue a response other than the formulation of a compliance agreement or providing information or technical assistance; and
2. The response the Secretary intends to issue.

The IHE shall inform the Secretary of the corrective action it has taken in order to comply with the terms of the Secretary's response within a period specified by the Secretary. If an IHE does not comply with the terms of a response issued by the Secretary, the Secretary may issue an additional response or impose a sanction on the IHE in accordance with the procedures in §86.304.

§ 86.304 What are the procedures used by the Secretary to demand repayment of Federal financial assistance or terminate an IHE's eligibility for any or all forms of Federal financial assistance?

A designated ED official begins a proceeding for repayment of Federal financial assistance or termination (or both) of an IHE's eligibility for Federal financial assistance by sending the IHE a notice by certified mail with return receipt requested. This notice:

1. Informs the IHE of the Secretary's intent to demand repayment of Federal financial assistance or to terminate, describes the consequences of that action, and identifies the alleged violations that constitute the basis for the action;
2. Specifies the amount of Federal financial assistance that must be repaid and the date by which the IHE must repay the funds;
3. Informs the IHE that the repayment of Federal financial assistance will not be required or that termination will not be effective on the date specified in the notice if the designated ED official receives appropriate documentation by the IHE.

Subpart E—Appeal Procedures

§ 86.400 What is the scope of this subpart?

The procedures in this subpart are the exclusive procedures governing appeals of decisions by a designated ED official to demand the repayment of Federal financial assistance or terminate the eligibility of an IHE to receive some or all forms of Federal financial assistance for violations of this part.

§ 86.401 What are the authority and responsibility of the ALJ?

The ALJ regulates the course of the proceeding and conduct of the parties during the hearing and takes all steps necessary to conduct a fair and impartial proceeding. The ALJ takes whatever measures are appropriate to expedite the proceeding. These measures may include, but are not limited to:

1. Scheduling of conferences;
2. Setting time limits for hearings and submission of written documents; and
3. Terminating the hearing and issuing a decision against a party if that party does not meet those time limits. The alj is not authorized to issue subpoenas.

The scope of the ALJ's review is limited to determining whether:

1. The IHE received any form of Federal financial assistance after becoming ineligible to receive that assistance because of failure to submit a certification; or
2. The IHE violated its certification.

§ 86.402 Who may be a party in a hearing under this subpart?

Only the designated ED official and the IHE that is the subject of the proposed termination or recovery of Federal financial assistance may be parties in a hearing under this subpart.

§ 86.403 May a party be represented by counsel?

A party may be represented by counsel.

§ 86.404 How may a party communicate with an ALJ?

A party may not communicate with an ALJ on any fact at issue in the case or on any matter relevant to the merits of the case unless the other party is given notice and an opportunity to participate. To obtain an order or ruling from an ALJ, a party shall make a motion to the ALJ. Except for a request for an extension of time, a motion must be made in writing unless the parties appear in person or participate in a conference telephone call. The ALJ, however, may require a party to reduce an oral motion to writing.

§ 86.405 What are the requirements for filing written submissions?

Any written submission under this subpart must be filed by hand-delivery, mail, or fax. If a party files a brief or other document, the party shall serve a copy of the filed material on the other party on the filing date by hand-delivery or by mail. If agreed upon by the parties, service of a document may be made upon the other party by fax. Any written submission must be accompanied by a statement certifying the date that the filed material was filed and served on the other party. The filing date for a written submission is the date the document is hand-delivered or mailed(a party filing by fax is responsible for confirming that a complete and legible copy of the document was received by ED).

§ 86.406 What must the ALJ do if the parties enter settlement negotiations?
If the parties to a case file a joint motion requesting a stay of the proceedings for settlement negotiations or for parties to obtain approval of a settlement agreement, the ALJ grants the stay. The following are not admissible in any proceeding under this part:

1. Evidence of conduct during settlement negotiations;
2. Statements made during settlement negotiations; or
3. Terms of settlement offers.

The parties may not disclose the contents of settlement negotiations to the ALJ. If the parties enter into a settlement agreement and file a joint motion to dismiss the case, the ALJ grants the motion.

§ 86.407 What are the procedures for scheduling a hearing?
If an IHE requests a hearing, the designated ED official sets the date and the place. The date is at least 15 days after the official receives the request and no later than 45 days after the request for hearing is received by ED. On the motion of either or both parties, the ALJ may extend the period before the hearing is scheduled beyond the 45 days. No termination takes effect until after a hearing is held and a decision is issued by the Department. With the approval of the ALJ and the consent of the designated ED official and the IHE, any time schedule specified in this section may be shortened.

§ 86.408 What are the procedures for conducting a pre-hearing conference?
A pre-hearing conference may be convened by the ALJ if the ALJ thinks that such a conference would be useful, or if requested by the designated ED official or the IHE. The purpose of a pre-hearing conference is to allow the parties to settle, narrow, or clarify the dispute. A pre-hearing conference may consist of a conference telephone call, an informal meeting, or the submission and exchange of written material.

§ 86.409 What are the procedures for conducting a hearing on the record?
A hearing on the record is an orderly presentation of arguments and evidence conducted by an ALJ. An ALJ conducts the hearing entirely on the basis of briefs and other written submissions unless evidentiary hearing is needed to resolve a material factual issue in dispute or oral argument is needed to clarify the issues in the case. The formal rules of evidence and procedures applicable to proceedings in a court of law are not applicable. The designated ED official has the burden of persuasion in any proceeding under this subpart. The parties may agree to exchange relevant documents and information. The ALJ may not order discovery, as provided for under the Federal Rules of Civil Procedure, or any other exchange between the parties of documents or information. The ALJ accepts evidence that is relevant and material to the proceeding and is not repetitious.

§ 86.410 What are the procedures for issuance of a decision?
The ALJ issues a written decision to the IHE, the designated ED official, and the Secretary by certified mail, return receipt requested, within 30 days after the last brief is filed, the last day of the hearing (if one is held), or the date on which the ALJ terminates the hearing. The ALJ's decision states whether the violation or violations contained in the Secretary's notification occurred, and articulates the reasons for the ALJ's finding. The Secretary reviews the decision on request of either party, or on his or her own initiative. If the Secretary decides to review the decision, the parties are informed of this by written notice sent within 15 days of the Secretary's receipt of the ALJ's decision. The Secretary's decision may affirm, modify, reverse or remand the ALJ's decision and includes a statement of reasons for the decision.

§ 86.411 What are the procedures for requesting reinstatement of eligibility?

An IHE whose eligibility to receive Federal financial assistance has been terminated may file with ED a request for reinstatement as an eligible entity no earlier than 18 months after the effective date of the termination. In order to be reinstated, the IHE must demonstrate that it has corrected the violation(s) on which the termination was based, and that it has met any repayment obligation imposed upon it. In addition, the IHE shall comply with the requirements and procedures for reinstatement of eligibility applicable to any Federal program under which it desires to receive Federal financial assistance.

PART 97—PROTECTION OF HUMAN SUBJECTS

Subpart A—Federal Policy for the Protection of Human Subjects (Basic ED Policy for Protection of Human Research Subjects)

§ 97.101 To what does this policy apply?

Except as provided in the second paragraph of this section, this policy applies to all research involving human subjects conducted, supported or otherwise subject to regulation by any federal department or agency which takes appropriate administrative action to make the policy applicable to such research.

Unless otherwise required by department or agency heads, research activities in which the only involvement of human subjects will be in one or more of the following categories are exempt from this policy:

1. Research conducted in established or commonly accepted educational settings, involving normal educational practices, such as research on regular and special education instructional strategies, or research on the effectiveness of or the comparison among instructional techniques, curricula, or classroom management methods.
2. Research involving the use of educational tests (cognitive, diagnostic, aptitude, achievement), survey procedures, interview procedures or observation of public behavior, unless information obtained is recorded in such a manner that human subjects can be identified (directly or through identifiers linked to the subjects), as well as any disclosure of the human subjects' responses outside the research could reasonably place the subjects at risk of criminal or civil liability or be damaging to the subjects' financial standing, employability, or reputation.
3. Research involving the use of educational tests (cognitive, diagnostic, aptitude, achievement), survey procedures, interview procedures, or observation of public behavior that is not exempt under the above statement of this section, if the human subjects are elected or appointed public officials or candidates for public office, or Federal statute(s) require(s) without exception that the confidentiality of the personally identifiable information will be maintained throughout the research and thereafter.
4. Research, involving the collection or study of existing data, documents, records, pathological specimens, or diagnostic specimens, if these sources are publicly available or if the information is recorded by the investigator in such a manner that subjects cannot be identified, directly or through identifiers linked to the subjects.
5. Research and demonstration projects which are conducted by or subject to the approval of department or agency heads, and which are designed to study, evaluate, or otherwise examine public benefit or service programs, procedures for obtaining benefits or services under those programs, possible changes in or alternatives to those programs or procedures, or possible changes in methods or levels of payment for benefits or services under those programs.
6. Taste and food quality evaluation and consumer acceptance studies (if wholesome foods without additives are consumed or agricultural chemical or environmental contaminants in the foods are at or below the level found to be safe by the FDA, approved by the EPA, or the Food Safety and Inspection Service of USDA).

Judgment on covered activities. Department or agency heads retain final judgment as to whether a particular activity is covered by this policy. Furthermore, Department or agency heads may require that specific research activities or classes of research activities conducted, supported, or otherwise subject to regulation by the department or agency but not otherwise covered by this policy, comply with some or all of the requirements of this policy.

Unless otherwise required by law, department or agency heads may waive the applicability of some or all of the provisions of this policy to specific research activities otherwise covered by this policy. Except when otherwise required by statute or E.O., the department or agency head shall forward advance notices of these actions to the Office for Human Research Protections, DHHS or any successor office, and shall also publish them in the Federal Register or in such other manner as provided in department or agency procedures. Note: Institutions with HHS-approved assurances on file will abide by provisions of title 45 CFR Part 46 Subparts A–D. Some of the other Departments and Agencies have incorporated all provisions of title 45 CFR Part 46 into their policies and procedures as well. However, the exemptions at 45 CFR 46.101(b) do not apply to research involving prisoners, Subpart C. The exemption at 45 CFR 46.101(b)(2), for research involving survey or interview procedures or observation of public behavior, does not apply to research with children, Subpart D, except for research involving observations of public behavior when the investigator(s) do not participate in the activities being observed.

§ 97.102 Definitions.

- *Department* or *agency head* - the head of any federal department or agency and any other officer or employee of any department or agency to whom authority has been delegated.
- *Institution* - any public or private entity or agency (including federal, state, and other agencies).
- *Legally authorized representative* - an individual or judicial or other body authorized under applicable law to consent on behalf of a prospective subject to the subject's participation in the procedure(s) involved in the research.
- *Research* - a systematic investigation, including research development, testing and evaluation, designed to develop or contribute to generalizable knowledge. Activities which meet this definition constitute research for purposes of this policy, whether or not they are conducted or supported under a program which is considered research for other purposes. For example, some demonstration and service programs may include research activities.
- *Research subject to regulation*, and similar terms are intended to encompass those research activities for which a federal department or agency has specific responsibility for regulating as a research activity, (for example, Investigational New Drug requirements administered by the Food and Drug Administration). It does not include research activities which are incidentally regulated by a federal department or agency solely as part of the department's or agency's broader responsibility to regulate certain types of activities whether research or non-research in nature (for example, Wage and Hour requirements administered by the DOL).
- *Human subject* - a living individual about whom an investigator (whether professional or student) conducting research obtains data through intervention or interaction with the individual, or identifiable private information.
- *Intervention* includes both physical procedures by which data are gathered (for example, venipuncture) and manipulations of the subject or the subject's environment that are performed for research purposes. Interaction includes communication or interpersonal contact between investigator and subject. "Private information" includes information about behavior that occurs in a context in which an individual can reasonably expect that no observation or recording is taking place, and information which has been provided for specific purposes by an individual and which the individual can reasonably expect will not be made public (for example, a medical record). Private information must be individually identifiable (i.e., the identity of the subject is or may readily be ascertained by the investigator or associated with the information) in order for obtaining the information to constitute research involving human subjects.
- *IRB* - an institutional review board established in accord with and for the purposes expressed in this policy.
- *IRB approval* - the determination of the IRB that the research has been reviewed and may be conducted at an institution within the constraints set forth by the IRB and by other institutional and federal requirements.
- *Minimal risk* - that the probability and magnitude of harm or discomfort anticipated in the research

are not greater in and of themselves than those ordinarily encountered in daily life or during the performance of routine physical or psychological examinations or tests.
- *Certification* - the official notification by the institution to the supporting agency, in accordance with the requirements of this policy, that a research project or activity involving human subjects has been reviewed and approved by an IRB in accordance with an approved assurance.

§ 97.103 Assuring compliance with this policy—research conducted or supported by any Federal Department or Agency.

Each institution engaged in research which is covered by this policy and which is conducted or supported by a federal department or agency shall provide written assurance (executed by the authorized individual) satisfactory to the department or agency head that it will comply with the requirements set forth in this policy. In lieu of requiring submission of an assurance, individual department or agency heads shall accept the existence of a current assurance, appropriate for the research in question, on file with the Office for Human Research Protections, HHS, or any successor office, and approved for federal-wide use by that office. When the existence of an HHS-approved assurance is accepted in lieu of requiring submission of an assurance, reports (except certification) required by this policy to be made to department and agency heads shall also be made to the Office for Human Research Protections, (HHS), or any successor office.

Departments and agencies will conduct or support research covered by this policy only if the institution has an assurance approved as provided in this section, and only if the institution has certified to the department or agency head that the research has been reviewed and approved by an IRB provided for in the assurance, and will be subject to continuing review by the IRB. Assurances applicable to federally supported or conducted research shall at a minimum include:

1. A statement of principles governing the institution in the discharge of its responsibilities for protecting the rights and welfare of human subjects of research conducted at or sponsored by the institution, regardless of whether the research is subject to federal regulation. This may include an appropriate existing code, declaration, or statement of ethical principles, or a statement formulated by the institution itself. This requirement does not preempt provisions of this policy applicable to department- or agency-supported or regulated research and need not be applicable to any research exempted or waived under §97.101 (b) or (i) as stated in the full Federal section.
2. Designation of one or more IRBs established in accordance with the requirements of this policy, and for which provisions are made for meeting space and sufficient staff to support the IRB's review and recordkeeping duties.
3. A list of IRB members identified by name; earned degrees; representative capacity; indications of experience such as board certifications, licenses, etc., sufficient to describe each member's chief anticipated contributions to IRB deliberations; and any employment or other relationship between each member and the institution; for example: full-time employee, part-time employee, member of governing panel or board, stockholder, paid or unpaid consultant. Changes in IRB membership shall be reported to the department or agency head, unless in accord with §97.103(a) of this policy, the existence of an HHS-approved assurance is accepted. In this case, change in IRB membership shall be reported to the Office for Human Research Protections, HHS, or any successor office.
4. Written procedures which the IRB will follow (i) for conducting its initial and continuing review of research and for reporting its findings and actions to the investigator and the institution; (ii) for determining which projects require review more often than annually and which projects need verification from sources other than the investigators that no material changes have occurred since previous IRB review; and (iii) for ensuring prompt reporting to the IRB of proposed changes in a research activity, and for ensuring that such changes in approved research, during the period the IRB approval has already been given, may not be initiated without IRB review and approval except when necessary to eliminate apparent immediate hazards to the subject.

5. Written procedures for ensuring prompt reporting to the IRB, appropriate institutional officials, and the department or agency head of (i) any unanticipated problems involving risks to subjects or others or any serious or continuing noncompliance with this policy or the requirements or determinations of the IRB and (ii) any suspension or termination of IRB approval.

§ 97.107 IRB membership.

Each IRB shall have at least five members, with varying backgrounds to promote complete and adequate review of research activities commonly conducted by the institution. The IRB shall be sufficiently qualified through the expertise and diversity of its members (including consideration of race, gender, and cultural backgrounds and sensitivity to such issues as community attitudes) to promote respect for its advice and counsel in safeguarding the rights and welfare of human subjects. In addition to possessing the professional competence necessary to review specific research activities, the IRB shall be able to ascertain the acceptability of proposed research in terms of institutional commitments and regulations, applicable law, and standards of professional conduct and practice. The IRB shall therefore include persons knowledgeable in these areas. If an IRB regularly reviews research that involves a vulnerable category of subjects, such as children, prisoners, pregnant women, or handicapped or mentally disabled persons, consideration shall be given to the inclusion of one or more individuals who are knowledgeable about and experienced in working with these subjects. An IRB should also make every effort to address the following points:

1. Every nondiscriminatory effort will be made to ensure that no IRB consists entirely of men or entirely of women, including the institution's consideration of qualified persons of both sexes, so long as no selection is made to the IRB on the basis of gender. No IRB may consist entirely of members of one profession.
2. Each IRB shall include at least one member whose primary concerns are in scientific areas and at least one member whose primary concerns are in nonscientific areas.
3. Each IRB shall include at least one member who is not otherwise affiliated with the institution and who is not part of the immediate family of a person who is affiliated with the institution.
4. No IRB may have a member participate in the IRB's initial or continuing review of any project in which the member has a conflicting interest, except to provide information requested by the IRB.
5. An IRB may, in its discretion, invite individuals with competence in special areas to assist in the review of issues which require expertise beyond or in addition to that available on the IRB. These individuals may not vote with the IRB.

§ 97.108 IRB functions and operations.

In order to fulfill the requirements of this policy each IRB shall:

1. Follow written procedures in the same detail as described in §97.103(b)(4) and to the extent required by §97.103(b)(5); and
2. Except when an expedited review procedure is used (see §97.110), review proposed research at convened meetings at which a majority of the members of the irb are present, including at least one member whose primary concerns are in nonscientific areas.

In order for the research to be approved, it shall receive the approval of a majority of those members present at the meeting.

§ 97.109 IRB review of research.

An IRB shall review and have authority to approve, require modifications in (to secure approval), or disapprove all research activities covered by this policy. An IRB shall require that information given to subjects as part of informed consent is in accordance with §97.116 (but the IRB may require that additional information be given to subjects it would meaningfully add to the protection of the rights and welfare of subjects). An IRB shall also notify investigators and the institution, in writing, of its decision to approve or disapprove the proposed research activity (or of modifications required to secure IRB approval). If the IRB decides to disapprove a research activity, it shall include a statement of the reasons for its decision and give the investigator an opportunity to respond. An IRB shall conduct continuing review of research covered by this policy at intervals appropriate to the degree of risk, but not less than once per year, and shall have authority to observe or have a third party observe the process and research.

§ 97.110 Expedited review procedures for certain kinds of research involving no more than minimal risk, and for minor changes in approved research.

The Secretary of HHS has established (and published as a Notice in the Federal Register) a list of categories of research that may be reviewed by the IRB through an expedited review procedure. The list will be amended, as appropriate after consultation with other departments and agencies, through periodic republication in the Federal Register. A copy of the list is available from the Office for Human Research Protections, HHS, or any successor office.

An IRB may use the expedited review procedure to review the following:

1. Some or all of the research appearing on the list and found by the reviewer(s) to involve no more than minimal risk, and/or
2. Minor changes in previously approved research during the period (of one year or less) for which approval is authorized.

Under an expedited review procedure, the review may be carried out by the IRB chairperson or by one or more experienced reviewers designated by the chairperson from among members of the IRB. In reviewing the research, the reviewers may exercise all of the authorities of the IRB except that the reviewers may not disapprove the research. A research activity may be disapproved only after review in accordance with the non-expedited procedure set forth in §97.108(b) of the full Federal section. Each IRB which uses an expedited review procedure shall adopt a method for keeping all members advised of research proposals which have been approved under the procedure.

§ 97.111 Criteria for IRB approval of research.

In order to approve research covered by this policy, the IRB shall determine that all of the following requirements are satisfied:

1. Risks to subjects are minimized by using procedures which are consistent with sound research design and which do not unnecessarily expose subjects to risk and, whenever appropriate, by using procedures already being performed on the subjects for diagnostic or treatment purposes.
2. Risks to subjects are reasonable in relation to anticipated benefits, if any, to subjects, and the importance of the knowledge that may reasonably be expected to result. In evaluating risks and benefits, the IRB should consider only those risks and benefits that may result from the research (as distinguished from risks and benefits of therapies subjects would receive even if not participating in the research). The IRB should not consider possible long-range effects of applying knowledge gained in the research (for example, the possible effects of the research on public policy) as among those research risks that fall within the purview of its responsibility.
3. Selection of subjects is equitable. In making this assessment the IRB should take into account the purposes of the research and the setting in which the research will be conducted and should be particularly cognizant of the special problems of research involving vulnerable populations, such as children, prisoners, pregnant women, mentally disabled persons, or economically or educationally disadvantaged persons.
4. Informed consent will be sought from each prospective subject or the subject's legally authorized representative, in accordance with, and to the extent required by §97.116.
5. Informed consent will be appropriately documented, in accordance with, and to the extent required by §97.117.

6. When appropriate, the research plan makes adequate provision for monitoring the data collected to ensure the safety of subjects.
7. When appropriate, there are adequate provisions to protect the privacy of subjects and to maintain the confidentiality of data.

When some or all of the subjects are likely to be vulnerable to coercion or undue influence, such as children, prisoners, pregnant women, mentally disabled persons, or economically or educationally disadvantaged persons, additional safeguards have been included in the study to protect the rights and welfare of these subjects.

§ 97.112 Review by institution.

Research covered by this policy that has been approved by an IRB may be subject to further appropriate review and approval or disapproval by officials of the institution. However, those officials may not approve the research if it has not been approved by an IRB.

§ 97.113 Suspension or termination of IRB approval of research.

An IRB shall have authority to suspend or terminate approval of research not conducted in accordance with the IRB's requirements or that has been associated with unexpected serious harm to subjects. Any suspension or termination of approval shall include a statement of the reasons for the IRB's action and shall be reported promptly to the investigator, institutional officials, and the department or agency head.

§ 97.114 Cooperative research.

Cooperative research projects are those projects covered by this policy which involve more than one institution. In the conduct of cooperative research projects, each institution is responsible for safeguarding the rights and welfare of human subjects and for complying with this policy. With the approval of the department or agency head, an institution participating in a cooperative project may enter into a joint review arrangement, rely upon the review of another qualified IRB, or make similar arrangements for avoiding duplication of effort.

§ 97.115 IRB records.

An institution, or when appropriate an IRB, shall prepare, maintain, and retain (for at least three years after completion of the research) adequate documentation of IRB activities, including the following:

1. Copies of all research proposals reviewed, scientific evaluations that accompany the proposals, approved sample consent documents, progress reports submitted by investigators, and reports of injuries to subjects.
2. Minutes of IRB meetings which shall be in sufficient detail to show attendance at the meetings; actions taken by the IRB; the vote on these actions including the number of members voting for, against, and abstaining; the basis for requiring changes in or disapproving research; and a written summary of the discussion of controverted issues and their resolution.
3. Records of continuing review activities.
4. Copies of all correspondence between the IRB and the investigators.
5. A list of IRB members (see §97.103(b)(3)).
6. Written procedures for the IRB (see §97.103(b)(4-5)).
7. Statements of significant new findings provided to subjects, as required.

§ 97.116 General requirements for informed consent.

Requirement of informed consent. Except as provided elsewhere in this policy, no investigator may involve a human being as a subject in research covered by this policy unless the investigator has obtained the legally effective informed consent of the subject or the subject's legally authorized representative. An investigator shall seek such consent only under circumstances that provide the prospective subject or the representative sufficient opportunity to consider whether or not to participate and that minimize the possibility of coercion or undue influence. The information that is given to the subject or the representative shall be in language understandable to the subject or the representative. No informed consent, whether oral or written, may include any exculpatory language through which the subject or the representative is made to waive or appear to waive any of the subject's legal rights, or releases or appears to release the investigator, the sponsor, the institution or its agents from liability for negligence.

Basic elements of informed consent. Unless stated otherwise in the full Federal section, the following information shall be provided to each subject in seeking informed consent:

1. A statement that the study involves research, an explanation of the purposes of the research and the expected duration of the subject's participation, a description of the procedures to be followed, and identification of any procedures which are experimental;
2. A description of any reasonably foreseeable risks or discomforts to the subject;
3. A description of any benefits to the subject or to others which may reasonably be expected from the research;
4. A disclosure of appropriate alternative procedures or courses of treatment, if any, that might be advantageous to the subject;
5. A statement describing the extent, if any, to which confidentiality of records identifying the subject will be maintained;
6. For research involving more than minimal risk, an explanation as to whether any compensation and an explanation as to whether any medical treatments are available if injury occurs and, if so, what they consist of, or where further information may be obtained;
7. An explanation of whom to contact for answers to pertinent questions about the research and research subjects' rights, and whom to contact in the event of a research-related injury to the subject; and
8. A statement that participation is voluntary, refusal to participate will involve no penalty or loss of benefits to which the subject is otherwise entitled, and the subject may discontinue participation at any time without penalty or loss of benefits to which the subject is otherwise entitled.

Additional elements of informed consent. When appropriate, one or more of the following elements of information shall also be provided to each subject:

1. A statement that the particular treatment or procedure may involve risks to the subject (or to the embryo or fetus, if the subject is or may become pregnant) which are currently unforeseeable;
2. Anticipated circumstances under which the subject's participation may be terminated by the investigator without regard to the subject's consent;
3. Any additional costs to the subject that may result from participation in the research;
4. The consequences of a subject's decision to withdraw from the research and procedures for orderly termination of participation by the subject;
5. A statement that significant new findings developed during the course of the research which may relate to the subject's willingness to continue participation will be provided to the subject; and
6. The approximate number of subjects involved in the study.

An IRB may approve a consent procedure which does not include, or which alters, some or all of the elements of informed consent set forth above, or waive the requirement to obtain informed consent provided the IRB finds and documents that:

1. The research or demonstration project is to be conducted by or subject to the approval of state or local government officials and is designed to study, evaluate, or otherwise examine public benefit of service programs, procedures for obtaining benefits/services under those programs, possible

changes in or alternatives to those programs or procedures, or possible changes in methods or levels of payment for benefits or services under those programs; and

2. The research could not practicably be carried out without the waiver or alteration.

An IRB may approve a consent procedure which does not include, or which alters, some or all of the elements of informed consent set forth in this section, or waive the requirements to obtain informed consent provided the IRB finds and documents that:

1. The research involves no more than minimal risk to the subjects;
2. The waiver or alteration will not adversely affect the rights and welfare of the subjects;
3. The research could not practicably be carried out without the waiver or alteration; and
4. Whenever appropriate, the subjects will be provided with additional pertinent information after participation.

§ 97.117 Documentation of informed consent.

Except as provided in the last paragraph of this section, informed consent shall be documented by the use of a written consent form approved by the IRB and signed by the subject or the subject's legally authorized representative. A copy shall be given to the person signing the form.

Except as provided in the last paragraph of this section, the consent form may be either of the following:

1. A written consent document that embodies the elements of informed consent required by §97.116. This form may be read to the subject or the subject's legally authorized representative, but in any event, the investigator shall give either the subject or the representative adequate opportunity to read it before it is signed; or
2. A short form written consent document stating that the elements of informed consent required by §97.116 have been presented orally to the subject or the subject's legally authorized representative. When this method is used, there shall be a witness to the oral presentation. Also, the IRB shall approve a written summary of what is to be said to the subject or the representative. Only the short form itself is to be signed by the subject or the representative. However, the witness shall sign both the short form and a copy of the summary, and the person actually obtaining consent shall sign a copy of the summary. A copy of the summary shall be given to the subject or the representative, in addition to a copy of the short form.

An IRB may waive the requirement for the investigator to obtain a signed consent form for some or all subjects if it finds either:

1. That the only record linking the subject and the research would be the consent document and the principal risk would be potential harm resulting from a breach of confidentiality. Each subject will be asked whether the subject wants documentation linking the subject with the research, and the subject's wishes will govern; or
2. That the research presents no more than minimal risk of harm to subjects and involves no procedures for which written consent is normally required outside of the research context.
3. In cases in which the documentation requirement is waived, the IRB may require the investigator to provide subjects with a written statement regarding the research.

§ 97.118 Applications and proposals lacking definite plans for involvement of human subjects.

Certain types of applications for grants, cooperative agreements, or contracts are submitted to departments or agencies with the knowledge that subjects may be involved within the period of support, but definite plans would not normally be set forth in the application or proposal. These include activities such as institutional type grants when selection of specific projects is the institution's responsibility; research training grants in which the activities involving subjects remain to be selected; and projects in which human subject's involvement will depend upon completion of instruments, prior animal studies, or purification of compounds. These applications need not be reviewed by an IRB before an award may be made. However, except for research exempted or waived under §97.101 (b) or (i), no human subjects may be involved in any project supported by these awards until the project has been approved by the IRB, as provided in this policy, and certification submitted, by the institution, to the department or agency.

§ 97.119 Research undertaken without the intention of involving human subjects.
In the event research is undertaken without the intention of involving human subjects, but it is later proposed to involve human subjects in the research, the research shall first be reviewed and approved by an IRB, as provided in this policy, a certification submitted, by the institution, to the department or agency, and final approval given to the proposed change by the department or agency.

§ 97.120 Evaluation and disposition of applications and proposals for research to be conducted or supported by a Federal Department or Agency.
The department or agency head will evaluate all applications and proposals involving human subjects. This evaluation will consider the risks to the subjects, the adequacy of protection against these risks, the potential benefits of the research to the subjects and others, and the importance of the knowledge gained or to be gained. On the basis of this evaluation, the department or agency head may approve or disapprove the application or proposal, or enter into negotiations to develop an approvable one.

§ 97.122 Use of Federal funds.
Federal funds administered by a department or agency may not be expended for research involving human subjects unless the requirements of this policy have been satisfied.

§ 97.123 Early termination of research support: Evaluation of applications and proposals.
When the department or agency head finds that an institution has materially failed to comply with the terms of this policy, he or she may require termination or suspension of any department or agency support. In making decisions about supporting or approving applications or proposals covered by this policy, the department or agency head may take into account factors such as whether the applicant has been subject to a prior termination or suspension and whether the applicant materially failed to discharge responsibility for the protection of the rights and welfare of human subjects (whether or not the research was subject to federal regulation).

§ 97.124 Conditions.
With respect to any research project or any class of research projects the department or agency head may impose additional conditions prior to or at the time of approval when in the judgment of the department or agency head additional conditions are necessary for the protection of human subjects.

Subparts B–C [Reserved]

Subpart D—Additional ED Protections for Children Who Are Subjects in Research

§ 97.401 To what do these regulations apply?
This subpart applies to all research involving children as subjects conducted or supported by the ED or research conducted by ED employees. Exemptions in §97.101(b)(1) and (b)(3-6) of the full Federal section are applicable to this subpart. The exemption in §97.101(b)(2) regarding educational tests is also applicable to this subpart. The exemption in §97.101(b)(2) for research involving survey or interview procedures or observations of public behavior does not apply to research covered by this subpart, except for research involving observation of public behavior when the investigators do not participate in the activities being observed.

§ 97.402 Definitions.

The definitions in §97.102 apply to this subpart as well as the following definitions:

- *Children* - persons not of legal age to consent to treatments or procedures involved in the research, under the applicable law of the jurisdiction in which the research will be conducted.
- *Assent* - a child's affirmative agreement to participate in research. Mere failure to object should not, absent affirmative agreement, be construed as assent.
- *Permission* - the agreement of parent(s) or guardian to the participation of their child or ward in research.
- *Parent* - a child's biological or adoptive parent.
- *Guardian* - an individual who is authorized under applicable State or local law to consent on behalf of a child to general medical care.

§ 97.403 IRB duties.

In addition to other responsibilities assigned to IRBs under this part, each IRB shall review research covered by this subpart and approve only research that satisfies the conditions of all applicable sections of this subpart.

§ 97.404 Research not involving greater than minimal risk.

ED conducts or funds research in which the IRB finds that no greater than minimal risk to children is presented, only if the IRB finds that adequate provisions are made for soliciting the assent of the children and the permission of their parents or guardians, as set forth in §97.408.

§ 97.405 Research involving greater than minimal risk but presenting the prospect of direct benefit to the individual subjects.

ED conducts or funds research in which the IRB finds that more than minimal risk to children is presented by an intervention or procedure that holds out the prospect of direct benefit for the individual subject, or by a monitoring procedure that is likely to contribute to the subject's well-being, only if the IRB finds:

1. The risk is justified by the anticipated benefit to the subjects;
2. The relation of the anticipated benefit to the risk is at least as favorable to the subjects as that presented by available alternative approaches; and
3. Adequate provisions are made for soliciting the assent of the children and permission of their parents or guardians, as set forth in §97.408.

§ 97.406 Research involving greater than minimal risk and no prospect of direct benefit to individual subjects, but likely to yield generalizable knowledge about the subject's disorder or condition.

ED conducts or funds research in which the IRB finds that more than minimal risk to children is presented by an intervention or procedure that does not hold out the prospect of direct benefit for the individual subject, or by a monitoring procedure which is not likely to contribute to the well-being of the subject, only if the IRB finds that:

1. The risk represents a minor increase over minimal risk;
2. The intervention or procedure presents experiences to subjects that are reasonably commensurate with those inherent in their actual or expected medical, dental, psychological, social, or educational situations;
3. The intervention or procedure is likely to yield generalizable knowledge about the subjects' disorder or condition that is of vital importance for the understanding or amelioration of the subjects' disorder or condition; and
4. Adequate provisions are made for soliciting assent of the children and permission of their parents or guardians, as set forth in §97.408.

§ 97.407 Research not otherwise approvable which presents an opportunity to understand, prevent, or alleviate a serious problem affecting the health or welfare of children.

ED conducts or funds research that the IRB does not believe meets the requirements of §97.404, §97.405, or §97.406 only if the IRB finds that the research presents a reasonable opportunity to further the understanding, prevention, or alleviation of a serious problem affecting the health or welfare of children. In addition, ED funds or conducts research that he Secretary, after consultation with a panel of experts in pertinent disciplines and following opportunity for public review and comment, has determined either:

1. The research in fact satisfies the conditions of §97.404, §97.405, or §97.406, as applicable; or
2. The research presents a reasonable opportunity to further the understanding, prevention, or alleviation of a serious problem affecting the health or welfare of children.

§ 97.408 Requirements for permission by parents or guardians and for assent by children.

In addition to the determinations required under other applicable sections of this subpart, the IRB shall determine that adequate provisions are made for soliciting the assent of the children, if in the judgment of the IRB the children are capable of providing assent. In determining whether children are capable of assenting, the IRB shall take into account the ages, maturity, and psychological state of the children involved. This judgment may be made for all children to be involved in research under a particular protocol, or for each child, as the IRB deems appropriate. Even if the IRB determines that the subjects are capable of assenting, the IRB may still waive the assent requirement under circumstances in which consent may be waived in accord with §97.116.

In addition to the determinations required under other applicable sections of this subpart, the IRB shall determine, in accordance with and to the extent that consent is required by §97.116, that adequate provisions are made for soliciting the permission of each child's parent(s) or guardian(s). If such permission is to be obtained, the IRB may find that permission of one parent is sufficient for research to be conducted under §97.404 or §97.405. If research is covered by §§97.406 and 97.407 (and such permission is to be obtained), both parents must give their permission unless one parent is deceased, unknown, incompetent, not reasonably available, or if only one parent has legal responsibility for the care and custody of the child.

In addition to waiver provisions contained in §97.116, if the IRB determines that a research protocol is designed for conditions or for a subject population for which parental permission is not a reasonable requirement to protect the subjects, it may waive the consent requirements (see the full section), provided an appropriate mechanism for protecting the children who will participate as subjects in the research is substituted, and provided further that the waiver is not inconsistent with Federal, State, or local law. The choice of an appropriate mechanism depends upon the nature of the activities described in the protocol, the risk and anticipated benefit to the research subjects, and their age, maturity, status, and condition.

§ 97.409 Wards.

Children who are wards of the State or any other agency, institution, or entity may be included in research approved under §97.406 or §97.407 only if that research is:

1. Related to their status as wards; or
2. Conducted in schools, camps, hospitals, institutions, or similar settings in which the majority of children involved as subjects are not wards.

If such research is approved, the IRB shall require appointment of an advocate for each child who is a ward, in addition to any other individual acting on behalf of the child as guardian or in loco parentis. One individual may serve as advocate for more than one child. The advocate must be an individual who has the background and experience to act in, and agrees to act in, the best interest of the child for the duration of the child's participation in the research and who is not associated in any way (except in the role as advocate or member of the IRB) with the research, the investigator or investigators, or the guardian organization.

PART 98—STUDENT RIGHTS IN RESEARCH, EXPERIMENTAL PROGRAMS, AND TESTING

§ 98.1 Applicability of part.

This part applies to any program administered by the Secretary of Education that:

1. Was transferred to the Department by the ED Organization Act (DEOA); and
2. Was administered by the Education Division of the Department of Health, Education, and Welfare on the day before the effective date of the DEOA.

This part applies to any program administered by the Secretary of ED that was enacted after the effective date of the DEOA, unless the law enacting the new Federal program has the effect of making section 439 of GEPA inapplicable.

The following chart lists the funded programs to which Part 98 does not apply as of February 16, 1984.

Name of program	Authorizing statute	Implementing regulations
High School Equivalency Program and College Assistance Migrant Program	Section 418A of the Higher Education Act of 1965 as amended by the Education Amendments of 1980 (Pub. L. 96–374) 20 U.S.C. 1070d–2)	Part 206.
Programs administered by the Commissioner of the Rehabilitative Services Administration	The Rehabilitation Act of 1973 as amended by Pub. L. 95–602 (29 U.S.C. 700, et seq.)	Parts 351–356, 361, 362, 365, 366, 369–375, 378, 379, 385–390, and 395.
College housing	Title IV of the Housing Act of 1950 as amended (12 U.S.C. 1749, et seq.)	Part 614.

§ 98.2 Definitions.

- *Department* and *ED* - the United States Department of Education.
- *Secretary* - the Secretary of ED or an official acting under authority for the Secretary.
- *Recipient* - an organization receiving financial assistance to carry out a project or program.
- *Act* - the General Education Provisions Act.
- *Office* - the information and investigation office specified in §98.5.

§ 98.3 Access to instructional material used in a research or experimentation program.

All instructional material (including teacher manuals, films, tapes, or other supplementary instructional material) used in connection with any research or experimentation project shall be available for inspection by the parents or guardians of the children engaged in such program or project. For the purpose of this part research or experimentation program or project means any program or project in any program under parts of §98.1 that is designed to explore or develop new or unproven teaching methods or techniques. For the purpose of the section children means persons not above age 21 who are enrolled in a program under some parts of §98.1) not above the elementary or secondary education level, as determined under State law.

§ 98.4 Protection of students' privacy in examination, testing, or treatment.

No student shall be required, as part of any program specified in §98.1 (a) or (b) of the full Federal section, to submit without prior consent to psychiatric examination, testing, or treatment, or psychological examination, testing, or treatment, in which the primary purpose is to reveal information concerning one or more of the following:

1. Political affiliations;
2. Mental and psychological problems potentially embarrassing to the student or his or her family;

3. Sex behavior and attitudes;
4. Illegal, anti-social, self-incriminating and demeaning behavior;
5. Critical appraisals of other individuals with whom the student has close family relationships;
6. Legally recognized privileged and analogous relationships, such as those of lawyers, physicians, and ministers; or
7. Income, other than that required by law to determine eligibility for participation in a program or for receiving financial assistance under a program.

§ 98.5 Information and investigation office.

The Secretary has designated an office to provide information about the requirements of Section 439 of the Act, and to investigate, process, and review complaints that may be filed concerning alleged violations of the provisions of the section. The name and address of this office is as follows: FERPA Office, U.S. Department of Education, 400 Maryland Avenue, SW., Washington, DC 20202.

§ 98.6 Reports.

The Secretary may require the recipient to submit reports containing information necessary to resolve complaints under section 439 of the Act and the regulations in this part.

§ 98.7 Filing a complaint.

Only a student or a parent (or guardian) of a student directly affected by a violation under Section 439 of the Act may file a complaint under this part. The complaint must be submitted in writing to the Office. The complaint must:

1. Contain specific allegations of fact giving reasonable cause to believe that a violation of either §98.3 or §98.4 exists; and
2. Include evidence of attempted resolution of the complaint at the local level (and at the state level if a state complaint resolution process exists), including the names of local and state officials contacted and significant dates in the attempted resolution process.

The Office investigates each complaint which the Office receives that meets the requirements of this section to determine whether the recipient failed to comply with the provisions of Section 439 of the Act.

§ 98.8 Notice of the complaint.

If the Office receives a complaint that meets the requirements of §98.7, it provides written notification to the complainant and the recipient or contractor against which the violation has been alleged that the complaint has been received. The notice to the recipient or contractor must:

1. Include the substance of the alleged violation; and
2. Inform the recipient or contractor that the office will investigate the complaint and that the recipient or contractor may submit a written response to the complaint.

§ 98.9 Investigation and findings.

The Office may permit the parties to submit further written or oral arguments or information. Following investigation, the Office provides to the complainant and recipient(s) written notice of its findings and the basis for its findings. If the Office finds that the recipient or contractor has not complied with section 439 of the Act, the Office includes in its notice under paragraph (b) of this full Federal section:

1. A statement of the specific steps that the Secretary recommends the recipient or contractor take to comply; and
2. Provides a reasonable period of time, given all of the circumstances of the case, during which the recipient or contractor may comply voluntarily.

§ 98.10 Enforcement of the findings.

If the recipient or contractor does not comply during the period of time set under §98.9(c), ED may either:

1. For a recipient, take an action authorized under 34 CFR Part 78, including issuing a notice of intent to terminate funds under 34 CFR 78.21; withholding funds under 34 CFR 78.21, 200.94(b), or 298.45(b); or issuing a cease and desist notice under 34 CFR 78.31, 200.94(c) or 298.45(c), depending upon the program under which the notice is issued.
2. For a contractor, direct the contracting officer to take an action authorized under the Federal Acquisition Regulations, including either issuing a notice to suspend operations under 48 CFR 12.5, or issuing a notice to terminate for default, either in whole or in part under 48 CFR 49.102.

PART 99—FAMILY EDUCATIONAL RIGHTS AND PRIVACY

Subpart A—General

§ 99.1 To which educational agencies or institutions do these regulations apply?

Except as otherwise noted in §99.10, this part applies to an educational agency or institution to which funds have been made available under any program administered by the Secretary, if the educational agency or institution:

1. Provides educational services or instruction, or both, to students; or
2. Is authorized to direct and control public elementary or secondary, or postsecondary educational institutions.

Note that this part does not apply to an educational agency or institution solely because students attending that agency or institution receive non-monetary benefits under a program referenced above, if no funds under that program are made available to the agency or institution.

§ 99.2 What is the purpose of these regulations?

The purpose of this part is to set out requirements for the protection of privacy of parents and students under Section 444 of GEPA, as amended.

§ 99.3 What definitions apply to these regulations?

The following definitions apply to this part:

- *Act* - the Family Educational Rights and Privacy Act of 1974, as amended, enacted as section 444 of GEPA.
- *Attendance* includes, but is not limited to:
  1. Attendance in person or by paper correspondence, videoconference, satellite, Internet, or other electronic information and telecommunications technologies for students who are not physically present in the classroom; and
  2. The period during which a person is working under a work-study program.
- *Biometric record*, as used in the definition of personally identifiable information, means a record of one or more measurable biological or behavioral characteristics that can be used for automated recognition of an individual. Examples include fingerprints; retina and iris patterns; voiceprints; DNA sequence; facial characteristics; and handwriting.
- *Dates of attendance* – The term means the period of time during which a student attends or attended an educational agency or institution. Examples of dates of attendance include an academic year, a spring semester, or a first quarter. The term does not include specific daily records of a student's attendance at an educational agency or institution.
- *Directory information* - information contained in an education record of a student that would not generally be considered harmful or an invasion of privacy if disclosed. Directory information includes, but is not limited to, the student's name; address; telephone listing; electronic mail address; photograph; date and place of birth; major field of study; grade level; enrollment status (e.g. , undergraduate or graduate, full-time or part-time); dates of attendance; participation in officially recognized activities and sports; weight and height of members of athletic teams; degrees, honors and awards received; and the most recent educational agency or institution attended. Directory information does not include a student's social security number or student identification (ID) number. Directory information includes a student ID number, user ID, or other unique personal identifier used by the student for purposes of accessing or communicating in electronic systems, but only if the identifier cannot be used to gain access to education records except when used in conjunction with one or more factors that authenticate the user's identity, such as a personal identification num-

ber (PIN), password, or other factor known or possessed only by the authorized user.

- *Disciplinary action or proceeding* - the investigation, adjudication, or imposition of sanctions by an educational agency or institution with respect to an infraction or violation of the internal rules of conduct applicable to students of the agency or institution.
- *Disclosure* - to permit access to or the release, transfer, or other communication of personally identifiable information contained in education records by any means, including oral, written, or electronic means, to any party except the party identified as that which provided or created the record.
- *Educational agency or institution* - any public or private agency or institution to which this part applies under §99.1(a).
- *Education records* - The term means those records that are directly related to a student and maintained by an educational agency or institution or by a party acting for the agency or institution. The term does not include:
    1. Records that are kept in the sole possession of the maker, are used only as a personal memory aid, and are not accessible or revealed to any other person except a temporary substitute for the maker of the record.
    2. Records of the law enforcement unit of an educational agency or institution, subject to the provisions of §99.8.
    3. Records relating to an individual who is employed by an educational agency or institution, that are made and maintained in the normal course of business, relate exclusively to the individual in that individual's capacity as an employee; and are not available for use for any other purpose.
    4. Records on a student who is 18 years of age or older, or is attending an institution of postsecondary education, that are made or maintained in connection with a medical treatment of a student and disclosed only to individuals providing any treatment.
    5. Records created or received by an educational agency or institution after an individual is no longer a student in attendance and that are not directly related to the individual's attendance as a student.
    6. Grades on peer-graded papers before they are collected and recorded by a teacher.
- *Eligible student* - a student who has reached 18 years of age or is attending an institution of postsecondary education.
- *Institution of postsecondary education* - an institution that provides education to students beyond the secondary school level; "secondary school level" means the educational level (not beyond grade 12) at which secondary education is provided as determined under State law.
- *Parent* - a parent of a student and includes a natural parent, a guardian, or an individual acting as a parent in the absence of a parent or a guardian.
- *Party* - an individual, agency, institution, or organization.
- *Personally Identifiable Information* - the term includes, but is not limited to:
    1. The student's name;
    2. The name of the student's parent or other family members;
    3. The address of the student or student's family;
    4. A personal identifier (i.e., student's social security number, student number, or biometric record);
    5. Other indirect identifiers (i.e., the student's birth date, place of birth, and mother's maiden name);
    6. Other information that, alone or in combination, is linked or linkable to a specific student that would allow a reasonable person in the school community, who does not have personal knowledge of the relevant circumstances, to identify the student with reasonable certainty; or
    7. Information requested by a person who the educational agency or institution reasonably believes knows the identity of the student to whom the education record relates.

- *Record* - any information recorded in any way, including, but not limited to, handwriting, print, computer media, video or audio tape, film, microfilm, and microfiche.
- *Secretary* - the Secretary of the U.S. Department of Education or an official or employee of the ED acting for the Secretary under a delegation of authority.
- *Student* (except as otherwise specifically provided in this part) - any individual who is or has been in attendance at an educational institution and regarding whom the agency or institution maintains education records.

§ 99.4 What are the rights of parents?

An educational agency or institution shall give full rights under the Act to either parent, unless the agency or institution has been provided with evidence that there is a court order, State statute, or legally binding document relating to such matters as divorce, separation, or custody that specifically revokes these rights.

§ 99.5 What are the rights of students?

The rights accorded to (and consent required of) parents under this part transfer from the parents to the student when the student becomes an "eligible student." Nothing in this section prevents an educational institution from disclosing education records, or personally identifiable information from education records, to a parent without the prior written consent of an eligible student if the disclosure meets the conditions in the first paragraph of §99.31 as stated in the full Federal section.

§ 99.7 What must an educational agency or institution include in its annual notification?

Each educational agency or institution shall annually notify parents of students currently in attendance, or eligible students currently in attendance, of their rights under the Act and this part. The notice must inform parents or eligible students that they have the right to:

1. Inspect and review the student's education records;
2. Seek amendment of the student's education records that the parent or eligible student believes to be inaccurate, misleading, or otherwise in violation of the student's privacy rights;
3. Consent to disclosures of personally identifiable information contained in the student's education records, except to the extent that the act and §99.31 authorize disclosure without consent; and
4. File a complaint with ED under §§99.63 and 99.64 concerning alleged failures by the educational agency or institution to comply with the requirements of the act and this part.

§ 99.8 What provisions apply to records of a law enforcement unit?

Law enforcement unit means any individual, office, department, division, or component of an educational agency (such as a unit of commissioned police officers or non-commissioned security guards) that is officially authorized or designated by that agency or institution to:

1. Enforce any local, State, or Federal law, or refer to appropriate authorities a matter for enforcement of any local, State, or Federal law against any individual or organization other than the agency or institution itself; or
2. Maintain the physical security and safety of the agency or institution.

Records of a law enforcement unit means those records, files, documents, and other materials that are created by a law enforcement unit, created for a law enforcement purpose, and maintained by the law enforcement unit.

Contacting law enforcement units (LEU). Nothing in the Act prohibits an educational agency or institution from contacting and requesting its LEU to investigate a possible violation of, or to enforce, any local, State, or Federal law. Records do not lose their status as education records and remain subject to the Act, including disclosure provisions of §99.30, while in the possession of the LEU. Note that the Act neither requires nor prohibits the disclosure by an educational agency or institution of its LEU records.

Subpart B—What Are the Rights of Inspection and Review of Education Records?

§ 99.10 What rights exist for a parent or eligible student to inspect and review education records?

Except as limited under §99.12, a parent or eligible student must be given the opportunity to inspect and review the student's education records. This provision applies to any educational institution and any SEA and its components. The educational institution or SEA shall comply with a request for access to records within a reasonable period of time, but not more than 45 days after it has received the request.

§ 99.11 May an educational agency or institution charge a fee for copies of education records?

An agency or institution may charge a fee for a copy of an education record for the parent or eligible student unless such a fee prevents them from exercising the right to inspect and review the student's education records. An agency may not charge a fee to search for or retrieve educational student records.

§ 99.12 What limitations exist on the right to inspect and review records?

If the education records of a student contain information on more than one student, the parent or eligible student may inspect and review or be informed of only the specific information about that student. However, a postsecondary institution does not have to permit a student to inspect and review education records that are:

1. Financial records, including any information those records contain, of his or her parents;
2. Confidential letters and statements of recommendation placed in the education records of the student before January 1, 1975, as long as the statements are used only for the purposes for which they were specifically intended; and
3. Confidential letters and statements of recommendation placed in the student's education records after January 1, 1975, if the student has waived his or her right to inspect and review those letters and statements (and those letters and statements are related to the student's admission, application to employment, or receipt of an honor).

Subpart C—What Are the Procedures for Amending Education Records?

§ 99.20 How can a parent or eligible student request amendment of the student's education records?

If a parent or eligible student believes the education records relating to the student contain information that is inaccurate, misleading, or in violation of the student's rights of privacy, he or she may ask the educational agency to amend the record. If the agency decides not to amend the record as requested, it shall inform the parent or eligible student of its decision and of his or her right to a hearing under §99.21.

§ 99.21 Under what conditions does a parent or eligible student have the right to a hearing?

An educational agency or institution shall give a parent or eligible student, upon request, an opportunity for a hearing to challenge the content of the student's education records on the grounds that the information contained in the education records is inaccurate, misleading, or in violation of the privacy rights of the student. If, as a result of the hearing, the educational agency or institution decides that the information is inaccurate, misleading, or otherwise in violation of the privacy rights of the student, it shall amend the record accordingly and inform the parent or eligible student of the amendment in writing. However, if the educational agency decides the information in the education record is not inaccurate, misleading, or otherwise in violation of the privacy rights of the student, it shall inform the parent or student of the right to place a statement in the record commenting on the contested information in the record or stating why he or she disagrees with the decision of the agency or institution, or both.

§ 99.22 What minimum requirements exist for the conduct of a hearing?

The hearing required by §99.21 must meet, at a minimum, the following requirements:

1. The educational agency or institution shall hold the hearing within a reasonable time after it has received the request for the hearing from the parent or eligible student.
2. The educational agency or institution shall give the parent or eligible student notice of the date, time, and place, reasonably in advance of the hearing.
3. The hearing may be conducted by any individual, including an official of the educational agency or institution, who does not have a direct interest in the outcome of the hearing.
4. The educational agency or institution shall give the parent or eligible student a full and fair opportunity to present evidence relevant to the issues raised under §99.21. The parent or eligible student may, at their own expense, be assisted or represented by one or more individuals of his or her own choice, including an attorney.
5. The educational agency or institution shall make its decision in writing within a reasonable period of time after the hearing.
6. The decision must be based solely on the evidence presented at the hearing, and must include a summary of the evidence and the reasons for the decision.

Subpart D—May an Educational Agency or Institution Disclose Personally Identifiable Information From Education Records?

§ 99.30 Under what conditions is prior consent required to disclose information?

The parent or eligible student shall provide a signed and dated written consent before an educational agency discloses personally identifiable information from the student's education records (except as provided in §99.31). The written consent must:

1. Specify the records that may be disclosed;
2. State the purpose of the disclosure; and
3. Identify the party or class of parties to whom the disclosure may be made.

When a disclosure is made:

1. The educational agency or institution shall provide him or her with a copy of the records disclosed if a parent or eligible student so requests; and
2. The agency or institution shall provide the student with a copy of the records disclosed if the parent of a student who is not an eligible student so requests.

§ 99.31 Under what conditions is prior consent not required to disclose information?

An educational agency or institution may disclose personally identifiable information from an education record of a student without the consent required by §99.30 if the disclosure meets one or more of the following conditions:

1. The disclosure is to other school officials or teachers within the institution that have legitimate educational interests (or, under special conditions, a contractor, consultant, volunteer, or other outsourced party).
2. The disclosure is, subject to the requirements of §99.34, to officials of another school, school system, or institution of postsecondary education where the student seeks or intends to enroll, or where the student is already enrolled so long as the disclosure is for purposes related to the student's enrollment or transfer.
3. The disclosure is, subject to the requirements of §99.35, to authorized representatives of the Comptroller General of the U.S., the Attorney General of the U.S., the Secretary, or State and local educational authorities.
4. The disclosure is in connection with financial aid for which the student has applied or received, if

the information is necessary to determine the eligibility, amount, and conditions for the aid;

5. The disclosure is to State and local officials or authorities to whom this information is specifically allowed to be reported or disclosed pursuant to State statute.
6. The disclosure is to Federal, State, local agencies, or independent organizations conducting studies for, or on behalf of, educational agencies or institutions to improve instruction, administer student aid programs, or validate predictive tests;
7. The disclosure is to accrediting organizations to carry out their accrediting functions.
8. The disclosure is to parents (see §99.3) of a dependent student, as defined in section 152 of the Internal Revenue Code of 1986.
9. The disclosure is to comply with a judicial order or lawfully issued subpoena.
10. The disclosure is in connection with a health or safety emergency (see §99.36).
11. The disclosure is information designated as "directory information" (see §99.37).
12. The disclosure is to the parent of a student who is not an eligible student or to the student.
13. The disclosure (subject to §99.39) is to a victim of an alleged perpetrator of a crime of violence or a non-forcible sex offense (which may only include the final results of disciplinary proceedings conducted by the postsecondary institution with respect to that alleged crime or offense);
14. The disclosure (subject to §99.39) is in connection with a disciplinary proceeding at an institution of postsecondary education.
15. The disclosure is to a parent of a student at a postsecondary education institution regarding the student's violation of any Federal, State, or local law, or of any policy of the institution governing the use or possession of alcohol or a controlled substance (see the full Federal section);
16. The disclosure concerns sex offenders and other individuals required to register under section 170101 of the Violent Crime Control and Law Enforcement Act of 1994, 42 U.S.C. 14071, and the information was provided to the educational agency or institution under 42 U.S.C. 14071 and applicable Federal guidelines.

De-identified records and information. An educational agency or institution, or a party that has received education records or information from education records under this part, may release the records or information without the consent required by §99.30 after the removal of all personally identifiable information provided that the educational agency or institution or other party has made a reasonable determination that a student's identity is not personally identifiable, whether through single or multiple releases, and taking into account other reasonably available information.

Reasonable methods. An educational agency or institution must use reasonable methods to identify and authenticate the identity of parents, students, school officials, and any other parties to whom the agency or institution discloses personally identifiable information from education records.

§ 99.32 What recordkeeping requirements exist concerning requests and disclosures?

An educational agency or institution must maintain a record of each request for access to and disclosure of personally identifiable information from the education records of each student, as well as the names of State and local educational authorities and Federal officials and agencies listed in §99.31(3) that may make further disclosures of personally identifiable information from the student's education records without consent under paragraph two of §99.33. The institution shall maintain the record with the education records of the student as long as the records are maintained.

In general, if an educational agency or institution discloses personally identifiable information from education records with the understanding authorized under the second paragraph of §99.33, the record of the disclosure required under this section must include:

1. The names of the additional parties to which the receiving party may disclose the information on

behalf of the educational agency or institution; and

2. The legitimate interests under §99.31 which each of the additional parties has in requesting or obtaining the information.

The following parties may inspect the record relating to each student:

1. The parent or eligible student;
2. The school official or his or her assistants who are responsible for the custody of the records;
3. Those parties authorized in §99.31(1) and (3) of the full Federal section for the purposes of auditing the recordkeeping procedures of the educational agency or institution.

§ 99.33 What limitations apply to the redisclosure of information?

An educational agency or institution may disclose personally identifiable information from an education record only on the condition that the party to whom the information is disclosed will not disclose the information to any other party without the prior consent of the parent or eligible student. The officers, employees, and agents of a party that receives such information under this paragraph may use the information, but only for the purposes for which the disclosure was made.

The first paragraph of this section does not prevent an educational institution from disclosing personally identifiable information with the understanding that the party receiving the information may make further disclosures of the information on behalf of the educational institution if:

1. The disclosures meet the requirements of §99.31 and the educational institution has complied with the requirements of the second paragraph of §99.32; or
2. A State or local educational authority or Federal official or agency listed has complied with requirements as stated in the full Federal section.

A party that receives a court order or lawfully issued subpoena and rediscloses personally identifiable information from education records on behalf of an educational agency or institution in response to that order or subpoena under §99.31(9) must provide the required notification.

If it is determined that a third party outside the educational institution improperly rediscloses personally identifiable information from education records in violation of this section, or fails to provide notification required under subpoena, the educational agency or institution may not allow that third party access to personally identifiable information from education records for at least five years.

§ 99.34 What conditions apply to disclosure of information to other educational agencies or institutions?

An educational agency that discloses an education record under §99.31(2) of the full Federal section shall make a reasonable attempt to notify the parent or eligible student at the last known address of the parent or eligible student, unless the disclosure is initiated by the parent or eligible student or the annual notification of the institution includes a notice that they forward education records to other agencies requesting records. An educational agency or institution may disclose an education record of a student in attendance to another educational institution if the student is enrolled in or receives services from the other agency, and the disclosure meets the requirements of the first paragraph of this section.

§ 99.35 What conditions apply to disclosure of information for Federal or State program purposes?

Authorized representatives of the officials or agencies listed in §99.31(3) of the full Federal section may have access to education records in connection with an audit or evaluation of Federal or State supported education programs, or for the enforcement of or compliance with Federal legal requirements. Authority for an agency or official listed in §99.31(3) to conduct an audit, evaluation, or compliance or enforcement activity is not conferred by the Act or this part and must be established under other Federal, State, or local authority.

Information that is collected under the previous paragraph must be:

1. Protected in a manner that does not permit personal identification of individuals by anyone other than the officials or agencies headed by officials referred to in paragraph one of this section, except that those officials and agencies may make further disclosures of personally identifiable information from education records on behalf of the educational agency or institution in accordance with the requirements of §99.33(b) of the full Federal section; and
2. Destroyed when no longer needed for the purposes listed in paragraph one, above.

§ 99.36 What conditions apply to disclosure of information in health and safety emergencies?

An educational agency or institution may disclose personally identifiable information from an education record to appropriate parties, including parents of an eligible student, in connection with an emergency if the information is necessary to protect the health or safety of the student or other individuals. Nothing in this Act or this part shall prevent an educational agency or institution from

1. Including appropriate information in the education records of a student concerning disciplinary action taken against the student for conduct that posed a significant risk to the safety or well-being of that student, other students, or other members of the school community;
2. Disclosing appropriate information maintained in the above statement to teachers and school officials within the agency or institution who have legitimate educational interests in the behavior of the student; or
3. Disclosing appropriate information maintained above to other school teachers and officials who have legitimate educational interests in the behavior of the student.

§ 99.37 What conditions apply to disclosing directory information?

Disclosure. An educational agency may disclose directory information if it has given public notice to parents of students in attendance and eligible students in attendance at the agency or institution of:

1. The types of personally identifiable information that the agency has designated as directory information;
2. A parent's or eligible student's right to refuse to let the agency designate any or all of those types of information about the student as directory information; and
3. The period of time within which a parent or eligible student has to notify the agency in writing that he or she does not want any or all of those types of information about the student designated as directory information.

Former Students. An educational agency may disclose directory information about former students without complying with the notice and opt out conditions in the previous paragraph. However, the agency must continue to honor any valid request to opt out of the disclosure of directory information made while a student was in attendance unless the student rescinds the opt out request.

Non-Directory Information. An educational agency may not disclose or confirm directory information without meeting written consent requirements in §99.30 if a student's social security number or other non-directory information is used or combined with other data to identify the student or their records.

§ 99.38 What conditions apply to disclosure of information as permitted by State statute adopted after November 19, 1974, concerning the juvenile justice system?

If reporting or disclosure allowed by State statute concerns the juvenile justice system and the system's ability to effectively serve, prior to adjudication, the student whose records are released, an educational agency or institution may disclose education records under §99.31. The officials and authorities to whom the records are disclosed shall certify in writing to the educational agency or institution that the information will not be disclosed to any other party, except as provided under State law, without prior written consent of the student's parent(s).

§ 99.39 What definitions apply to the nonconsensual disclosure of records by postsecondary educational institutions in connection with disciplinary proceedings concerning crimes of violence or non-forcible sex offenses?

As used in this part:

- *Alleged perpetrator of a crime of violence* - a student who is alleged to have committed acts that would, if proven, constitute any of the following offenses or attempts to commit offenses that are defined in Appendix A to this part.
- *Alleged perpetrator of a nonforcible sex offense* - a student who is alleged to have committed acts that, if proven, would constitute statutory rape or incest.
- *Final results* - a decision or determination, made by an honor court or council, committee, commission, or other entity authorized to resolve disciplinary matters within the institution. The disclosure of final results must include only the name of the student, the violation committed, and any sanction imposed by the institution against the student.
- *Sanction imposed* - a description of the disciplinary action taken by the institution, the date of its imposition, and its duration.
- *Violation committed* - the institutional rules or code sections that were violated and any essential findings supporting the institution's conclusion that the violation was committed.

Subpart E—What Are the Enforcement Procedures?

§ 99.60 What functions has the Secretary delegated to the Office and to the Office of Administrative Law Judges?

The Secretary designates the Office to:

1. Investigate, process, and review complaints and violations under the Act and this part;
2. Provide technical assistance to ensure compliance with the Act and this part; and
3. Act as the Review Board required under the Act to enforce applicable programs.

§ 99.61 What responsibility does an educational agency or institution have concerning conflict with State or local laws?

If an agency cannot comply with the Act due to a conflict with State or local law, it shall notify the Office within 45 days, giving the text and citation of the conflicting law.

§ 99.62 What information must an educational agency or institution submit to the Office?

The Office may require an educational agency or institution to submit reports, information on policies and procedures, annual notifications, training materials, and other information necessary to carry out its enforcement responsibilities under the Act or this part.

§ 99.63 Where are complaints filed?

A parent or eligible student may file a written complaint with the Office regarding violations under the Act by contacting Family Policy Compliance Office, 400 Maryland Avenue SW., Washington DC 20202.

§ 99.64 What is the investigation procedure?

A complaint must contain specific factual allegations giving reasonable cause to believe that a violation has occurred. The Office investigates a complaint filed by a parent or eligible student, or conducts its own investigation when no complaint has been filed, to determine whether an educational agency or institution has failed to comply with a provision of the Act or this part. If the Office determines that an educational agency or institution has failed to comply with a provision of the Act or this part, it may also determine whether the failure to comply is based on a policy or practice of the agency or institution

§ 99.65 What is the content of the notice of investigation issued by the Office?

The Office notifies the complainant and any educational agency or institution in writing if it initiates an investigation. The notice to the educational agency or institution will:

1. Include the substance of the allegations against the educational agency or institution; and
2. Direct the agency or institution to submit a written response and other relevant information (including information about its policies and practices regarding education records).

§ 99.66 What are the responsibilities of the Office in the enforcement process?

The Office reviews a complaint submitted by the educational agency or institution and considers all relevant submitted information. Following its investigation, the Office provides a written notice to the educational agency of the basis for its findings. If the educational agency or institution has not complied with a provision of the Act or this part, it may also find that the failure to comply was based on a policy or practice of the agency or institution.

§ 99.67 How does the Secretary enforce decisions?

If an educational agency or institution does not comply during the prescribed period of time, the Secretary may legally enforce action in accordance with Part E of GEPA, including withholding further payments under any applicable program, issuing a compliant to compel compliance through a cease-and-desist order, or terminating eligibility to receive funding under any applicable program.

Appendix A to Part 99—Crimes of Violence Definitions

- *Arson* - Any willful or malicious burning or attempt to burn, with or without intent to defraud, a dwelling house, public building, motor vehicle or aircraft, personal property of another, etc.
- *Assault Offenses* - An unlawful attack by one person upon another. Note: By definition there can be no "attempted" assaults, only "completed" assaults.
    - *Aggravated Assault* - An unlawful attack by one person upon another for the purpose of inflicting severe or aggravated bodily injury. This type of assault usually is accompanied by the use of a weapon or by means likely to produce death or great bodily harm.
    - *Simple Assault* - An unlawful physical attack by one person upon another where neither the offender displays a weapon, nor the victim suffers obvious severe or aggravated bodily injury involving apparent broken bones, loss of teeth, possible internal injury, severe laceration, or loss of consciousness.
    - *Intimidation* - To unlawfully place another person in reasonable fear of bodily harm through the use of threatening words or other conduct, or both, but without displaying a weapon or subjecting the victim to actual physical attack. Note: This offense includes stalking.
- *Burglary* - unlawful entry into a building or structure with intent to commit a felony or theft.
- *Criminal Homicide—Manslaughter by Negligence* - the killing of another person through gross negligence.
- *Criminal Homicide*—Murder and Nonnegligent Manslaughter - willful (nonnegligent) killing of one human being by another.
- *Destruction/Damage/Vandalism of Property* - willfully or maliciously destroy, damage, deface, or otherwise injure real or personal property without the consent of the owner or the person having custody or control of it.
- *Kidnapping/Abduction* - the unlawful seizure, transportation, or detention of a person, or any combination of these actions, against his or her will, or of a minor without the consent of his or her custodial parent(s) or legal guardian. Note: Kidnapping/Abduction includes hostage taking.
- *Robbery* - the taking of, or attempting to take, anything of value under confrontational circumstances from the control, custody, or care of a person or persons by force or threat of force or violence or by putting the victim in fear. Note: Carjackings are robbery offenses where a motor vehicle is taken through force or threat of force.

- *Sex Offenses, Forcible* - any sexual act directed against another person, forcibly or against that person's will, or both; or not forcibly or against the person's will where the victim is incapable of giving consent.
    - *Forcible Rape* (Except "*Statutory Rape*") - The carnal knowledge of a person, forcibly or against that person's will, or both; or not forcibly or against the person's will where the victim is incapable of giving consent because of his or her temporary or permanent mental or physical incapacity (or because of his or her youth).
    - *Forcible Sodomy* - Oral or anal sexual intercourse with another person, forcibly or against that person's will, or both; or not forcibly or against the person's will where the victim is incapable of giving consent because of his or her youth or because of his or her temporary or permanent mental or physical incapacity.
    - *Sexual Assault With An Object* - To use an object or instrument to unlawfully penetrate, however slightly, the genital or anal opening of the body of another person, forcibly or against that person's will, or both; or not forcibly or against the person's will where the victim is incapable of giving consent because of his or her youth or because of his or her temporary or permanent mental or physical incapacity. Note: An "object" or "instrument" is anything used by the offender other than the offender's genitalia.
    - *Forcible Fondling* - The touching of the private body parts of another person for the purpose of sexual gratification, forcibly or against that person's will, or both; or not forcibly or against the person's will where the victim is incapable of giving consent because of his or her youth or because of his or her temporary or permanent mental or physical incapacity. Note: Forcible Fondling includes "Indecent Liberties" and "Child Molesting."
    - *Nonforcible Sex Offenses* (Except "*Prostitution Offenses*") - Unlawful, nonforcible sexual intercourse.
        - *Incest* - Nonforcible sexual intercourse between persons who are related to each other within the degrees wherein marriage is prohibited by law.
        - *Statutory Rape* - Nonforcible sexual intercourse with a person who is under the statutory age of consent.

Index

J

K

L

M

N

O

P

Q

R

S

Suspension 3, 2, 3, 13, 14, 15, 39, 71, 75, 84, 89, 107, 108, 109, 111, 112, 115, 116, 117, 118, 119, 120, 121, 122, 123, 126, 127, 128, 129, 130, 142, 144, 147

T

U

V

W

X

Y

Z

www.ingramcontent.com/pod-product-compliance
Lightning Source LLC
LaVergne TN
LVHW082336200926
848481LV00012B/3365
* 9 7 8 0 9 8 3 7 6 2 2 4 9 *